UNHEALED
WOUNDS

A drawing that appeared in the French weekly, *L'Express*, and that sums up the controversy surrounding the Barbie affair. Half the population wants to open the book on that fateful year; the other half wants it shut as tightly as possible. (*drawing by* TIM)

UNHEALED WOUNDS

France and the Klaus Barbie Affair

ERNA PARIS

Grove Press, Inc., New York

First published in 1985 by Methuen Publications, Canada.

First Grove Press Edition 1986
First Printing 1986
ISBN: 0-394-55390-X
Library of Congress Catalog Card No. 86-298

First Evergreen Edition 1986
First Printing 1986
ISBN: 0-394-62216-2
Library of Congress Catalog Card No. 86-298

Library of Congress Cataloging-in-Publication Data

Paris, Erna
  Unhealed wounds.

  Reprint. Originally published: Agincourt, Ontario,
Canada: Methuen, 1985.
  1. Barbie, Klaus, 1913-   . 2. War criminals—
Germany—Biography. 3. World War, 1939-1945—
Atrocities. 4. World War, 1939-1945—France.
5. France—History—German occupation, 1940-1945.
I. Title.
DD247.B32P37 1986   940.54'05 86-298
ISBN 0-394-55390-X
ISBN 0-394-62216-2 (Evergreen: pbk.)

Printed in the United States of America

GROVE PRESS, INC., 196 West Houston Street,
New York, N.Y. 10014

5 4 3 2 1

To Thomas More Robinson

CONTENTS

ACKNOWLEDGMENTS

During the years I spent writing this book, dozens of people on both sides of the Atlantic generously offered assistance in many ways. They directed me in libraries and archives, opened their files, talked history and politics, challenging me in ways that made me clarify or redirect my thinking, wrote me letters of introduction and shared their personal experiences, although these were sometimes painful in the recollection. To name all of these people would require a book in itself, but as they read this story each will recognize his or her essential contribution.

I would, however, like to name a few individuals whose help and encouragement meant a great deal to me. Professor Michael R. Marrus and Professor Robert Spencer, both of the history department of the University of Toronto, each took the time to read draft chapters of the book and to comment in ways I found particularly helpful. I would also like to thank my friends David Lewis Stein and Heather Robertson, both political journalists, for reading and commenting on parts of the manuscript at an early stage. Thanks are due as well to Margaret Woollard, who edited the manuscript with wonderful professionalism and care.

In Europe, I owe special thanks to Jean-Claude Buhrer, correspondent in Switzerland for *Le Monde*, for his ongoing assistance and for reading selected chapters. Nelly Gutman, director of the Centre d'études et de recherches sur l'antisémitisme contemporain (CERAC), was helpful throughout, as were Yves Jouffa, president of the illustrious Ligue des droits de l'homme, and Dr. Marc Aron of Lyons. My Paris friends, Geneviève-Dominique de Salins, and Ruth and Berry Hayward, provided important opportunities to discuss my research.

I would also like to thank the following for help in various ways: Lucie Aubrac, Henry Bulawko, Jacques Derogy, Charles Favre, Carole Garber, Marion Hebb, Beate Klarsfeld, Serge Klarsfeld, Charles Korman, Michelle Lapautre, Jean-Pierre Lévy, Tanya Long, Gilles Najman, Pascal Ory, Léon Poliakov, Jean-Marc Théolleyre, Jacques Vergès.

Naturally, I remain solely responsible for all interpretations and any errors that have occurred in the text.

To my husband, companion and friend, Tom Robinson, a participant in this book from the first moment to the last, I owe a writer's greatest debt: for his consistent and unfailing encouragement when I needed it, and for sensitive editorial criticism that always stopped short of interference. My son Roland's interest in and commitment to what I was doing touched me deeply, and his magical ability to keep the computer working was essential. From across an ocean, my daughter, Michelle, encouraged me as well. It is hard to write a book without the support of one's family and friends: and in that I am blessed.

PREFACE

I began this book out of a sense that there was more than met the eye
in the strange, passionate response of the French to the return of their
most infamous war villain, the Nazi whom they held responsible for
the death of French Resistance hero Jean Moulin. The courageous role
played by the French Resistance in opposing the Nazis and in the
eventual liberation of France is an important and well-known story,
but it soon became apparent that for legal reasons the trial of Klaus
Barbie was going to deal exclusively with a less well-known aspect of
the Occupation: the deportation of the Jews. I was also interested in
the hope being expressed by many French Jews that the trial might
lead to an open, public recognition of these deportations and of the
role the French themselves had played in collaborating with Nazis like
Barbie. There seemed to be much that was still hidden in this story.

My own lengthy association with France led me to think that I
might be in a unique position to explore the Barbie affair with an in-
sider's understanding, but an outsider's eye. During the 1960s I lived
in France, as a French citizen. It was a time when the Algerian war
raged and when few ever talked about the taboo subject of the wartime collaboration. Certainly no one ever talked about the fate of
76,000 Jews, some of whom were French citizens of ancient vintage,
others of whom had more recently sought refuge in the bosom of the
very land that had appeared to shine a beacon of hope to all mankind.

The research revealed the existence of not one, but two distinct
Frances, each with a long historical tradition. One tradition, steeped
in xenophobic nationalism and conservative values, culminated in the
figurative crowning of Marshal Philippe Pétain in 1940 as leader of
the collaborative government of Vichy France. The other looked back
to the Revolution and the cry of "Liberty, Equality, Fraternity" for
its inspiration. Klaus Barbie had appeared on the scene as the two
Frances were engaged in what amounted to civil war.

Forty years later Barbie's return to French soil liberated the demons of those terrible days. In fact, his presence soon became a new torture to the Resistance he had tried to destroy so long ago.

The research also pinpointed the Barbie affair as one of the connecting links among European extremist groups. Neo-nazism is very much alive and in association with unlikely companions. But above all, the "affair" is a story of obsession and the settling of scores, as well as a search for justice. It is, in particular, a story of racism, a racism that has altered the lives of all the major participants in the trial — the defendant, of course, but also the prosecution and the defense. And racism continues to play an important role, for the Barbie trial will take place in a France that is witnessing the rise of a new, extreme right-wing movement that attacks Arabs with the very vocabulary that was once reserved for Jews.

Beneath the surface turmoil of the Klaus Barbie affair is the reality of a nation that has not yet come to terms with its own recent past. From every perspective, it is the story of wounds that have never healed.

ERNA PARIS
Paris, May 1985

UNHEALED
WOUNDS

· 1 ·

FRANCE REACTS IN SHOCK

For forty years the name of Klaus Barbie has burned scarlet and unrequited on an unfinished page of French history. An older generation that knew the war not only never forgot him, but passed on vivid stories of his brutalities to their children. So when the news came through that the man himself was being transported across the Atlantic to face justice on the very soil where he had served the Third Reich, a not unpredictable collective shudder seized the nation. It was a mixed shudder of elation and dread: elation on the part of the former Resistance fighters who had survived Barbie's bullwhip and water-torture and execution squads; elation on the part of the families of those who did not survive; and elation, of course, on the part of the Jews. In the region of Lyons, almost every Jew alive had lost someone to the Nazi death machine headed by "the butcher of Lyons," as they called him.

There was also dread, however, because for most of those same forty years it had been tacitly understood in France that the dark days of the German Occupation and the collaborationist Vichy regime would be interred as quietly as possible. On June 14, 1944, the day General Charles de Gaulle landed at Bayeux, a mythology began to sprout: France was now a nation of valorous Resistance fighters who had strenuously opposed the enemy occupier. Only a tiny handful of traitors had sold out to the enemy, and these were duly tried and pilloried as examples of treachery. Then in August 1953, the National Assembly passed a general amnesty law, and the disturbing business of 1940 to 1944 was hurriedly shoved into the back closet of history. The new attitude was sharply revealed at the 1954 trial of Karl-Albrecht Oberg. Oberg had been the most powerful ss official in occupied France, a man who answered only to ss chief Heinrich Himmler and whose very presence in France underlined the importance the Nazis had attached to the Final Solution (for which they needed French assistance); but the trial created scant interest, either inside or outside the courtroom. *Le Monde* reported archly that this was a trial "without passion" and that the French were "preoccupied with more timely problems."

The back closet of history, however, could not entirely contain its unlovely contents. As in Ionesco's play *Amédée*, in which a charming young couple has hidden in the cupboard a corpse that proceeds to grow and extend grotesque members at absurd and unlikely moments, the truth about Vichy and the cheerful participation of millions of French men and women in the roundup, deportation and even killing of their fellow citizens had a disconcerting tendency to ooze out of the dark into the respectable light of day. It wasn't until filmmaker Marcel Ophuls' 1969 documentary, *The Sorrow and the Pity*, that the French began to take notice of their recent history. Ophuls shocked the nation to its roots. In 1979, the sanitized Hollywood serial, "The Holocaust," further jolted sensibilities. Still French school texts ignored the Occupation except to honor the underground Resistance. Professional historians who had taken their cue from the national agreement to "forget" were far from happy when foreign scholars began to muck around in archives and produce carefully footnoted tomes that demonstrated beyond question that the land of liberty, equality and fraternity, the country that had so proudly provided refuge for the unwanted and homeless, had collaborated with the Nazis in a way that was quite unequalled in the history of the war. No one really wanted to know that the Germans had had only 2,500 Gestapo police in the whole of France and that the entire business of suppression and oppression had been the official state policy of Marshal Pétain and actually legislated into the law of the land; or that up to 5,000 auxiliary French police had carried out the necessary tasks of enumerating Jews (the Germans used the lists for deportations), issuing large yellow stars the size of a palm with "*JUIF*" written across them in black letters, appropriating property for the state coffers and guarding transports of cattle cars sealed shut on a human cargo destined vaguely for "the East." No one wanted to know that the French and German police were helped by up to 30,000 *miliciens*, a paramilitary force of French fascists who operated with considerable autonomy in pursuing the enemies of Vichy, as well as countless numbers of bureaucrats and pro-fascist civilians who freely volunteered their services. Anonymous denunciations rained upon local prefects and other officials of Vichy France: so and so was really a Jew and living under an assumed identity with false papers;

this one was a communist; that one was in the Resistance. No one wanted to know such things; but, with the passage of decades, the truth was becoming more difficult to conceal or rationalize.

The arrival of Klaus Barbie on French soil thus brought with it the fear that he would point a finger at people who had helped him, people who, having undergone a sudden transformation from collaborator to Resistance fighter, from traitor to hero, had been living in relative obscurity for almost half a century. Barbie had actually claimed in an interview that the only things he remembered from his halcyon days of youth and power were the names of those erstwhile "friends." He claimed to have remained in contact with veterans of the Charlemagne Division, a group of Frenchmen who voluntarily joined the Waffen ss to fight the communist menace on the Russian front. The trial would be his last hour on a public stage, and Klaus Barbie intended to play each scene to advantage. He did not plan to go down alone.

The trial loomed ahead like an irresistibly beautiful iceberg in a fog-shrouded sea; but at the outset, the French (at least those who spoke publicly in the newspapers and before the microphones of the nation) seemed prepared to maintain their course. The door of the closet into which the truth about Vichy had been hurriedly pushed forty years ago had already begun to open, and most were aware it would not close again until its contents had seen the light of day. With a few prominent exceptions, the French seemed prepared to air their history and, they hoped, complete the unwritten page.

Of the gallons of newspaper ink deployed to describe, dissect and agonize over the complex reaction to the capture of Klaus Barbie, no one put this point of view better than journalist Guy Baret writing in *France Soir* on February 7, 1983. With the wonderful linguistic sonority that marks French journalism at its most literary, Baret wrote the following under the heading "Are We Ready?"

Forty years after the death of Jean Moulin, Klaus Barbie will appear before his judges. Are we ready? No, we are not ready to hear the atrocious accounting that night and fog will never engulf. We are not ready to hear, in sorrow and pity, the witness whose eyes are still filled with horror. The history of genocide will become current news again.

Are we ready to look at the true face of France, at the dark years reflected in the mirror of this trial?

Are we ready to see old wounds reopened and the unextinguished fire of yesterday's passion relit?

Are we ready to end the Manichean myths that nourished civil wars?

Are we ready to renounce the image of Epinal whereby the entire population of France rose against the occupier and only a handful collaborated?

Are we ready to recognize that at certain times the most difficult thing is not *doing one's duty, but rather to know what it is?*

Are we ready, forty years later, to reconcile ourselves not in compromise, but in truth?

All this will be a part of the trial of Klaus Barbie. It will be an ordeal for our country . . . but it will be to our honor to attempt to confront [our past].

In 1942, at the age of twenty-eight and fresh from a year-long posting with the anti-Jewish service in Holland, ss-Obersturmführer Klaus Barbie was reassigned to France. The new placement was a promotion, a reward for having led a commando squad that had successfully quelled an uprising in the Amsterdam ghetto.

Barbie's zone of responsibility was Lyons, and his task as chief of the second largest Gestapo force in France was primarily the destruction of the Resistance, as well as the obligatory rounding up and deportation of Jews. He was known as an exceptionally cruel man, even for the ss. A fellow officer allowed that "Barbie's excesses were not always reported to Paris," which is to suggest (with little evidence) that his behavior might have been curbed. Another colleague later described him as "the very soul of the Gestapo."

Klaus Barbie's interrogations were famous for their savagery and consisted mainly of various methods of torture, which he reputedly enjoyed administering. The drowning technique was his favorite. Barbie also beat people with his own personal bullwhip, and the instrument became as notorious as its owner. And for every attack on a German, large numbers of hostages were shot.

Notable though his cruelty was, however, the memory of Klaus Barbie festered in the hearts of the French for forty years primarily because of his symbiotic relationship with one man — Jean Moulin, the martyred hero of the French Resistance. Under Moulin, who was Charles de Gaulle's representative in France, the warring parties of the

Resistance were united into the National Resistance Council (Conseil national de la résistance). This was no mean task. The French have a penchant for splintering on the political Right and Left. There were serious rivalries between groups, even among those who shared similar ideologies, and there were personal rivalries between leaders of the various networks.

On June 12, 1943, Moulin held a meeting of the unified Resistance in a suburb of Lyons. Someone informed the Gestapo.

One man escaped that day under questionable circumstances. René Hardy was arrested and tried twice after the Liberation, and both times he was acquitted; but there are many people who continue to believe he betrayed Moulin and that the truth has never been told. Barbie, for one, has given notice that he intends to resurrect the Hardy affair during his own trial.

Jean Moulin became the symbol of the mythological France in which every Frenchman was a Resistance fighter between 1940 and 1944, and it's hard to find a town without a street or a monument to his memory. In 1964, twenty-one years after his death, his remains were transferred from the Père Lachaise cemetery in Paris to the Pantheon, the highest honor France could offer its martyr. It was a cold, dreary day, but thousands of people wept silently to hear André Malraux describe Moulin as "the poor, tortured king of the shadows" and "the chief of the people of the night." In 1981, when François Mitterrand took office as president of France, one of his first official acts was to pay homage to Moulin.

As the destroyer of Jean Moulin, Klaus Barbie is perceived as the enemy of all that is most noble in the French spirit. Devil and superstar, their names will be forever linked. Barbie himself claims he respected Moulin and thought they had a great deal in common. He also claims to have nothing but warm feelings for the French. In 1975 he was tracked down in Bolivia by Michel Goldberg, a young Jew whose father had been deported to "the East" in February 1943. Goldberg impersonated a journalist and interviewed Barbie. (Later he planned to kill him, but retreated.) During the course of their conversation, Barbie protested that he had nothing at all against the French — indeed, his son was married to a Frenchwoman — and that during a trip to Europe some years earlier he had done some sightseeing in Paris, one of his favorite cities.

Klaus Barbie believes the western world ought to be a little more grateful for the role he played in ending Jean Moulin's career. "By arresting Jean Moulin I changed the course of history," he bragged to Michel Goldberg. "Jean Moulin . . . was so intelligent that had he lived it is he and not de Gaulle who would have presided over the destiny of France after our departure. France would probably have become communist."

All evidence suggests that Moulin was a radical socialist and not a communist, but Barbie wasn't wrong in implying that there were truly massive political and ideological divisions within the Resistance. For that very reason, not all former Resistance fighters were overjoyed at the news that Barbie would be tried in Lyons. There were Gestapo spies within the Lyons Resistance networks, many of whom had never been exposed, and there were Resistance spies in the Gestapo who were, in fact, double agents working for the Germans. Klaus Barbie gleefully promised to denounce them all.

Since the specific charges to be brought against Barbie related to "crimes against humanity," in particular to crimes against the Jews, some former *résistants* found themselves uneasily evaluating the state of their personal consciences. The French Resistance was by no means anti-Semitic, but it didn't specifically help the Jews either, although there were many Jews fighting within its ranks. Only the organized Jewish Resistance specifically helped the Jews, by hiding children, setting up escape routes into Spain and Switzerland and generally working in cooperation with hundreds of courageous and humane individuals, including many priests and nuns. The communists didn't become a major factor in the French Resistance until after Germany invaded Russia in 1941. The underground Maquis wasn't able to recruit large numbers of people until February 1943, when the Germans obliged the French government to institute a forced labor draft in which young Frenchmen were sent to work in Germany. But the oppression of the Jews had begun long before: indeed, it had begun immediately after the Occupation, in the summer of 1940.

In the days following his imprisonment in Fort Montluc, Klaus Barbie, like Alice in Wonderland, grew alternately larger and smaller in the eyes of the public. In his larger-than-life incarnation, he was depicted as a monster with a ravenous, inhuman appetite for cruelty and as a perverted sadist who got his thrills by fondling women's breasts as he smashed his whip against bleeding bodies. In his smaller-than-life depictions he was described as personally beyond the pale and inconsequential. The death penalty was abolished in France in 1981 and, although the prospect of Klaus Barbie on trial sent fresh adrenalin coursing through the veins of the pro-capital-punishment lobby, and calls for his execution were heard from former Resistance fighters (in particular, from Jean Moulin's widow), it was unlikely that the law would be rescinded even for this special occasion. Others asked what point there was in sentencing a sick, old man to life imprisonment — except for vengeance; except as a symbolic gesture.

Oh yes, a symbolic gesture. Within days of his arrival in France, Klaus Barbie and his prospective trial had become a metaphor for the past, present and future of France and, on occasion, of the rest of the world. The issues he was seen to symbolize were varied and all-encompassing. Perhaps the most prevalent was the expressed desire to use the trial to condemn nazism itself, "an ideology that concluded logically with crimes against humanity because it excluded entire ethnic groups," as the late, respected commentator Raymond Aron wrote in *L'Express*.[1] In other words, all Nazi crimes would crowd invisibly into the dock when Klaus Barbie stood before his judges in Lyons. But Aron and several others went further still. The court should try not just Nazi ideology, but all political ideologies, whether left- or right-wing. "From the most humane doctrine in the world came the Gulag," continued Aron, "[and] the communist utopia cost Cambodians millions of lives . . . Pol Pot is still recognized as the legitimate government by a number of states."

Others followed suit. A deputy from the department of Ain who was not born until after the war ended wrote that the trial should be a testimonial to what happens when power is unchecked and when democracies give up before a totalitarian system. Most of all, it should show how the monstrous actions of Klaus Barbie epitomize the logical outcome of any political ideology, of the Left or the Right.

National Socialism dreams of a perfect society founded by a pure race. Therefore it gets rid of the "impure" races . . . Communist ideology dreams of a perfect society ruled by the superior proletarian class. It needs no war to get rid of the others . . . Massacres of race, massacres of class, the horror that we banish through Klaus Barbie in fascism still exists wherever communism triumphs . . . The youth of France must see not only a bloody brute who was allowed by default to torture and exterminate other people. They must also see that the very future is in question because this terror is brought about by totalitarian ideologies.[2]

Some commentators conceded that it was perhaps important to try the real man, Klaus Barbie, on real charges for real crimes against real people, but such individuals appeared to be in a minority. Jacques Julliard writing in the *Nouvel Observateur*[3] thought the importance of the trial was to silence recent attempts to deny that the Holocaust existed and to expose efforts to romanticize it with the fancy conceits of psychoanalysis. "The men and women who staffed the concentration camps were not 'fallen angels,' but degenerate brutes," he wrote. (Two of the most notorious books claiming to debunk the "myth" of the Holocaust were written by Frenchmen, Paul Rassiner and Robert Faurisson.) Also on trial, according to Julliard, would be the false image of collective French heroism during the Occupation. The truth about France's tragedy would emerge, and it would trigger an important and necessary catharsis.

The real accused sitting in that Lyons courtroom would not be Klaus Barbie, however, but terror itself. Not just the particular terror inflicted by Barbie in the Lyons region in 1943 and 1944, or the more general terror orchestrated by the Nazi machine as it swept across Europe, but TERROR as a large, metaphysical abstraction. On trial in a small courtroom in Lyons would be the entire "inheritance" of nazism, here held responsible for:

- The underground resistance fighter in Afghanistan who is asphyxiated in a tunnel.
- The Salvadoran peasant who has his skin torn off because he was born in a suspicious place.
- The pregnant woman who is disemboweled in Guatemala.
- The murdered victims of the Irish political-religious wars.
- The Vietnamese woman who is drowned after she is raped.
- The Iranian and Iraki who are obliged to kill each other.
- The Ugandans whose limbs are broken in the [state] dungeons.
- The Russian intellectual injected by police doctors.

"All this is more important than the fate of a retired monster like Barbie," concluded the writer.

From the beginning it was clear that Barbie was planning to use the same broad arguments of "human culpability" in his trial defense.

He asked his lawyers to compile a list of wartime atrocities committed since World War I. According to court sources he intended to argue that what he did was no different from the actions of many soldiers before and after his time. But Barbie's ace in the hole, according to such reasoning, would be the behavior of the French themselves. During the Algerian war, torture was commonplace. More important, everyone was amnestied after that war was over.

The thrust of Barbie's arguments would be to minimize his personal culpability. Why remember one war when there have been more than a hundred others since? "I have forgotten," he told journalists on the airplane that flew him to France. "If they [the rest of the world] have not forgotten, it is their business."

Not for Klaus Barbie the prostrate *mea culpa*, or the suicide of remorse. Barbie remained a proud Nazi, even as he learned that the destination of the airplane was France and not Germany as he had hoped. So proud that in 1966 he was expelled from the German club in La Paz for shouting "*Heil Hitler*" at the envoy of the German Federal Republic.

For Klaus Barbie, the war had never ended.

The Barbie trial was certain to be compared and equated with the celebrated show trial of Adolf Eichmann in 1962, and already parallels were emerging. There was, in Israel, a similar attempt to use the trial for propaganda purposes. The prosecutor, Gideon Hausner, representing the government of David Ben-Gurion, had in mind a case that was built not so much on what Eichmann did, but on what the Jews had suffered. He wanted to raise questions of apparently greater import than the guilt of one man, questions like: How could such a thing happen? What role did the Allies play in the ultimate tragedy of the Jewish people? Why the Jews? Why, for that matter, the Germans? There was a great deal of talk about lessons for the future generation. But as Hannah Arendt correctly pointed out in her landmark book *Eichmann in Jerusalem*, justice insisted on the central importance of Adolf Eichmann, the middle-aged man in the glass booth. Justice insisted that the accused be prosecuted, defended and judged, and that all other questions, important as they were, be left outside the courtroom proper. The presiding judge, Moishe Landau, did his best to insure that they were.

In France, although the journalists may have been preparing to try nazism, communism, the Iranian revolution, the Vietnam war, the French in Algeria, the French under Marshal Pétain and humankind itself, and although the defense was preparing a case along similar diffuse lines, the state prosecutor was quietly putting together a dossier against one man. The charges against Barbie would be specific and substantiated by witnesses, and they would be "crimes against humanity" as opposed to "war crimes."

Some journalists did understand that justice consists of bringing specific charges against a specific person, then proving them with evidence. "I need the specifics of a situation in order to understand it. The dirty linen is still crawling with Nazi vermin [and it is] a very specific plague," stated one writer who was prepared to buck the trend of lumping all postwar atrocities together. "But what a stroke of luck all this is for the television channels," she added, sarcastically. "A bad one who is even worse than J. R. [Ewing]. Absolute and unrepentant evil. Nazism as entertainment. Hitler? Never heard of him. Then suddenly, fifty years later, Hitler blackens the newspapers, fills the television screens and continues to fascinate. Who can make sense of it?"[4]

In 1983, after their government had effected the popular, international coup of bringing Barbie back, few in France were prepared to deplore the prospect of a trial, at least in public. But a short letter to *The Guardian*[5] surely spoke for hundreds of thousands of conservative French men and women whose point of view was only temporarily out of fashion, people who maintained a historical affinity for the right wing of the political spectrum.

. . . I don't care what Barbie did during the war. That was the war. Sure, crimes were committed during World War II, on both sides. But the major flaw in the Nazi-hunting campaigns of [Simon] Wiesenthal, [Beate] Klarsfeld and company is that you have to be on the loser's side in a war to be prosecuted for war crimes . . .

Political movements firmly rooted in the tradition of the Resistance will benefit from the coverage of the Barbie trial, especially the Gaullist Party (which reveres the "man of June 18th, 1940") to the Communist Party (which boasts of having lost 75,000 of its members in the struggle against nazism) and to the preachy, moralizing Left in general (of which the Socialist Party is a good example). No, after 40 years, there is no justice to be expected from the Barbie trial. It is plain, disgusting revenge. Let's make no mistake about it.

Just as Klaus Barbie continued to defend the "ideals" of National Socialism, so were there French people who maintained their own wartime sympathies, including support for the Nazi campaign against the communists and perhaps the Jews.

The most visible and widely quoted intellectual to take a position against the trial of Barbie was Jean-Edern Hallier, a writer of Breton origin and a frequenter of fashionable Paris salons. Hallier, who was characterized by John Ardagh as an example of "intellectual dandyism at its most flamboyant," has described himself both as a "*monstre sacré*" and "the only living Frenchman who fulfills the role of a great writer in the nineteenth-century sense. I'm a historic leader of the far Left, yet the Right, too, finds me fascinating," he added modestly.

According to Ardagh, Hallier's sympathy for the Left has cooled noticeably since the heyday of May 1968, which might account for his provocative comments on the Barbie "crisis."

"When will France stop trying to win the last war? When will we stop creating hatred?" he asked with a flourish. "I feel nauseous when I contemplate the barbarous ritual sacrifice we're preparing. I wouldn't have hesitated to kill Barbie with my bare hands some years ago, but today I'd prefer a little more charity and some moral [self-] questioning."[6]

In opposing the Barbie capture and trial, the conservative right wing echoed the opinions of Klaus Barbie himself. From his formerly safe perch in Bolivia, Barbie gave at least six major interviews to the international press during the past decade, and in each he stressed his attachment to moral relativism. "Those who lose a war are called war criminals. The winners become the redressers of wrongs," he said in January 1972. Eleven years later, on discovering that the plane carrying him out of Bolivia was heading for France, Barbie once again voiced the identical sentiment. "*Vae victis*," he said bitterly. "Woe to the vanquished."

The most thoughtful note sounded against the trial of Barbie—and perhaps the saddest—came from Simone Veil, the former president of the Judicial Commission of the European Parliament; it was sad because Veil, a Jew who was denounced in the south of France in 1944 and sent to Auschwitz, was so afraid and so widely misunderstood.

Madame Veil was quoted as saying that nothing valuable was likely to come out of such a trial. She said that the very fabric of France might be torn apart again as the old questions about the Occupation and the Resistance were raised anew. But underlying her remarks was a serious apprehension that was shared by other French Jews. As a survivor of Auschwitz, Veil was depressed by the lump-them-all-together vogue in which the crimes of Nazis were being compared to every other abomination on the face of the earth. "We haven't sufficiently stressed that the Nazi regime was not limited to political repression," she said in an interview. "It was a different kind of totalitarianism, quite atypical, and for that reason it is wrong to compare it with the Soviet Gulag, even if millions of people died from Stalinist repression. Since Barbie arrived on French soil we have heard very little about the essential point, which is the specific nature of nazism and crimes against humanity. We have been witnessing a trivializing of the Hitler phenomenon, from the professor who has 'explained' to us that there were no gas chambers in Auschwitz to the politicians who compare the Hitler state to Argentina or El Salvador, to the people who talk about nazism in [the Lebanese refugee camps of] Sabra and Shatila. As if any of that had anything to do with the real nature of nazism.

"If a trial allows us to analyse in depth the Hitlerian phenomenon, then it will be useful. But I'm afraid that will have to be done by historians."[7]

Veil correctly perceived that quite different issues were more likely to preoccupy the French—the collaboration, for example, and the perennial question of who killed Jean Moulin. As for the latter, Veil thought it was a useless pursuit. "I do not believe that this is the real problem today. I just can't see members of the jury, who may be quite ignorant of the entire period, or perhaps too knowledgable, discussing the case of someone, a Resistance fighter, who perhaps broke down and gave information under torture." On collaboration, she wondered aloud how much further ahead French men and women would be when it had been demonstrated that there were, in occupied France, a certain number of despicable bastards and a certain number of weak people who gave information. Yet, and it was an important hesitation, she also expressed the contradictory wish that the trial of Klaus Barbie address the question of "how it could happen that so many respectable heads of families were able to participate without question in this work of death [that was organized] on an industrial scale?"[8]

Madame Veil never once mentioned the Jews, but it was to them and to their fate that she was alluding. Seventy-six thousand French

Jews were deported during the Occupation, and 90 percent of them were arrested by the *French* police, not the Germans. Of the 76,000, only 3,000 returned.

In suppressing the truth about the Occupation, the French have also suppressed the shame of betrayal and complicity. As a result, the fate of the deported Jews has rarely been a subject of overt concern. Although Klaus Barbie has been charged with the arrest and murder or deportation to the death camps of some 7,591 Jews, it is the arrest and killing of 4,342 maquisards and, in particular, the ordeal of Jean Moulin, that interests France. With a few important exceptions, the fate of the Jews as such accounted for little in the reams of newsprint dedicated to the forthcoming trial. One journalist referred scornfully to the omission. "The really big deal is Jean Moulin," he wrote in the *Nouvel Observateur.* "One might have thought it was the Jews."

France, of course, has a sad history of anti-Semitism, in spite of being the first country in Europe to emancipate the Jews, and in spite of a long tradition of welcoming the homeless refugee. Anti-Semitism erupted with virulence with the Dreyfus affair at the end of the nineteenth century and persisted under the patronage of right-wing political movements until the Nazis came along. Most contemporary observers agree that overt anti-Semitism more or less disappeared after 1945, but they also agree that the strain remains present (though usually latent) in French society. According to a recent opinion poll, 10 percent of the French admit to being anti-Semitic, and less than 25 percent think Jews are ordinary people just like anyone else.

Spokesmen for the 600,000 Jews in France (the largest Jewish community in Europe outside the Soviet Union) were publicly thankful to the Mitterrand government for bringing Klaus Barbie "home" a decade after he had been tracked down in Bolivia by Beate Klarsfeld, a German Protestant, married to a French Jew, who has dedicated her life to bringing Nazis to justice. Her husband, lawyer Serge Klarsfeld, thanked "those in the Elysée who answered our appeal and effected Barbie's return to France where he can be judged at the scene of his crimes." Other leaders echoed his remarks and made a point of insisting that they, like the officials of the government, were seeking justice and not revenge. Jean-Jacques Bloch, the president of the Jewish Council for the Rhône-Alpes-Center, said that the Jewish community was counting on French justice to judge and make known the horrors that Klaus Barbie had committed. He asked that French youth who did not live through this barbaric period draw a lesson from the trial that would enable them to become more vigilant and to hold even more tenaciously to the ideals of freedom, human dignity and mutual respect among people.

Behind the scenes there was less unanimity. French Jews were still reeling from the aftermath of the rue Copernic bombings in late 1980, when a bomb exploded outside a synagogue, killing four people. There was widespread outrage at that event in French society followed by a massive protest march during which non-Jews were seen wearing signs saying, "*Nous sommes tous des juifs français.*" But a comment made by Premier Ramond Barre continued to rankle. Barre condemned the attackers for an incident that could have harmed "innocent passers-by." The rabbi of the synagogue, English-born Michael Williams, has remained cynical. "There were no arrests, and no one ever questioned anyone in the synagogue about anything he might have seen or heard before, during or after the incident. I don't think we can trust the authorities further than we can spit," he said bluntly and bitterly.

Most remain convinced that the rue Copernic attack, the machine gunning at Jo Goldenberg's restaurant in the summer of 1982 that killed six people and wounded twenty-two, as well as the attacks on other Jewish targets, among them schools, meeting halls, commercial establishments and a former Rothschild bank, are the work of international terrorists and not local anti-Semites; but the result is that the "Jewish question" has been in the air again, and it has been making a lot of people nervous.

"I'm not very much in favor of stirring things up," said a survivor of Auschwitz who is now an international lawyer. Rabbi Williams best put Jewish fears in context. "The Jewish community has a very traumatic history in this country," he noted, with typically British understatement.

In Lyons, itself, the news of Barbie's capture brought a strong emotional reaction from Jews and former Resistance fighters of all persuasions. For symbolic reasons, Barbie was taken first to Fort Montluc. This was where the wartime internment took place, including the ultimate agony of Moulin. In the courtyard of the fort, a sort of shack reserved for the Jews was permanently moored. Thousands of men, women and children were brought to Montluc and, if they were suspected of being in the Resistance or being wealthy, were frequently shot on the spot. More often they were held as a ready pool of hostages to be killed whenever reprisals were called for. For those who escaped immediate death, Fort Montluc was a first station on the way to Drancy, the holding camp near Paris, and then to Auschwitz.

For some, the return of Barbie was an unbearable *dénouement* to their lives. Among the throngs of former victims and the merely curious who waited tensely at the airport of Lyons-Satolas for the arrival of Barbie's plane was a forty-four-year-old woman hiding a .22 carbine rifle under a sheet. Two policemen noticed and bolted forward and arrested her.

She told reporters she had been taken to Drancy with her parents when she was five years old. They never returned. "I swore revenge," she said. "This morning when I heard Klaus Barbie was being brought to Lyons, I went out and bought bullets for this rifle that I owned. The clerk showed me how to use it and I came directly to the airport."

Fearing just such an attempt on Barbie's life, the authorities had decided to land the plane in secret at Orange. There, Barbie was transferred to a Puma helicopter, which carried him 250 kilometers to the tiny air base of Corbas just south of Lyons.

Emotions flared among the ranks of former Resistance fighters — Jews and gentiles — who had no difficulty remembering their life and death struggle with the sometime Gestapo chief. Lise Lesèvre, now eighty-two, was permanently disabled after being tortured by Barbie for nine consecutive days in 1944. She had been arrested while carrying messages for the Resistance. Raymond Aubrac, who was arrested along with Moulin, recalled eating the papers they were examining in Dr. Dugoujon's office as soon as the noise of the Gestapo raid reached their ears. "Have you ever eaten paper?" he asked. "You know, it's not bad when you start, but it's dreadful by the time you've finished." Aubrac was condemned to death, but was rescued in a daring coup plotted and carried out by his wife, Lucie.

Serge Klarsfeld, however, has suggested that the "heroes of the Resistance" did little to help extradite Barbie during the twelve years it took to get him back to France after Beate Klarsfeld discovered him in Bolivia. He suggested that the reason France was interested in Barbie "had less to do with the murder of Jews than with Mr. Barbie's mistake of killing the hero of the Resistance, Jean Moulin. If he hadn't, no one would have heard of him, and he'd still be living a quiet life in Bolivia.

"What interests us now are 'crimes against humanity,' which until recently have been hushed up or ignored," he added. "One of the darkest chapters in French history was the role of the French in the deportation of the Jews."

The prospect of a Pandora's box of embarrassing revelations prompted hundreds of nervous Frenchmen to settle scores and scurry for cover. René Hardy announced that he would testify at the trial if called, but that he had "nothing to say." Then he disappeared from view. Moulin's wife, Renée, was challenged by four former resistance leaders, who said she knew nothing of the underground movement and in fact had never even seen her husband since their divorce in 1928. Madame Moulin insisted that she and Moulin had met privately and claimed she was a target of a campaign of lies. Socialist minister Gaston Deferre claimed he had warned Moulin not to attend the fateful meeting, but the man at whose office it was held said he doubted whether Deferre had ever met Moulin. And the newspaper *Le Matin* reported that the conservative mayor of Nice had told friends he had photos of an official of a rival conservative party giving the Nazi salute during a wartime rally in France. At a lower level, hundreds of French *concierges* who had informed on people hiding in their premises or living on false papers now began to tremble at the prospect of new denunciations, with themselves on the receiving end.

In Germany, by contrast, the trial of Klaus Barbie was greeted with unmistakable glee. West Germans were disdainful of France's national reluctance to examine the myth of the all-pervasive, all-noble French Resistance. After the Barbie arrest, German television commentators suggested that France should start to come to terms with its role during the war just as Germany had recently been trying to do. Far from retreating in shame over the terrible tales of Barbie's atrocities, the Germans fastened onto stories of French collaborators who helped Barbie do his job. "The dimension of collaboration should be totally uncovered," claimed a writer for *Die Zeit*. "The police and gendarmes who gave away Jews and sometimes members of the Resistance to the Germans; all these good, upright Frenchman without whom a few hundred [*sic*] Nazi officials in France would not have been able to do what they did."

France was not the only nation likely to be embarrassed at the Barbie trial. In August 1983, charges that the United States had employed Barbie as an anticommunist agent immediately after the war, protected him from the French, then arranged for his escape via one of the notorious "rat lines" out of Europe were substantiated. The U.S. government "apologized" to the French while emphasizing that it was not the central administration that was responsible but an intelligence agency (the forerunner of the CIA) acting independently. Days later, Serge Klarsfeld accused the French government itself of hiring a former Gestapo agent to help identify informers. Other revelations of an equally embarrassing nature were likely to emerge.

Beyond the joy, the fear and the general mud-slinging that emerged, as unhealed war wounds were painfully reopened, waited the central figure of the drama. Klaus Barbie was old and frail. He had left the graves of his son and his wife of forty-two years in Bolivia. Yet he remained, above all else, a stalwart Nazi, steadfastly loyal to the beliefs of his youth.

I am a convinced Nazi. I am proud to have been a commanding officer of the best military outfit in the Third Reich, and if I had to be born a thousand times again, I would be a thousand times what I've been. For the sake of Germany and Bolivia . . .

I am not a fanatic. I am an idealist.

Forty years after the war, Klaus Barbie's hatreds had not abated, nor had his cynicism. For Barbie, the desire of all those who suffered from the terror and inhumanity of the Nazis to see a measure of justice brought back into the world was totally incomprehensible. "The 'Nazi hunt' isn't done out of vengeance, nor out of patriotism, but for money," he once proclaimed. "[It] is simply a question of financial interest . . .

"I am sorry about every Jew I did not kill."

Forty years after the war, he would be entitled to due process in a democratic country. Through the person of Klaus Barbie, France might open the closet door, at last, to begin a courageous and painful examination of its wartime past. But a trial date had yet to be set. And much could happen in the interim . . .

· 2 ·

THE EARLY LIFE AND TIMES OF
KLAUS BARBIE

No document of the early Nazi years conveyed the mesmerizing influence of Adolf Hitler with greater immediacy than Leni Riefenstahl's dazzling film, *Triumph of the Will*. Riefenstahl is fond of calling her work a documentary, but in reality it is one of the most significant propaganda films ever made. Financed by the Nazis and produced with the direct approval of both Hitler and Goebbels, *Triumph of the Will* is a precise and accurate representation of the mood, the ambiance and the message the Nazi movement wished to convey to the German people in 1934.

Triumph of the Will represents a radical transformation of history into theater.[1] Riefenstahl went to Nuremberg with 30 cameras and 121 technicians, and the plans for the rally itself were coordinated with plans for the film. When original footage was accidentally spoiled, Julius Streicher, Alfred Rosenberg, Rudolf Hess and Hans Frank were ordered to reconsecrate themselves to Hitler the following week, without an audience. (They replayed their parts with appropriate histrionics.) Significantly, however, the delay did not matter, for the pageant at Nuremberg was conceived to straddle the worlds of fantasy and reality and to conjure up echoes of other collectively ecstatic events in the history of mankind. To watch thousands move and march as one, then pledge their loyalty in a single roaring voice — the voice of the "nation" raised in joyous submission to the triumphant will of the nation's leader — is, even now, to experience other images from the past: a medieval pageant in pomp and riotous color, banners waving in symbolic homage to the glory of God; or a swell of collective rapture as believers pledge themselves to a holy crusade against the infidel. Our movement is "a holy order" cries Hitler to the faithful who listen with rapturous attention. "I believe I am acting in accordance with the will of the Almighty Creator; by defending myself against the Jew I am fighting for the work of the Lord," he had written in *Mein Kampf*, establishing the all-important religious metaphor.

Triumph of the Will presented a central ideal of the Nazi movement: the iron-willed individual whose strength of character, self-control and personal discipline were such that he was able to overcome individualism and offer himself in submission to a greater power. This idea struck a sympathetic chord with a Christian population. Hitler attempted to build a non-Christian, neo-pagan form of religion using the symbols of a remote Teutonic past, but it was his reliance on the familiar forms of Christianity that made the new "faith" so comfortable for so many.

Although it has been fashionable (both inside and outside of Germany) to think of the Nazi movement as a short aberration in the life of an ultracivilized country, nazism was, in reality, a direct product of a century of German cultural history; for although German *Kultur* had come to represent a pinnacle of artistic achievement, particularly in the realm of music, it had also focused on images and ideas that favored the development of Aryan ideology. The intellectual bedrock for such ideas came initially from the writings of the philosopher Johann Gottlieb Fichte (1762–1814), who has subsequently been called both the father of German nationalism and the father of German anti-Semitism. Much of Fichte's thinking was inspired by Germany's bitter defeat during the Napoleonic Wars, after which both Napoleon and France came to represent everything modern and evil. The French ideals of liberty, equality and fraternity that inspired the 1789 French Revolution were anathema and, more serious still, un-German. German thought took another direction altogether; it set its sights on the past, the remote past of mythic heroes and grandeur, and rejected the modern world as envisioned by the Enlightenment.

In defeat, Fichte glorified Germans and Germanness.

Among all modern peoples it is you in whom the seed of human perfection most decidedly lies, and you who are charged with progress in human development. If you perish in this your essential nature, then there perishes together with you every hope of the whole human race for salvation from the depths of its miseries.[2]

As for the Jews within Germany, Fichte had been opposed to their emancipation at least since 1793, when he argued that they were a destructive state within a state and that their ideas were as disreputable as French ideas. (Few things were worse in Germany than being compared to the French.)

Fichte set a tone that was adopted by leaders in several spheres. For example, after Bismarck's victory over France in the Franco-Prussian war of 1870, it was widely believed that the battle had been won because of German *moral* superiority. Superior arms and tactics were simply taken for granted. One contemporary pundit described the event as "a divine judgment . . . inscribed in letters of fire upon the tablets of history."[3]

The renowned philosopher Georg Wilhelm Friedrich Hegel (1770–1831) also had an important impact on German political thinking. At the center of Hegelian thought was an all-embracing mind or spirit that was the same as, and made concrete in, the political state. Individuals had political existence only insofar as they participated in this spirit or belonged to the state. As a direct consequence, the king or emperor, who represented mind, spirit and divinity, included and subsumed the individuality of his subjects.

The philosophical conceits of Friedrich Wilhelm Nietzsche (1844–1900) were different in substance, but not totally dissimilar in their conclusions. Nietzsche was an isolated visionary who eventually went mad, but his iconoclastic, romantic ideas precipitated a veritable cult in late-nineteenth-century Germany that was rivalled only by the cult of the Kaiser himself.

According to Nietzsche, man becomes heroic through the proper use of the will. His theory of a superior class of *Übermenschen*, with its echoes of Plato's Philosopher King and a ruling elite whose role it is to lead mankind along the road to social and moral perfection, struck just the right chord in *fin de siècle* Germany, where antiliberal, antidemocratic, pro-national sentiments had been evolving for decades. Nietzsche considered democracy a barrier to the establishment of his ideal state, calling the attitudes of the masses a "slave morality." Leaders must aspire to live by another ethos altogether, a "master morality" that extended beyond the boundaries of tradition. Unlike the Philosopher King of Plato's *Republic*, who was obliged to adhere to the same laws as ordinary people but with even greater vigilance, Nietzsche's superman was held to be under no such constraints. He lived beyond the so-called good and evil of ordinary men. The superman was duty bound to create his own laws. The moral shackles of history were not for him.

Many Germans (unlike the French) took Nietzsche literally. The idea that the strong had innate rights over the weak was appealing; indeed, it seemed self-evident to many that the supreme *Übermensch* was already in their midst. The energetic Kaiser was clearly the embodiment of the Nietzschean (and Hegelian) ideal. Kaiser Wilhelm II was not one to dispute this flattering notion, and he certainly did nothing to discourage the hero worship that followed in its wake. Indeed, he believed firmly in the divine right of kings. The Kaiser's main interests seemed to be clothes and military parades, in which he loved to strut in full regalia accompanied by stirring martial music. He was fun-loving and given to practical jokes, but he also advocated expansionism and enjoyed saber rattling, which made his neighbors exceedingly nervous.

Kaiser Wilhelm made a special point of supporting the arts. *Kultur*, he believed, ought to contribute to the moral fiber of the nation. The arts must represent the Ideal, which "only the German people" could preserve. Indeed, art that chose to represent the unlovely aspects of life sinned "against the German people," he pronounced.[4]

Major artists reflected such views. The mythological heroes and heroines of Richard Wagner carried within their bodies the seed of the future German race, a race of flaxen-haired Nordic gods and demigods. And the composer Richard Strauss actually proposed himself (indirectly) for the title of Nietzsche's superman when his musical autobiography, *A Hero's Life*, was premiered on March 3, 1893.

Nineteenth-century German nationalism also gave rise to the mystical concept of *Volk*. *Volk* meant more than a people bound together by common ties of language, territory and custom; it conveyed something quite deliberately unspecified, something transcendent that touched upon the inner essence of the group, both collectively and individually. Through membership in the *Volk*, men and women hoped to overcome the sense of separateness and alienation that is inherent in the human condition.

The role of the *Volk* was elaborated as early as 1810: "A state without *Volk* is nothing, a soulless artifice; a *Volk* without a state is nothing, a bodiless airy phantom, like the Gypsies and the Jews. Only state and *Volk* together can form a Reich, and such a Reich cannot be preserved without *Volkdom*," wrote one of the originators of the idea.[5] More than a century later, the centralized, spiritual universe of Hegel in combination with Nietzsche's *Übermenschen* and the ineffable mysteries of *Volk* did indeed produce a particular world-view that Hitler needed only to draw upon and develop.

Jews and Gypsies were excluded from participation in the mystical state of being and, by implication, from the political state as well. As the nineteenth century progressed, Jewishness as an abstract principle became the antagonist of Germanness as an abstract principle, a negative measuring stick of one's right to belong to the German *Volk*.

Until the 1870s, hatred of Jews had expressed itself primarily through myths that had been propagated over the centuries (not least by the lower Christian clergy) and incorporated in a collective consciousness. Jews were accused of poisoning wells, baking the blood of Christian children into Passover *matzohs* and other like abominations. But the nineteenth century ushered in a frightening new world of industrialization that threatened a centuries-old traditional way of life. Peasants left their fields and headed for the cities to work in factories, capital assumed a new importance and the rise of a new bourgeoisie filled the old landed classes with fear.

In 1873, a financial crash rocked Germany, and anti-Semitism (which had been dormant since the 1820s) assumed a new political dimension. Jews were identified with that frightening new arbiter of people's lives, the stock market, and with a presumed domination of unearned capital. In 1875 an article appeared linking Jews and liberals, to the great satisfaction of those who despised both.[6] And the myth of "the Jewish conspiracy" made an appearance on the political scene. The myth originated without a Jewish context in an 1864 French novel purporting to retail a dialogue between Machiavelli and Montesquieu[7] and became a "Jewish story" four years later in a German novel called *Biarritz*.[8] At the end of the century, this latter work was the source for the notorious *Protocols of the Elders of Zion*, which was fabricated in Czarist Russia; and in the 1920s, the *Protocols*, in turn, became a *pièce de résistance* of Hitler's anti-Semitic ideology.[9]

In November 1879, Heinrich von Treitschke, professor of history at the university of Berlin, penned a phrase that would echo widely in the years to come. "The Jews are our national misfortune," he wrote. The following year, a second author suggested that Berlin be renamed the capital of the Jewish Reich;[10] and an "Anti-Semites' Petition" was circulated and addressed to Bismarck.[11]

As one historian with a descriptive flair has put it, anti-Semitism after 1873 soon functioned "like a political magic rabbit."[12] When a candidate pulled it out of his hat, voter support increased. Whole towns were occasionally embroiled in anti-Semitic controversy, as when the citizens of Düsseldorf debated whether to honor their famous son, Heinrich Heine, in spite of his Jewish birth. (They decided not to.) But nineteenth-century anti-Semitism was not yet specifically racial in nature. Jews were described as alien nonparticipants in the *Volk*, as controlling the press and as a subversive element within the Reich; but the focus was on conversion, and Jews who heeded this advice were assured that they might then become good German patriots.

Hitler had a German legacy of more than one hundred years of pro-Aryan, anti-Semitic ideology to draw upon as he stood before an enraptured crowd in the Nuremberg stadium; and, at their core, the ideas he espoused were comfortably familiar to those who paid homage on that day. "Our movement will not die so long as one of us has breath," he cried to the believers. They answered with a terrible, unified roar. But it was Goebbels who touched the nerve center of truth that September afternoon: "In order to last, a movement must reach the hearts of men — their minds, yes, but especially their hearts," he said. It was an accurate psychological insight. And in September 1934, one of those overjoyed hearts beat in the breast of the young Klaus Barbie, a recent graduate from the Friedrich Wilhelms Gymnasium in Trier.

Nikolaus (Klaus) Barbie was born on October 25, 1913, in the little Rhineland town of Bad Godesberg, near Bonn. The Barbie family came from Merzig, in the Saar. In origin, they were probably a French Catholic family called Barbier that had left France as refugees at the time of the Revolution. Ironically, it was precisely this group of refugees, along with the Huguenots and the Jews, who formed a cultural and economic elite in a developing modern Germany and who had helped raise Berlin, for example, into a metropolis of international stature.

In spite of flamboyant patriotism and chauvinism, growing anti-Semitism and a monarch who was inspired with his own divinity, Germany in the year of Klaus Barbie's birth remained a highly civilized country, the proud birthplace of Goethe, Beethoven, Bach, Kant, Zweig and Heine. The arts and the universities flourished. The Jews, though disliked, were fully acculturated and highly assimilated. (Roughly one-third of those born Jews intermarried, and many others had been baptized or were Jews in name only.) Among those who continued to practice their religion, it was a cliché to speak of being "a Jew at home and a German in the street." But the year of 1914 was a watershed. Before young Klaus Barbie was one year old, war erupted, his father went off to battle, and nothing was ever the same again in the household, or, indeed, in the country. The elder Barbie returned an angry, bitter man. He had been wounded in the neck at Verdun and taken prisoner by the French, whom he hated. He never recovered his health. And his son never forgave.

Nikolaus Barbie was a schoolteacher, and young Klaus was a student in his father's school until he was ten years old. The elder Barbie soon began to drink heavily and to abuse his family. His relationship with his son was difficult and brutal, so it was with relief that Klaus went off to Trier in 1923 to continue his education. "Thus an entirely new period began for me," wrote the student in a reflective essay submitted just before his graduation in 1934. "I was finally independent."[13]

Klaus was small and quiet. He was passably intelligent without being brilliant. He was reasonably popular without being considered a leader. He was neither a troublemaker nor a rebel. He was, in other words, not the sort of person one remembered clearly, an unremarkable individual, except for a talent for languages that would come in handy in his later career.

Barbie was not an insensitive boy. While still in school he joined a Catholic charity organization that visited prisoners and distributed food to the hungry. But the inner brutalization that had already begun in the family would destroy this aspect of his personality. Before long his parents moved to Trier, and Barbie was forced to return home.

These were difficult times. "The terrible sufferings I had to endure during the years when I passed from the upper third level to the upper first must forever remain my secret and a warning for my future," he wrote revealingly in his essay. "I can say that these years made me a wise man. These years taught me how bitter life can be, and how terrible destiny."

The "terrible sufferings" Barbie referred to no doubt concerned a tragedy that was occurring within his family. His younger brother, Kurt, died of a chronic illness in June 1933 at the age of eighteen. And his father's sickness was diagnosed as cancer. Nikolaus Barbie also died in 1933, just four months after his younger son. Significantly, perhaps, Klaus attributed his father's death to "the effects of a war wound." In his eyes, it was the French who were responsible. Indeed, years later in Lyons, Barbie cited his father's death as his main reason for hating the French.

Growing up in the Rhineland, Barbie had plenty of other opportunities to assimilate an ancestral hatred for the French. Louis XIV had destroyed many of the churches; Napoleon had annexed the territory; and, according to the terms of the Treaty of Versailles, Trier itself was occupied first by the Americans and then by the French. The locals particularly feared the French, especially the Algerian cavalry army, which was considered particularly brutal. Nineteen twenty-three, the year the young Barbie moved to Trier, was an especially terrible year for skirmishes between occupier and occupied.

By 1923, too, the "stab-in-the-back" theory, according to which Germany's enemies within its borders had caused the defeat of the nation, had gained credence. The Jews were thought to be among the main culprits. The intellectual community also collaborated in this mood of black despair. Few historians examined the "stab-in-the-back" theory; on the contrary, the best known among them set about to disprove charges of war guilt. Since the state was central in the affairs of men and transcended all individual interest, such disproof was of urgent importance for national pride.[14]

Economically, chaos reigned, with inflation raging at a ludicrous rate. In 1923, 1,783 printing presses ran twenty-four hours a day to create the necessary number of banknotes. People were paid twice a day so they could buy what they needed before the next quotation on the dollar. Sickness reigned, tuberculosis spread. In that same year, it was estimated that 24 percent of schoolchildren were undernourished.

But the most serious consequence of World War I was invisible, for human beings had been brutalized in new, far-reaching ways that extended beyond the battlefields. During the war, hatred and killing had been praised as noble virtues. Afterwards, suffering and despair infiltrated the lives of millions on a hitherto unknown scale.

Klaus Barbie's entire youth was thus marked by disturbance, both inside and outside his family; and it was easy to project the origins of this misery on to the French. The Great War was seen as but one more example of Gallic treachery. But 1933, the year the Barbie family finally fell apart, also marked the beginning of the Hitler era. "The events of this year have not left me a moment of rest," wrote Barbie on November 30, just weeks after his father's death.

In 1933, there was, however, consolation available, a place where a bereft young man might drown his troubles. A tidal wave of optimism was washing over the nation. "The powerful national upsurge attracted me, as it did every true young German, and today I can serve all those who follow the Führer," wrote the young man. By April of that year, Klaus Barbie had joined the Hitler Youth movement, and by the time he wrote his essay in November he had already risen to the rank of Youth Leader. He was barely twenty years old.

Barbie became a quick convert to the ideology of the Nazi movement, but he probably joined initially for lack of other alternatives. He graduated from high school, but his marks were mediocre, and he did not receive permission to go on to higher education. Such a move would not have been possible in any case, for Barbie's circumstances had been greatly reduced by his father's death. "I must say that destiny, through the death of my father, has reduced my most cherished hopes to nothing," he wrote. "I wanted to become a philologist, but my present situation forbids this."

As it happened, Klaus Barbie was to put his interest in language and linguistics to other uses, first in France and later in Bolivia. As a young man with limited career options, however, he signed up for the Voluntary Work Service — a public job-creation project that had come under the control of the Nazis — and set out for the town of Niebüll on the North Sea coast where he stayed from April until the last day of October 1934. Following this tour of duty, Barbie returned to Trier to rejoin the Hitler Youth.

By 1934, the Hitler Youth had assumed an important role in the country. Schoolchildren were the obvious focus of a regime that was counting on a one-thousand-year reign. The essence of the teaching program was a consciousness of race, blood and soil, and to this end children were given assignments asking them to observe Jews and describe their "mannerisms," among other things. They learned that the future of humanity depended on them as Aryans, and that only Aryans might be regarded as fully human. As pure Aryans, the children were also taught that part of their future duty was to perpetuate the race for the Reich. (Some couldn't contain their patriotism, and forests and fields sheltered writhing young bodies zealously getting a head start on their duties.)

Earlier values of intellectual independence and self-sufficiency were radically revised, for the child who matured in the "new order" needed to embody obedience and submission to the state. An article on the Hitler Youth published in Germany in the 1930s explained this in the clearest of terms. "The youngster who enters the movement of Adolf Hitler soon learns to subordinate his own petty will to the laws which have built states and made whole nations happy, but the violation of which results in the loss of freedom and the collapse of the *Volk*," wrote the author. "As he grows older, he learns that discipline and subordination are not arbitrary inventions called into play by a few power-hungry men . . . but, rather, the premises for his own and his people's existence."[15]

Because men needed to be physically strong to fight the battle against the enemy, the muscular male body was idealized, and physical training occupied a large part of the school day and weekends as well. So much so that, in 1934, the director of a Stuttgart high school complained to the minister of education that the Hitler Youth had created a 33 percent loss of competency in Latin, Greek, modern languages and mathematics among his students.[16]

Hatred, defiance and passion were the "genuine" qualities of the *Volk*, according to Alfred Baeumler, professor of philosophy at the University of Berlin and one of the leading theoreticians of the Third Reich. These were the Nordic, soldierly virtues that needed to be inculcated into the young. Adolescents were scolded by their elders, who warned that the German people had forgotten how to hate and that "virile strength" had been replaced by "female lamentations." "He who is unable to hate cannot love, either," chided SA leader Ernst Röhm in 1928. "Fanatical love and hate—their fires kindle flames of freedom . . ." he added.[17]

By 1934, the Nazi party virtually controlled admissions to the universities. A proportion of the faculty embraced Hitlerism with enthusiasm, having found the new ideology little more than an offshoot of intellectual trends that had been widely accepted for more than a century. (Those who could not support the regime quit or were fired.) To the intellectuals who followed him, Hitler looked like the latest in a line of leaders incarnating the state and all its subjects, as Hegel had determined. Nietzsche, too, offered a familiar and comfortable set of beliefs to the intellectual world, and some of its members (in particular Professor Baeumler) set about tailoring the great philosopher to the exigencies of National Socialism. Baeumler stressed Nietzsche's emphasis on the will and on the rule of an elite community of

Übermenschen, while conveniently ignoring the philosopher's hatred of nationalism.

For more than a hundred years, the intellectual community had created a framework of academic respectability for the political infrastructure of a German society that stressed militarism and exaggerated patriotism, so that part of the Nazi program surprised no one. Hitler's virulent anti-Semitism bothered more than a few, but, like many other reasonably minded citizens, they thought it was an exaggeration the Führer would get over. Like the population at large, the intellectuals of the Third Reich needed to feel proud of their country once again. They wanted to be rescued from the alienation brought about by defeat and the social chaos that had followed in its wake.

During his inaugural address as rector of the University of Freiburg in 1933, the renowned philosopher Martin Heidegger praised Hitler as a leader chosen by destiny to incarnate the essence of the German soul. (Heidegger was subsequently trotted out by the Nazis for ceremonial occasions.) Many of the major historians also complied readily, as did numbers of social scientists. (Indeed, in the summer of 1984, a heated debate raged in Germany as a result of excerpts from a forthcoming book that charged that psychiatrists had collaborated with the Hitler regime — doing very well financially during lean times — and that many of these people had become leaders in their profession in the postwar years. According to the author, psychotherapy adopted the official Nazi ideology, holding that Aryans who had neurotic conflicts, "given the proper guidance of an innate German will," could correct mental distress.[18])

With the advent of Hitler, intellectual activity of the sort that had made Germany famous withered away. Up to 50 percent of university lecturers, deans and researchers were fired as Jews or "white Jews" (people who sympathized with their victimized colleagues, were married to Jews or opposed the regime). Hitler himself described nuclear physics as "Jewish physics," and Einstein's theory of relativity as "Jewish bluff." Inevitably, less competent people filled their places. The new rector of the University of Berlin (a veterinarian by profession and a storm trooper) initiated twenty-five courses in racial science and eighty-six courses in veterinary science.

This was the climate in which the young Klaus Barbie was raised and the atmosphere he experienced after his return to Trier in November 1934. Shortly thereafter, Barbie began to cooperate closely with

Karl Horrmann, the head of the regional section of the Nazi party, as secretary to the chief of the Trier section. Within weeks, Horrmann broached the subject of Nazi police work. The hardness that would later chill many of Barbie's victims to the core was already apparent to the older, more experienced man, and he considered young Klaus a good prospect for either the Gestapo or the security forces of the Sicherheitsdienst (SD).

Barbie was thrilled at the prospect and applied immediately, but he was left to cool his heels for more than six months before Reinhard Heydrich, then chief of the SD, interviewed him in Berlin. Heydrich was also favorably impressed, and on September 25, 1935, Klaus Barbie became SS No. 272,284 and took up his assignment as an assistant in the central office of the SD, the IV-D. He pledged his loyalty to Hitler, in a special ceremony, with the following oath:

I swear to you, Adolf Hitler
As Führer and Chancellor of the German Reich
Loyalty and valor.
I pledge to you
And to the superiors whom you will appoint
Obedience unto death
So help me God.

Suspecting he had innate talents that might be developed, Barbie's superiors dispatched him to police headquarters in Berlin's Alexanderplatz for training as an interrogator. This was basic education Barbie would put to good use, over the next half century, in the service of several governments. But his initial sense of his future came from an assignment to the police vice squad in Berlin in 1936. This job involved arresting Jews, homosexuals and prostitutes and gave him his first opportunity to physically attack the "enemy."

Barbie rose quickly in the esteem of his superiors, and on May 1, 1937, he was welcomed into the Nazi party as a full-fledged member. Also in 1937, Barbie underwent training at the SD school in Bernau and took the elite leadership course in Berlin. In October, he was transferred to the administrative staff of the SD. His career, as an SS officer seemed assured.

The SS (Schutzstaffel, or Blackshirts) had been formed in 1925 by Hitler's order as a select and totally dependable collective bodyguard for the Nazi elite; but until Heinrich Himmler took over in 1929, the unit, with 280 members, was visibly weaker than the 60,000-strong SA (Sturmabteilung—storm troopers—or Brownshirts) organization, which was also attached to the Nazi party. Under Himmler, the SS was transformed into a tightly disciplined body that was instantly responsiv: to the will of the Führer and became characterized by the same racial obsessions that gripped Hitler himself. Recruits were carefully screened to ensure they came from appropriately pure Aryan stock, as were their prospective wives. Training inculcated a racial mystique. The same ancient Teutonic symbolism that had once inspired Richard Wagner's operatic genius now informed the value structure of a powerful police organization.

Before the end of 1930, Himmler had built the SS into an elite army of 3,000 dedicated soldiers, and before the war came to an end, the SS would number over a million men. Their responsibilities divided into three branches: the concentration camps; the police; and a party army that included recruits from outside Germany.

Hardness of body and mind was an SS ideal. The latter often had to be taught, just as hatred had to be taught to schoolchildren. One SS official at Auschwitz hung a sign over his desk that read, "Sympathy is Weakness,"[19] perhaps to convince himself and anyone else who was having trouble adjusting to his or her gruesome daily chores. Another former SS officer recounted how terribly upset he was the first time he saw a beating. He said he went "hot and cold all over," but added that by the time he witnessed his first execution some years later, he was much less bothered by the whole business. That man was Rudolf Hoess, later commandant in chief at Auschwitz.[20]

Klaus Barbie's father and his younger brother had recently died, his mother had no money, and he himself had no prospects. The bitterness in the population found a direct parallel in his own life, for in the mind of this young man, the war, the French and ultimately the Jews (who were seen to be responsible for all woes) had caused his family's ruin and his father's death. From the ashes of his despair rose the Nazi party, phoenix-like, promising a career in which the meek became strong and the disadvantaged might overcome their handicaps. And crowning the new pyramid of power was the SS, where a seemingly mystical inversion of traditional values had occurred. In the SS, violence was beautiful. Fifty years after the cult of Nietzsche had appeared upon the stage of modern Germany, the SS was the ultimate incarnation of the superman theory (which allowed elite individuals to live according to their own moral lights) and the right hand of Hitler himself. Fifty years earlier Richard Wagner had transformed Teutonic mythology in high art. The ss, with its related rites and symbolism, and Leni Riefenstahl's beautifully staged "documentary," *Triumph of the Will*, were fruit from the same vine.

Although there were undoubtedly members of the ss who found it difficult to adjust to the glorification of violence, Klaus Barbie was not one of them. Physical brutality was not new to him: his father's rages had merely reflected the national rage he perceived all around him in his defeated country. Securely ensconced in the ss, he perceived his years of suffering to have come to an end. In the ss his deeply ingrained hatreds were sanctified. The past crumbled away. Young Barbie had found a comfortable home at last.

Was it any wonder that forty years later he continued to describe himself as an "idealist" and to extol with pride the virtues of his Nazi youth? "Do you really know what an ss soldier is? He is a Superman . . ."[21]

In April 1939, Barbie became engaged to Regina Margareta Maria Willms, the twenty-three-year-old daughter of a postal clerk. Regina had not finished high school, but she had taken a six-month course in cooking and had worked as a maid in Berlin. In 1937 she moved to Düsseldorf where she cared for children in a daycare center run by the Nazi Women's Organization. She was also a member of the Nazi party.

In order to marry, Klaus and Regina had to present evidence of their racial purity. Regina submitted character references as well, and both passed medical examinations, replied to questions about family medical history and supplied pictures of themselves in bathing suits so they could be scrutinized for possible racial defects.

The wedding took place on April 25, 1940, in Berlin, and was witnessed by Emil Goebel and Paul Neukirchen, two of Barbie's ss associates.[22] Since it was spring, the special ss ceremony probably took place under a lime tree (winter ceremonies took place in an ss building). The symbolism of Nazi weddings was Teutonic. Traditional wedding flowers were replaced by sunflowers and fir twigs representing the natural world. The couple exchanged rings and received a gift of bread and salt representing the fruitfulness and purity of the earth. An eternal flame burned in an urn before them.

The Barbies had both been raised as Catholics, but they accepted the new religion of the ss and signed themselves, accordingly, as "believers in God." This willingness to abandon Catholicism was another indication of Barbie's intense faith in the new ideology. Only one out of three ss men renounced their Christianity.

To add to the young couple's happiness, Barbie was promoted to ss-Untersturmführer (Second Lieutenant) on April 20, just five days before his marriage.

The honeymoon did not last long. On May 10, 1940, the German army began to roll through western Europe. On May 25, after a brief service with the troops in France, Barbie was assigned to duty in Holland, to the sD-Security Police Bureau for Jewish Affairs in The Hague. Barbie impressed his superiors there with his dedication to his job. In October 1940, a report sent back to Germany described him as "especially hardworking and responsible," and a "lover of life, and truth and a good comrade."[23] In November 1940, he was promoted to Obersturmführer (First Lieutenant), then transferred to the Zentralstelle für Jüdische Auswanderung, the Central Office for Jewish Emigration in Amsterdam. Germany was on the march, and the defeated peoples of Europe would soon come to experience the "ideals" of the ss at very close hand.

On the eve of the German invasion there were 140,000 Jews living in Holland, including 30,000 refugees from Germany. Nearly 60 percent lived in Amsterdam. Dutch Jews were acculturated, and intermarriage rates were high. They enjoyed complete civic equality, and many of their institutions received government support. They were also a highly educated community, and many of them played important roles in the political and social life of Holland.

Almost immediately, the occupiers began to impose restrictions on this community. By October 1940, the Reichskommissar, Seyss-Inquart, had come up with a definition of the term "Jew" that followed the principles laid out at Nuremberg in 1935. Jewish businesses were obliged to register, then liquidated or "Aryanized." In January 1941, individuals themselves were obliged to register, with a threat of five years in jail for failing to do so. Other anti-Jewish decrees followed along familiar lines, with dismissals from jobs and a prohibition on professional practice.

Physical violence broke out on February 12, 1941, when military formations of the Dutch Nazi party mounted an attack on Jewish homes and businesses "in extension of training exercises."[24] To their surprise, they met with resistance from Jews and non-Jews alike, and one of the attackers was killed, trampled beyond recognition. In retaliation, Hans Rauter, the high command of the ss in Holland, killed six of the defenders, evacuated non-Jewish inhabitants and ordered the old Jewish section sealed off. Canals leading into the quarter were closed, with the exception of one that could be closely monitored. The fighting went on for weeks, and when calm was finally restored, the Jews of the old quarter of Amsterdam found themselves living in a permanently sealed ghetto.

During these disturbances, the German command ordered the formation of the Joodse Raad, the Jewish Council, with two men in charge: Abraham Ascher, a merchant, and David Cohen, a professor. The council called upon the Jews of the old quarter to surrender their weapons. And with this act, the Jews of the new ghetto became truly defenseless.

Klaus Barbie was directly involved in this action, but his outstanding contribution to the period of unrest occurred on February 19 in the more affluent south end of the city. Two young German-Jewish refugees had opened an ice-cream shop and had dared to beat off bully attacks from Dutch Nazis with a few makeshift weapons. Barbie arrived on the scene and with typical ruthlessness far exceeded his orders, which were to arrest but not harm the owners. Instead, he smashed an ashtray over one of the partners' heads. The men were sentenced to death (Barbie was in charge of the firing squad). In acknowledgment of his zeal, Barbie's superiors rewarded him with the Iron Cross, second class.

A few days later the ss seized more than 400 Jewish men aged twenty to thirty-five and deported them summarily to Mauthausen. The raid sent shock waves through the Dutch population, which responded courageously with a general strike that paralyzed the country. But the German crackdown was swift and relentless. Martial law was imposed, order was restored and no further overt resistance ever disturbed the occupation of Holland. None of the young men sent to Mauthausen ever returned.

On June 11, 1941, Barbie knocked on the door of the Jewish Council office. He introduced himself to David Cohen and Abraham Ascher, then politely asked after the whereabouts of 300 young Zionists who had been removed from a colony in the countryside and placed in Amsterdam homes under the auspices of the council. Barbie explained that the German command had decided to allow the boys to return to their farm.

Since there had been an official request to the command regarding this very issue, the council leaders complied. Barbie thanked them politely, then left. Two days later, the Germans conducted a raid using the council lists and arrested more than 230 men. All were deported; none returned.[25]

On June 30, 1941, less than three weeks after Barbie had dispatched these youngsters to a concentration camp, Regina Barbie gave birth to a daughter in Trier. They called her Ute Regina.

Barbie received instructions to report to Germany for training in counterinsurgency techniques. Resistance groups had sprung up in all of the occupied areas. In June 1942, Barbie was sent to settle an "emergency" in the area of Gex, a tiny town on the French-Swiss border in the German-occupied zone. His job was to capture three spies. Barbie devised an intriguing, rather comical scheme to make his arrests by actually living in a house that stood on the border and had doors into either country; but his quarry escaped, and Barbie returned empty-handed.

Meanwhile, the war was starting to go badly for Germany. On October 23, 1942, the British Eighth Army attacked General Rommel's lines at El Alamein. On November 8, British and U.S. troops landed at Oran, Algiers and Casablanca. In the third week of November, the Russians initiated a devastating offensive around the city of Stalingrad and eventually encircled the German troops.

On November 11, 1942, in the midst of these events, Germany swept away the so-called independent Vichy regime and occupied the whole of France. In any case, Barbie wasn't one to worry. "We are happy to know that the future belongs to us completely," Adolf Hitler had shouted triumphantly to an audience of thousands at the Nuremberg Rally of September 1934. Barbie was a believer then, and time had not altered his passion. He had risen in the ss hierarchy and been awarded an Iron Cross. Although the outcome of the war looked less sure, new opportunities beckoned.

He received a plum assignment: head of the Gestapo of Lyons, the capital of the French Resistance. Barbie crossed the border with the highest of personal expectations. He would not be disappointed. In France he would discover a nation with a most intriguing past of its own.

· 3 ·

THE TWO FACES OF FRANCE

Although German intellectuals traditionally thought of the French, with their bloody Revolution and their absurd insistence on republican forms, as both frivolous and dangerously radical, such generalizations were not precisely borne out by facts.[1] For although the French Revolution had effectively opened the door to a new era in modern history, there remained a large, articulate and influential population in France that felt as appalled at the course of events in their own country as any German nationalist watching in horror from the other side of the Rhine. The French Revolution was a serpent that swallowed an elephant; and somehow, digestion never properly took place. The population proclaimed a republic, but it could not transform all of its citizens into republicans, and for the next two hundred years periodic hiccups convulsed the nation, setting citizen against citizen along the lines of a deeply ingrained political schism. An emotional longing for the Ancien Régime and for the traditional values it had incorporated during a thousand years of history surged and swelled in the serpent's throat. In 1983, the arrest of Klaus Barbie threatened to precipitate a new attack of national indigestion.

From 1789 until 1940, when the German army swept into France to begin a courteous *pas de deux* with officials of the Vichy regime, two streams of moral and political commitment struggled for supremacy in the republic. Twice, the monarchists triumphed; but, in the main, liberal France prevailed. At its root, the conflict between the "conservatives" and the "liberals" was always the same. During the 1790s, France became the first country in Europe to grant full civil rights to its Jewish population; but exactly one hundred years later the pendulum threatened to swing violently in the opposite direction. The Dreyfus affair, a cataclysmic event that divided France, provided new momentum for the rise of modern anti-Semitism. However, at the same time as the Dreyfus affair rocked the country and, indeed, the world, France also became a haven for refugees fleeing the pogroms of Czarist Russia. (In a mellow essay entitled "My Paris," Saul Bellow recalled that for thousands of east-European Jews, perfect happiness was summed up by the phrase, "*Wie Gott in Frankreich.*") And an open-door policy approved by a majority of French citizens remained in effect throughout most of the Third Republic (which emerged in 1871) in spite of mounting xenophobic pressures. Indeed, the Third Republic, with all its contradictions, saw France assume the title of the world's most sophisticated nation in its sponsorship of the arts, its prosperity and the rise of Paris as a cosmopolitan capital without equal anywhere in the world.

In Germany, nineteenth-century opinion-makers fought the tide of modernity with all their force; and, when they could not succeed, they blamed the Jews for the changes that many so greatly feared. In late-nineteenth-century France, the appearance of new capital and industry caused a similar social disorder. Throughout Europe, the old agrarian order was dissolving. The new power of money derived from industry and from stocks and other financial operations, replacing the old forms of income from land and rents. The rise of the cities and a growing political awareness among the industrialized working classes brought frightening new forms of anarchism and socialism in their wake. The late nineteenth century was a truly revolutionary time, and the propertied classes were justifiably terrified. So was the Catholic church, which was traditionally tied to the landed nobility. Like the noble estate, the Catholic church proclaimed the enduring values of a simpler world that had been swept away with the Ancien Régime, a world in which the ideal virtues of authority, dogma and order held sway. Both the nobility and the clergy refused the new "reign of money," as they called it, which they associated with Jews, financiers, parliaments, Freemasons, industrialization, urbanization, democracy and, of course, the republic.

After the economic depression of the early 1890s, a new group of nervous converts joined the ranks of the political Right: they were the newly unemployed, peasants forced off their land, small business people forced into bankruptcy and whole populations who lived in those areas of the provinces that were traditionally anti-republican and that were served primarily by a Catholic press that was deeply xenophobic and anti-Semitic.

As in Germany, anti-Semitism was the stock answer to *fin-de-siècle* woes, but in a new and different form. Medieval well-poisoning accusations gave way to modern charges of subverting the economy and destroying old values, and for the threatened classes the jump to a further claim that the Jews were ruining France was as easy as a phrase. But a crucial difference emerged in this new anti-Semitism as it evolved in France and in Germany. French anti-Semitism was cultural and nationalistic as opposed to "racial," although one of the first exponents of the racial theory was, in fact, a Frenchman. Joseph Gobineau's *Essay on Racial Inequality*, written in 1853, had less influence in France than in Germany, where his ideas coexisted comfortably with the indigenous philosophies of Fichte, Hegel and Nietzsche.

While resentments smoldered and anti-Semitism gained ground as a fashionable focus for a frightening new era, and while anarchist bombs terrorized the aristocracy and fevered socialists seethed with revolutionary ardor, the Dreyfus affair broke upon France. For more than a decade — from 1895, when Alfred Dreyfus's ribbons and medals were torn off his uniform in a ceremony called the "Parade of Judas," until 1906, when the same man was awarded the Cross of the Legion of Honor in the same courtyard of the Ecole Militaire where he had been dishonored — France was torn asunder in a devastating national crisis.

In brief, the Dreyfus affair concerned an unremarkable Jewish army officer from an old Alsatian family who, as a result of a series of byzantine happenings involving forged documents, wastepaper baskets and a cleaning lady, was unjustly convicted of treasonous conduct beneficial to Germany. The ensuing conflict, which eventually threatened the stability of the nation, pitted those who wanted to reopen the case for the sake of justice against those who, for the sake of *la patrie*, fought a reopening of the case. As a Jew and an Alsatian, Dreyfus fitted the bill as a likely traitor. (Dreyfus's family had opted for France after the humiliating French loss of Alsace in the Franco-Prussian war of 1870; but the fact that Alsatians spoke German and may still have had family and possessions in what was now Germany made them suspect in the eyes of their fellow countrymen.) The fact that Dreyfus by all accounts lacked charm further established a presumption of guilt.

When it became apparent that neither motive for nor proof of treason was forthcoming, the army officers conducting the inquiry fabricated the necessary documents, thus beginning a process in which the army, supported by the government, found itself entrapped in an ever-widening web of lies. In what became a media circus, with newspapers publishing attacks and counterattacks based on daily rumors of fabulous dimension, Dreyfus the man soon became almost irrelevant —except of course, that it was he who was suffering, he who was imprisoned on a solitary island and his life that hung in the balance. Dreyfus the Jew became a focus for the raging discontents of the age, for a renewal of the bitter schism that had rocked France a century earlier, for an attempted redefinition of the nation itself and for an articulation, on both sides, of what it was to be French at the end of the nineteenth century. Right-wing elements composed of an unhappy aristocracy, anti-Semites, nationalists, monarchists, the army, the church and the millions of sympathizers these sectors attracted perceived themselves as France incarnate. To demand a judicial review (known as "*Révision*"), thereby suggesting that the army might have been (at the very least) mistaken was to attack the very soul of the nation. In the minds of this population, only the army could restore honor to the defeated *patrie*. France was the army and the army was France. To be in favor of *Révision* was thus to betray the nation itself; to play into the hands of Germany, the enemy; to be a traitor, *just like Dreyfus*.

At the heart of the issue was the fact that, for his military judges, Dreyfus's guilt or innocence was simply not paramount. Of far greater importance was the fate of the nation, which transcended the fortunes of a mere individual. "I am convinced that Dreyfus is innocent," said a French officer, "but if I had to judge him I would condemn him once again, for the honor of the Army."[2] As Jean-Denis Bredin pointed out in his thoughtful book, *L'Affaire*, Dreyfus was "guilty" in three connected ways. First, he was guilty because the evidence pointed to his guilt. Second, he was guilty because, once he had been designated as such, the honor of the army and the interests of France demanded that he remain condemned. Third, he was guilty of becoming an instrument for what his opponents sincerely believed were "the forces of evil."

In 1845, Benjamin Disraeli described Britain as a country of "two nations" in an accurate reference to the British class system. Half a century later, French historian Ernest Lavisse spoke of "*les deux France*," of two distinct value systems separating those who prized order above justice and the nation-state above its members from those whose priorities were the reverse. In nineteenth-century and pre-Hitler Germany, the first value system prevailed easily, of course; but in France the ongoing ideological schism provided fertile soil for the transformation of the Dreyfus case into the Dreyfus affair. "The Dreyfus affair is a devastatingly faithful mirror reflecting our eternal characteristics, the best and the worst," wrote François Mauriac in 1962. "The affair is merely the most significant episode of a civil war that continues to this day."[3]

Of the dozens of courageous people who committed themselves to the cause of justice during the last turbulent years of the nineteenth century, none was more daring than the writer Emile Zola. Zola's outrage and his passion for truth led him to publish an extraordinary attack, entitled *J'accuse*, in which he named two ministers of war and two chiefs of the army general staff as "accomplices in one of the greatest iniquities of the century" and accused them of suppressing proof of the innocence of Alfred Dreyfus. He further charged that the army courts-martial had been illegal, and accused the army of directing the press to mislead the public.

Zola was charged with libel and publicly reviled. Excrement was mailed to his home; he was burnt in effigy; and, in keeping with the xenophobic mood of the times, he was referred to as a "foreigner" because his father had been Italian.

His trial lasted sixteen days. When the necessary verdict of guilty was announced, the mob surged about the doors and windows of the courthouse slavering with joy. Riots broke out all over the country. But the Dreyfusards, as the pro-revisionists came to be called, organized their forces to form the League for the Rights of Man (one of the originators was Marcel Proust, whose father refused to speak to him for a week) and circulated a petition for *Révision*. The first to sign was Anatole France, followed by others who were united by their disgust at the spectacle of irrationality that was consuming the nation.

From the ranks of the Dreyfusards emerged a man who would assume a crucial role in the subsequent history of France. Georges Clemenceau was known as "*l'homme sinistre*" by his opponents. He did not suffer fools gladly, and his tongue and pen were as sharp as his dueling sword. Both anti-German and anti-clerical (he accused the Jesuits of controlling the army and of being at the root of the Dreyfus affair), he had his own vision of what constituted patriotism. "There can be no patriotism without justice," he wrote. "As soon as the right of one individual is violated, the right of everyone is jeopardized . . . The true patriots are we who fight to obtain justice and to liberate France from the yoke of gold-braided infallibility."[4]

In the end, liberal France triumphed (although in part because the government feared an international boycott of the Paris Exposition of 1900); and in 1899, after he had been imprisoned for more than four years, Alfred Dreyfus was retried in the city of Rennes. At 7:00 A.M. on the morning of August 7, all eyes turned to the courtroom door to see a spectral-looking creature enter the hall. This was the man whose life had been caught in an eddy of history and whirled away in a tornado's embrace. Even his enemies were moved by pity. "One was overcome by a flood of pain that [seemed to] enter the courtroom," wrote Maurice Barrès, one of the most prestigious writers in the nationalist camp. "This poor human reject [standing] there in broad daylight, a ball of living flesh, torn between two camps, who had not had a moment's rest for six years . . ."[5]

The new verdict was a compromise that satisfied no one. Dreyfus was found "guilty" again, but with "extenuating circumstances." He had already served a sentence, so there would be no question of further incarceration.

Neither side was pleased; treason, after all, does not admit "extenuating circumstances." Dreyfus was offered a pardon, which he accepted because he simply could not bear any more, and all legal actions on both sides came to an end. Dreyfus was reinstated, promoted to the rank of major and decorated with the Legion of Honor.

Although it is certain that the outcome of the Dreyfus affair signalled the defeat of the Ancien Régime as a viable possibility and the strengthening of republicanism in France, it is also true that it led in a direct line to the semi-fascist government of Marshal Pétain at Vichy half a century later and to the threat of a "Klaus Barbie affair" almost another half century after that. For during the course of the Dreyfus affair, ideological positions were articulated with a previously unknown clarity. The essential humanism of modern France was pronounced and even institutionalized in the League for the Rights of Man, which was a milestone in the evolution of civil liberties everywhere; but xenophobic nationalism as a coherent political philosophy also made its appearance during the controversy, and in 1940 some of the same men whose careers had blossomed as anti-Dreyfusards assumed major roles in the government of Vichy France. Thousands more who shared the familiar ideology collaborated willingly, then shrewdly changed their stripes as General de Gaulle reentered France at the Liberation. Many years later, these were the men and women Klaus Barbie threatened to recognize with a wink and a recital, if and when France dared to bring him to trial.

As for the Dreyfus affair itself, the murky conclusion at Rennes ensured that it would never end. "Dreyfus" remains a loaded word and a symbol for both of "*les deux France*." Books continue to appear examining the case and its significance. Some are written by modern anti-Dreyfusards, although the subject at hand is, of course, no longer revision. Contemporary anti-Dreyfusard literature generally attempts to rehabilitate the officers who falsely inculpated Dreyfus by describing them as loyal patriots who erred on the side of devotion. One writer has shifted the accusation of treason to other men, now long dead. And the rampant anti-Semitism of the Dreyfus era is still evident in these writings. In 1950, Henri Giscard d'Estaing wrote that Dreyfus was lucky to be a Jew and thus to benefit from "Jewish financing." Giscard d'Estaing wasn't entirely sure that Dreyfus was innocent, and proposed the novel hypothesis that the man might have been a double agent in the service of both France and Russia. The author excoriated the anti-Semitic press of the Dreyfus era, but only because its excesses provoked a rallying of the pro-Dreyfusard camp and an eventual reopening of the case; and he concluded by reiterating views that had been at the heart of nationalist ideology half a century earlier. The Dreyfus affair deteriorated, he wrote, because people who were "legitimately exasperated by the . . . intrusion of France's enemies, which had been brought about under the aegis of a false humanitarianism," were driven to a regrettable excess. But, he continued, it was "Jewish intellectuals" and "Jewish money" that truly exploited the affair. Without the Jews, the Dreyfus case would have "stayed in the family," among the French, among Christians.[6]

Dreyfus never fails to fascinate the French precisely because the case continues to speak to them of themselves. As one writer put it, the modern anti-Dreyfusard militants reveal "the existence of a long cycle that has not yet come to an end."[7]

The thread that connected the Dreyfus affair with the regime of Marshal Philippe Pétain in the middle of the next century came principally from two prescient men who were able to exploit the hysteria of the Dreyfus era to shape the events of their time. Edouard Drumont belonged to that category of individuals whom history occasionally catapults into place at precisely the right moment. Born in Paris in 1844, he was a sophisticated and cultured man who became aware, perhaps earlier than most, of the social and economic threat contained in the incipient breakdown of the old order.

In 1886, Drumont published his seminal, two-volume work, *La France juive*. In it he described the Ancien Régime in idyllic terms. These were the halcyon days before the Revolution, before France was ruined by an invasion of Jews.

La France juive, which was essentially a polemical attack on modern civilization, was enormously successful. Like his counterparts in Germany, Drumont was quick to realize that anti-Semitism had a potential for mass appeal that could transcend class barriers, and he shrewdly united the anti-capitalism of the Left with the fears of the Right while including a whole population of lower-middle-class shopkeepers and artisans who were happy to blame their woes on a Jewish conspiracy. Drumont also succeeded in getting himself elected to parliament, from Algiers, on an anti-Semitic ticket.

In 1892, with his royalties from *La France juive*, Drumont founded *La Libre Parole*, a paper that inaugurated a new form of no-holds-barred journalism. Its message was crude anti-Semitism, and its target was Alfred Dreyfus.

Like the other anti-Dreyfusard papers (they were a majority) the issue at hand was neither guilt nor innocence, but the survival, perhaps better described as the revival, of the old order. Even the presumed act of treason itself was seen to devolve from a collective source. Dreyfus, according to *La Libre Parole*, shared the desire of his race for the ruin of France. Jews were identified with Germany and accused of having betrayed the nation in 1870, much in the way they were later accused, in post-1918 Germany, of betraying the German nation from within.

Mob behavior was not new to society, and certainly, given the events of the Revolution, not to French society; but as Hannah Arendt has pointed out, Drumont was one of the first to shape attitudes by means of the press. *La Libre Parole* mobilized a wide cross-section of rowdies, as well as the sincerely discontented, and incited them to riot. The cry "Death to the Jews" swept France.

From our perspective, one of Drumont's most interesting acts was his subscription campaign for the widow of Colonel Henry, who had committed suicide in prison after his role as the fabricator of the forgery was discovered. The diverse names and occupations of the subscribers offer us a fascinating window into rightist France of the Dreyfus era. Within a month, 15,000 individuals had contributed 130,000 francs. They included counts and duchesses, teachers, Catholic clerics, army officers of high and low degree, simple working people and civil servants. Their comments, too, have been preserved. Hatred was the main staple, for Jews and foreigners in general, but also for the Dreyfusards. Someone spoke of France's ancient "500-year-old hate for England," and there was a contribution with distinctly modern North American overtones from an individual who wanted "God in the schools."[8]

But the appeal of virulent anti-Semitism diminished after the Dreyfus pardon, which was followed by the "Sacred Union" of the World War I effort. *La Libre Parole* eventually disappeared from the scene after having been unsuccessfully offered for sale in 1907. Drumont himself had lost his parliamentary seat as early as 1902, and in 1906 Georges Clemenceau became prime minister of France, an important victory for republicanism.

The second principal traveller on the road that led to Vichy was Charles Maurras. Drumont died in 1917, but Maurras lived from 1868 until 1952 and was influential until public disgrace ended his career in 1945.

Charles Maurras was born into a royalist family that had been loyal to Napoleon III. At that time, the Catholic church was taking action to preserve its authority in the face of increasing social ferment. Just four years before Maurras's birth, the papal *Syllabus of Errors* had been published in an attempt to counteract growing liberal trends both inside and outside the Catholic church. The *Syllabus* was all-inclusive in its attack. It stated that the Catholic church was a complete society that was superior to and independent of all temporal governments, and it claimed the exclusive right to educate and to use force if it had to. All liberal freedoms were denounced: freedom of the press, freedom of speech and freedom of worship for non-Catholics. Other "errors" described included the false belief that the church ought to reconcile its teachings with progress and modern civilization.

Maurras was not a believer; in fact, his agnosticism was to cause Pope Pius XI to condemn his movement, Action Française, in 1926 (though it was reinstated in 1939 by Pope Pius XII). However, Maurras did support the authority of the church as established in the *Syllabus of Errors*.

Action Française was created in 1899, at the height of the Dreyfus affair, as the voice of integrist nationalism; and for more than forty years thereafter, Charles Maurras remained an inspiration to the Right. For Maurras and his followers, who included some of the brightest minds in France, the Third Republic incarnated everything that was decadent and most worthy of contempt. Theirs was a peculiarly French form of fascist thinking. Maurras was no mass murderer, to be sure, but rather an aesthete, a snob, a worshipper of the ancient world, a masculinist (he was reportedly brutal in his relationships with women) and an elitist in every sense of the word. He admired Plato and dreamed of installing a monarch in France who would enforce the rule of the elite. His membership in the Académie Française was a measure of the respect in which he was held.

Maurras's anti-Semitism was an integral part of this world view: "State anti-Semitism" he called it, in defense of national interests. State anti-Semitism was precisely what came to be under the rule of Vichy. Nothing universally revolting like the Nazi gas chambers, just an ordering of priorities in the perceived interests of a non-pluralistic society. For pluralism never has been a French idea. Even the liberal tradition has historically promoted assimilation to an indistinguishable common denominator that, for lack of a better term, might be called simply "Frenchness."

Like Drumont, Maurras demonstrated a remarkable ability to interest ordinary people in his ideas. After 1908, Action Française included a militant wing of young toughs known as the Camelots du roi, and well into the 1930s this loose confederation engaged in pitched street fights with its enemies, mostly young Jews, in an ongoing battle that the Camelots described as a "holy war."

"Those of us who were the children of Jews who had come to France to escape anti-Semitism were terribly upset by the success of nazism in Germany and the spur it gave to the fascists in France," recalled Henry Bulawko, a journalist who was deported to Auschwitz in 1943 and survived. "I was only fifteen years old in 1933, but I was already active in politics. Everyone was politicized in the thirties. There were constant fights with the Camelots on the rue des Rosiers and the boulevard Saint-Michel."

During the 1920s, Maurras's style of anti-Semitic nationalism fell temporarily out of fashion, and during the 1930s he was imprisoned for "incitement to murder" following his attacks on the Jewish premier, Léon Blum. But his time would come again. After the fall of France in June 1940, Maurras fled to the unoccupied zone, where he had "the honor and pleasure" of meeting a female astrologer who interpreted current events for him and recommended that he collaborate with the Nazis.[9] Although Maurras's nationalism had made him viscerally anti-German, the astrologer made him understand the importance of his collaboration for the future of France. A new world was in the making, a world that would effectively incorporate much of what he had dedicated his life to bringing about.

Charles Maurras immediately offered himself to Marshal Philippe Pétain, but the failure of the Vichy regime and the end of the war signaled the end of his personal career. In 1945 when republican France had once again seized the reins of power, Maurras was barred from the Académie Française — but apparently with some reluctance. The Académie decided not to fill his seat immediately, as was their usual procedure. Maurras was seemingly irreplaceable. The government had changed and so had the propaganda, but the familiar schism remained.

In 1940, with General Charles de Gaulle in London and Marshal Philippe Pétain in Vichy, *les deux France* were delineated as sharply as they had ever been. Both men claimed to incarnate the nation, the one in the republican mode that was born with the Revolution, the other in the mode of the old regime as symbolized by Charles Maurras and Action Française. Indeed, Maurras's oft-quoted dictum of the day was, "Our worst defeat has had the good result of ridding us of democracy."

The overwhelming acceptance among the French of Pétain and the Vichy government was no more an isolated bleep in French republican history than nazism was in Germany. In France, the decade leading up to the German invasion had been divisive to the point of unarmed civil war. "The cursed years," as the late Raymond Aron called them, had ravaged the country. Incompetent governments succeeded each other, economic decline sapped strength at both the national and individual levels, and partisan rivalry reached a level of ferocity that recalled the Dreyfus years.

Between 1935 and 1939, a majority of politicians and "intellectuals" opted for one or the other ideological camp. On the Left, the communists were engaged in a struggle-to-the-death against fascism — and against the socialists; on the opposite side of the political spectrum,

Charles Maurras was feverishly propagating his favorite themes. In his view, for example, the Italian invasion of Ethiopia was none of France's business, and a reprisal of any sort would only serve the interests of Freemasons, England (the historical enemy) and the Soviets, who wanted war in order to unleash their promised revolution.

With the election of the Popular Front in 1936 and the ascendancy of Léon Blum, a Jew and a socialist, anti-Semitism exploded with renewed virulence. "Rather Hitler than Blum," went the popular saying. Like Dreyfus before him, Blum became the focus of mindless slogans and hatred. Bolshevism, Blum, the Jews — all were one for the opposition. Anti-Semitic papers referred to Blum's "Talmudic cabinet."[10]

Nineteen thirty-six was a watershed year. The Popular Front came to power in France, Nazi Germany remilitarized the Rhineland, and civil war broke out in Spain. The fact that General Franco was receiving support from both Hitler and Mussolini extended the fascist encirclement of France. But within France, rightists and leftists continued to drown the national interest in factional dispute; governments succeeded one another in comic-opera style; and somehow the really serious question of the day was never properly addressed: how to deal with the growing giant on the eastern border — Germany flexing its muscles under Adolf Hitler.

The nature of French partisan squabbling changed abruptly on August 22, 1939, the day Stalin and Hitler signed a non-aggression pact; for suddenly hundreds of thousands of French communists were obliged to catch their breath and stop attacking the fascist pigs of yesterday. By August 23 they were denouncing the war effort more vigorously than Action Française. This new "agreement" between Right and Left intensified the turmoil of the ailing Third Republic and further confused the public. As millions of ordinary people felt a growing sense of helplessness and despair, the stage was set for the defeat that lay just beyond the horizon.

Nothing more clearly symbolized the French unreadiness for battle with the new Germany than the vaunted Maginot Line that stretched along the eastern border of the country. Back in the fourteenth century, the noble estate of warriors had definitively lost the Battle of Agincourt because, mired in self-glorifying tradition, they had failed to adapt themselves to new conditions of warfare. Six hundred years later, similar conditions prevailed. The French army was vaunted as one of the best if not the best in the world and was still led by the very men who had brought honor to the *patrie* during the 1914–18 war. But in spite of urgings to the contrary, principally from Charles de Gaulle, the French were assured that the Ardennes forest could not be penetrated and the Maginot Line did not need to be extended north to the English Channel.

On September 1, 1939, the Nazis invaded Poland; on September 17, the Red Army invaded Poland from the east. In France, political chaos intensified. Communist parliamentarians were stripped of their mandates and physically attacked in the Chamber of Deputies. Anticommunist police terror spread to the streets.

In May 1940, the German *Blitzkrieg* swept relentlessly through Holland and Belgium and into northern France (bypassing the Maginot Line altogether), and on May 19, General Maxime Weygand flew back to France from Syria to be named commander in chief of the French forces. Weygand, seventy-three years old, had played a key role during World War I as a major general and a protégé of the French commander in chief, Marshal Ferdinand Foch.

In the eyes of rightist France, Weygand's most important credentials stemmed from his resistance to the Red Army during the Polish-Soviet war of 1920. His anticommunism was obsessional: as the Nazis rolled into the north of France, General Weygand's priority was to preserve the French military for an eventual battle against the real enemy — the communists.

In Weygand, France had a leader who incarnated the thinking that had both created and sustained the anti-Dreyfusard movement fifty years earlier. France was the army; and he, General Weygand, would protect the former by preserving the latter. With this reasoning, the extraordinary capitulation of France before the Nazis could be described as an act of patriotism *in extremis*. Weygand obstinately refused to "dishonor" his totally unprepared forces, and in this he had the direct approval of Charles Maurras and the Action Française movement. Weygand's recommendation was, instead, to surrender. "If an armistice is not immediately demanded, disorder will spread to the armies as it already has to the population," he warned a cabinet meeting presided over by Prime Minister Paul Reynaud on June 12. Weygand's anticommunism also led him to declare, falsely, that Paris had been taken over by the communists and that they had installed their leader, Maurice Thorez, in the president's office at the Elysée. (Weygand later confided to friends that he had had the information from Pétain.)[11]

When it became known that Paris would not be defended, people with cars or the money to buy a train ticket left the capital as quickly as they could. They pushed and shoved for places on the trains heading south and streamed out of the city on every available road. Only the poor, the infirm and those who had nowhere to go remained.

On June 14, the German army marched triumphantly into Paris. There was no open resistance to the smart-looking soldiers on their motorcycles with their shiny boots and their clean uniforms. They waved and smiled at the girls who had come with their grim-faced parents to witness the occupation of the capital, the heart of the country. By the end of the day, the German army had taken possession of all the major points of the city and set up headquarters next to the American embassy in the Hotel Crillon. A swastika flew from the Arc de Triomphe. "They're not so bad," people began to whisper as the days passed. Who could fault such politeness, such courtesy? Why, they even offered old ladies their seats in the Métro. A poster went up all over the city on walls that formerly had displayed revolutionary slogans and other evidence of France's seething internal discontent. It showed an attractive German soldier protecting three children. "Abandoned people," the caption read, "have faith in the German soldier."

On June 16, the government of Paul Reynaud fell and 569 of France's 649 deputies and senators voted in favor of giving the revered Marshal Philippe Pétain what amounted to dictatorial powers — to salvage the honor of the nation.

In 1940, Philippe Pétain was eighty-four years old. He had been a symbol of patriotic France since 1916, when he had struggled on under terrible odds and won the battle of Verdun. There were a few doubters: Georges Clemenceau, for one, insisted on saying that during the war "Pétain constantly wanted to negotiate with the enemy."[12] But no one was listening. On the army's most glorious day, Philippe Pétain had been its most glorious leader; and in the minds of those for whom the army was the nation, the Marshal had become the incarnation of France itself.

When the nation needed a savior once again, it turned almost unanimously to the man who had inherited the mantle of Joan of Arc. This was no time for democracy; this was a time for strength, for faith, for a miracle. Salvation, if it were to happen, would come through the aegis of the beloved Marshal.

Not surprisingly, the terminology was religious and monarchistic. The new Pétainists spoke of the "restoration" of a France that had been too long ignored, a France where the enduring values of work, church and family would once more prevail. The new order was revolutionary, but a revolution of the Right in which the national soul would be saved from the sins of secular liberalism and the evils of communism.

Pétain himself came as close to being revered as a saint as a living man could. Women wept for joy when he passed, and he was photographed endlessly with little children playing at his knees. In spite of later propaganda suggesting that from the beginning a sizable resistance to Pétain sprang into being, the reality was quite the contrary. In 1940, the large majority of French saw the Victor of Verdun as a symbol of hope. As the church saved individual souls, so Pétain would save the *patrie*. It is not without interest that, on November 19, 1940, the man who would later play a major role in protesting the deportation of the Jews, Cardinal Gerlier, welcomed the Marshal to Lyons with the following words: "France needed a leader to conduct her toward her eternal destiny [and] God allowed you to be there . . . France *is* Pétain: all of France is behind you." And in September 1941, Monsignor Cholet used words that might have been lifted verbatim from a Nazi primer for schoolchildren. "We have no right to criticize the Leader himself or his orders," he said. "The subordinate obeys without question or enquiry."[13]

On June 17, the Marshal addressed the nation in a quavering voice that befitted both his advanced age and the circumstances. "I offer to France the gift of my person that I may ease her sorrow," he began. "It is with a heavy heart that I tell you that we must halt the combat. Last night I asked the adversary whether he is ready to seek with us, in honor, some way to put an end to the hostilities."

Forty-six years after the Dreyfus affair had illuminated *les deux France* and carved a deep ideological and moral chasm between the two, the integrist, nationalist camp had, at last, achieved power. And when Marshal Pétain vowed to take up a righteous sword against liberalism, communism and "selfish capitalism" and "to rid our country from the most miserable reign of all, that of money,"[14] Charles Maurras knew that his astrologer had been right after all.

Under the terms of the armistice, the Germans occupied three-fifths of France, including the northern sector and the Atlantic coast, and a quasi-independent French government was established in the town of Vichy. In the occupied zone, German orders were enforced by the French administration. As for the Vichy regime in the south, its laws were valid for both the occupied and unoccupied zones provided they did not counteract German regulations.

The Vichy government was founded on the very ideals that Charles Maurras had been propounding for half a century, and the men who surrounded and advised the Marshal came directly from the Maurras camp, in particular, Raphael Allibert (a former member of the ultrarightist terrorist Cagoulard group), who occupied the powerful ministry of justice. Nationalism was xenophobic and anti-Semitic. An "armistice army" of 100,000 men was created. This "army" paraded around a great deal accompanied by drumrolls and other martial theatrics designed to obscure the reality that it had not resisted the German invaders. A stunned population was reeling from a national defeat. Two million French soldiers were prisoners of war, and the economy was being pillaged by the German war effort.

Within months, a dissenting group of hard-line fascists in occupied Paris had breathed new life into the Parti Populaire Français, a frankly pro-Nazi organization formed in 1936. These men (one of whom had recently been a militant communist) proposed the eventual absorption of France into the New European Order of Hitler along with a homegrown national socialism within France itself, and they urged a close collaboration between the Nazis and Vichy.

For two years, various combinations of pro-Nazi fascists struggled to supplant the "softer" Vichy philosophy. In the end, they effectively won the day. As Raymond Aron described it, "Vichy in 1944 with [fascists] Déat and Doriot, no longer had much in common with Vichy of 1940 with its royalists such as Raphael Allibert."[15]

The Pétain government had been willing to collaborate with the Nazis from the very beginning, but it had hoped to do so on its own terms. The rationale was simple. Until late 1942 it was widely believed that Hitler would win the war; and France wanted to be on the winning side. The second reason involved trade-offs. "If we give a little here, they will give a little there. The occupation will be easier to bear if we make a few concessions."

From mid-1942, one of Vichy's main cards was the Jews. The Nazis wanted them, and the French did not. However, from the very beginning legal anti-Semitism may have seemed unsurprising to a population that had been conditioned by Action Française, among others, to

hate the "foreigner," the "communist," the "capitalist," the non-Catholic
and the Jew, in particular, as harbingers of an urban modernity that
was anathema to the deeply felt values of old, anti-Republican France.

The anti-Jewish laws of Vichy went into effect almost immediately. As early as July 22, 1940, just four short weeks after his government was created, the Marshal established a commission to revise the
naturalizations of Jews. On August 27, an antihate law prohibiting
racist comment in the press was revoked. On October 3, the French
equivalent of the Nuremburg laws came into effect; if anything, they
were more stringent in their definition of who was and was not a Jew
than their Nazi counterpart. Jews were excluded from the public service and from many of the professions. Most important, these indigenous Vichy laws established the notion of a Jewish race, whereas the
German authorities had been careful to refer only to the Jewish religion for fear of offending French public opinion. On October 4, a law
permitted the authorities to intern foreign Jews in special camps. On
October 7, a seventy-five-year-old law granting French citizenship to
Algerian Jews was repealed, leaving this entire population denuded of
its civic rights.

The anti-Jewish laws of Vichy were, of course, entirely foreign to
the traditions of *republican* France, the state that had illuminated a
path for the rest of the world in the area of human rights. But now the
other half of *les deux France* held the reins of power, and its leaders
had an entirely different set of priorities. Indeed, in 1947, it was discovered that in 1940 there had been no orders from the Germans to
instigate anti-Jewish legislation. The Vichy government had taken
action independently — in order to please the occupier and in the hope
of gain.

Until mid-1941, the Germans merely dumped unwanted Jews from
the occupied zone into the unoccupied zone (Marrus and Paxton, authors of *Vichy France and the Jews*, relate how the military commander
of Bordeaux sent a load of German Jews over the Demarcation Line
and told them they would be "free" on the other side), but this move
only angered Vichy, and many of those transferred were instantly shut-
tled into special internment camps at Gurs, Rivesaltes and elsewhere.
The French concentration camps were not death camps, to be sure,
but living conditions were inhumane. Death ravaged the starving,
disease-ridden inmates. In response, the population seemed to be neither for nor against the measures. For the most part, the French were

thinking about other things than the fate of the unpopular, foreign Jews in their midst; and in this atmosphere of indifference, extraordinary policies were initiated and carried out.

By mid-1941, however, German pressure to increase the persecution of Jews had intensified, and top echelons in Germany were well aware that Vichy France was indigenously and independently anti-Semitic. A new General Commission for Jewish Affairs was created, under the direction of hard-line anti-Semite Xavier Vallat, and by mid-1941 was actively involved in expropriating Jewish property. From the beginning, however, the ultimate fate of French Jews lay in the hands of top administrators, both French and German, who were not, in the main, fanatical anti-Semites. Crucial decisions were taken by Germans who were more interested in the economic exploitation of France for their war effort and by Frenchmen who were, in essence, consummate opportunists. The French politicians and administrators had convinced themselves that what they were doing would actually prevent further ravages to the country (some argued after the war that they were actually *protecting* Jews) and that whatever gains they might achieve in the long term justified whatever methods they might have to employ in the short term.

Germany was feeling the pinch of war, and pressures of many sorts were being applied to Vichy, in particular, demands for manpower and material for the Reich. Prime Minister Pierre Laval was asked for 250,000 men for the war effort within Germany. He complied in principle with a program that involved the return of one French prisoner of war for every three skilled workers who agreed to leave for Germany. Propaganda newsreels showed smiling Frenchmen leaning out of train windows blowing kisses at happy mothers, wives and girlfriends as they headed toward Germany. After February 1943, when the numbers were insufficient to satisfy the Germans, Laval instituted an obligatory program of work in Germany, and it was this deeply unpopular move (which many French continue to think of as the real deportations) that finally destroyed the credibility of the Vichy government in the eyes of the public.

As a reward for their collaboration, Laval and Pétain hoped to wring as many concessions as they could from their German overlords. On January 20, 1942, the Final Solution had been elaborated at the Wannsee conference in Berlin, and by June 1942, the policy was being applied to occupied territories in the west and, of course, unoccupied France.

At the end of June 1942, Adolf Eichmann, European-wide organizer of the deportation process, came to Paris. All Jews in France were to be deported, he announced, regardless of their nationality. During the week that followed this visit, Laval and his chief of police, René Bousquet, played a deadly poker game with the chief Gestapo officers in Paris. The issue under discussion was the following: the Germans wanted a major roundup of foreign Jews for deportation —numbers were important; they needed to fill trains and meet established quotas, but they didn't want to do the job themselves. For one thing, they simply lacked the personnel; second, they suspected that the sight of German police arresting helpless people would upset the population more than the sight of French police doing the same thing.

René Bousquet, who negotiated this request on behalf of the French government, had no comment regarding the actual roundups and deportations, but he did report that the Marshal and Pierre Laval had decided that the occupying forces would have to do the job themselves in the occupied territory. However, he added, hoping to soften the refusal, the French police would round up and deliver foreign Jews from the unoccupied zone.

On the German side of the negotiating table was Helmut Knochen, a brilliant young man of thirty who was commander of the security police in France. Knochen held his breath for a moment, struck by the audacity of these men who seemed to have forgotten that his country had defeated their country; but he quickly regained his composure and tried out his first ploy. A refusal by the French police to participate in the roundup of Jews in the occupied zone would be interpreted as a direct act of provocation against Hitler himself, he threatened.

Immediately intimidated by the threat of danger to Vichy autonomy and the fear that France would be excluded from playing an important role in the New European Order once Hitler had won the war, René Bousquet did not play the game. He capitulated immediately. The resultant agreement was that 20,000 adult Jews would be arrested in Paris and 10,000 delivered from the unoccupied zone. The date was July 2, 1942. With this agreement, Vichy France turned a corner and became a direct collaborator in the fate of 76,000 Jews who were deported from France.

On July 3, both Pétain and Laval confirmed the agreement. "The Marshal believes that this distinction [between foreign and French Jews] is just and will be understood by the public," wrote Laval.[16] As for Laval, his personal attitudes were clear enough and directly in line with the xenophobic thinking of his government. In the unoccupied zone a distinction had to be made between French Jews and "the garbage sent here by the Germans themselves," he remarked.[17]

The next day, on July 4, Laval blurred the very distinction he had been at pains to make. In a meeting with Knochen and Karl-Albrecht Oberg, chief of the ss and the German police in France, he independently proposed the deportation of children under the age of sixteen. Laval correctly guessed that the children were going to become a serious administrative problem. Moreover, it was very difficult to hide their suffering from the public.

The fact that the majority of these children would have been French citizens could not have escaped Laval's attention. His suggestion was made on his own initiative, and it preceded any request of the sort from the Nazis, who were, in fact, not ready for such action in spite of the fact that Oberg had arrived in Paris fresh from the Polish city of Radom, where 98 percent of the large Jewish population had already been exterminated. As Marrus and Paxton have pointed out, there is some indication that the Germans actually disapproved of the suggestion at this time, in part out of fear of public opinion.[18] However, the conclusion of the meeting was that families in the unoccupied zone who wanted their children to accompany them on their voyage "to the East" could do so. And French police took charge of assigning the children to the convoys.

In order to make the deportation of children acceptable to the public, Laval resorted to familiar propaganda. The "National Revolution" of the Vichy regime, with its catchwords of "Work, Family, and Country," was, of course, based on the sanctity of the family, so was it not obvious that children should remain with their parents? Although Pétain, Laval and Bousquet did not have positively corroborated information on the nature of the death camps, the story of "work camps" must have seemed just a little bit odd. What kind of "work" could men of eighty and babes in arms possibly be recruited for? And as Serge Klarfeld has pointed out, Laval was certainly aware of Hitler's speech of January 1, 1942, in which he proclaimed for the second time that "the result of this war will be the destruction of Judaism."[19]

Laval, however, had already declared himself in favor of Hitler. On June 22, he broadcast a speech to the nation in which he said, "I hope for the victory of Germany because without her, communism would take over everywhere in Europe."[20]

The Friday, July 10, 1942, edition of *Le Petit Parisien*, one of the large-circulation, collaborationist papers of the country, conveyed, as usual, a particular slant on the news. The lead front-page story proclaimed German advances on the eastern front, and an editorial reported the text of a morale-boosting speech delivered to French volunteers fighting communists alongside the Nazis. "By your abnegation and sacrifice, you are helping to stem the tide of bolshevism, the curse of our towns and countryside. You are defending European interests and, as such, French interests," exhorted Secretary of State Benoist-Méchin in an appeal to the bedraggled men who had enlisted out of religious-political passion and had seen their ranks decimated by the enemy and the sufferings imposed by a Russian winter. A second front-page story described the happy adventure of 1,000 skilled workers who had just left for Germany. Both German and French dignitaries saluted them as their train pulled out of the Gare du Nord. A center-page picture showed Field Marshal Erwin Rommel reviewing British prisoners at the Libyan port of Tobruk before despatching them to a camp. A small article reported on the debate in the Canadian parliament in which the bill authorizing Canadian troops to fight in Europe was passed by only four votes with all French-speaking members of the House voting in the negative. Two further articles reported the escapades of "Jewish thieves" in the capital, while another informed the public of new restrictions to be placed on Jews. As of July 10, they would no longer be allowed to walk along the grand boulevards of Paris. And certain shops and restaurants would be closed to them.

But the editorial cartoon on this particular day was, with hindsight, especially ironic. A Jew with a hooked nose, frizzy hair and a yellow star on his shirt is engaged in conversation with a French laborer.

"I'd rather die than go to work in Germany," says the Jew, ignoring his likely fate.

"Let's get right down to it. Have you ever worked anywhere?" retorts the laborer, expressing the view of the Jew as lazy and parasitical.

On the morning of that very same day, Prime Minister Laval had informed a cabinet meeting in Vichy that, for humanitarian reasons, he had been successful in obtaining permission to deport Jewish children between the ages of two and sixteen from the unoccupied zone. "They [the Germans] have accepted that now," he reported. Minutes from the meeting reveal that no opposition to the new policy was registered from the ministers present, including Marshal Pétain.[21]

At a meeting in Paris that same afternoon, the date for the roundup in the occupied zone was fixed: Thursday, July 16, starting at 4:00 A.M. Once arrested, people were to be taken to an indoor sports arena known as the Vélodrome d'Hiver where it was estimated that 25,000 people could be interned. Paris municipal police were instructed to survey Jews to prevent them from leaving the city in the days ahead.

Still on the same day, arrangements were finalized for a roundup of Jews elsewhere in the occupied zone. Trains from Bordeaux in the south, Rouen and Angers in the north, Nancy in the east and Orléans in the Loire Valley would deliver their human freight to the holding camp at Drancy. Also to be included were French Jews who had been convicted of various infractions of the regulations, like failing to obey one of the anti-Jewish laws or attempting to escape to the unoccupied zone.

When Adolf Eichmann learned that the number of Jews rounded up in the provinces was inferior to the target set by the Gestapo, and that a deportation departure date had been missed, he grew furious. "This is a matter of prestige," he shouted. Such inefficiency was nothing short of humiliating after he had so carefully negotiated a schedule of available trains with the French minister of transportation.[22] In his anger, Eichmann wondered aloud whether France would simply be dropped from the list of countries who were to be favored with the Final Solution. He was, however, appeased by his subordinates.

During the six days between July 10 and the July 16 roundup in Paris, sporadic warnings leaked out like tiny puffs of smoke. Individual police officers were horrified by their secret assignment and privately warned their intended victims. In the early hours of July 16, a few visited as many apartments as they could to say they would be returning shortly to make arrests. An underground Jewish paper warned people to escape or hide. Some escaped, but many did not. Where were people with small children to go? And most important, who could really believe that the *French* police would carry out such an action?

The massive strike began at 4:00 A.M. as planned, but what was supposed to be an orderly action that would not disturb the sensibilities of the local population soon turned into a scene of terror. In the predawn hours, families awoke to hear screams of anguish as people were assaulted with blows from rifle butts, then dragged from their homes. Some individuals committed suicide; children were hidden behind false walls, under beds and in cupboards.

By 5:00 P.M. the following day, 12,884 people had been interned at the Vélodrome d'Hiver, where no provision had been made for food, water or toilet facilities. Hardly a German had made an appearance. Nothing but French uniforms were to be seen. Who could believe it?

There was some complicity on the part of the French population —the ultra-fascist PPF of Jacques Doriot helped in the roundup, and a certain number of greedy *concierges* rushed into apartments after the occupants were removed and appropriated their property — but horror at the arrest of parents and children and outrage at the use of French police was a dominant reaction.

Four thousand children between the ages of two and sixteen were interned at Drancy and in camps outside of Paris. Without food or sanitary facilities, they huddled together on dirty straw. Diarrhea and psychological trauma decimated their numbers. Within two weeks of captivity, many were quietly buried in local cemeteries.

In camps like Drancy, mothers and children were interned together, and when the mothers were deported to Auschwitz, the children remained behind. The separation created a problem for the authorities, for the terrible cries of screaming parents and children being torn apart by guards wielding clubs upset the local population.

During the roundups in the unoccupied zone in August 1942, other local populations witnessed the anguish of parents and their children as the adults were sealed in cattle cars for their second-last train ride — to Drancy. Within the first week of August, 2,000 mothers were ripped from their children, but the children did not remain behind for long. On August 13, Adolf Eichmann approved the deportation of the children. In the name of "family unity," they were to be deported to the same place as their parents, but not at the same time. Children would "find their parents at the destination," according to both Nazi and Vichy officials.

During the second half of August 1942, 4,000 children who had previously been separated from their parents were brought to Drancy in sealed cattle cars, then packed off to Auschwitz. An internee by the name of Odette Daltroff-Baticle was placed in charge of them. When she was liberated in 1943, Odette wrote the following account:

*The buses arrived carrying children in an unimaginable state. Clusters
of insects surrounded them. The odor was terrible. They had traveled
in sealed freight cars for days and nights, 90 to a car with one woman
[in charge] . . . They ranged in age from 15 months to 13 years.*

*We immediately organized showers [but] for 1,000 children we
had only four towels. Once naked, they were even more frightful. They
were all terribly skinny and almost all of them had pus-filled bruises.
Another catastrophe; they almost all suffered from dysentery. Their
underwear was unbelievably dirty and their little packages were no
better . . . They all belonged in the infirmary, but this was impossible
since they were to leave for an unknown destination. With great cow-
ardice we told them that they would be reunited with their parents,
and with that they could bear what was happening.*

*I shall never forget the faces of those children: endlessly they pa-
rade before my eyes . . . The horror of the experience they are enduring is branded in their faces.*

*They show us their most precious possessions: the pictures of their
mothers and fathers which their mothers gave them when they parted.
Hastily, the mothers wrote a tender inscription. [Some] ask if they will
be lucky enough to hold on to a bracelet, a medallion, a souvenir of
happier days . . . A girl of five says to me, "They won't take the medallion, will they? It's not made of gold."*

*Like children, sometimes they play. They play at searches and
deportation.*

*Many have contagious diseases, but they leave [for the new
destination] anyway, with scarlet fever and diphtheria.*

*We try to make a list of their names and are surprised by a tragic
fact. The little ones do not know their names. A small boy . . . repeats
endlessly, "I am Pierre's brother." Opposite their numbers on the deportation lists is a question mark.*

*After the departure of 3,000 or 4,000 children without parents,
80 who were too sick to travel remained behind, but soon they, too,
must leave. They range in age from two to twelve years. Like the adults
they were placed in those unforgettable stairwells before their departure. For three or four days before each convoy, the 1,000 persons
scheduled to leave were isolated from the rest of the camp. Men, women
and children groaned on the wet, dirty straw including the blind and
the dying who would be carried to the train on stretchers.*

At 3:00 A.M. on the day of their departure, a friend and I began to prepare the 80 children. They were infected with dysentery, asleep in the straw and clinging to each other. I didn't know where to start. They were supposed to go down into the courtyard at 5:00 A.M., but a real revolt took place. They began to scream, they refused to move. It was an instinct of conservation. It wouldn't be easy to lead them to the slaughter.

The guard climbed the stair and made them move, but the youngest ones were not big enough to carry their own package. As they left there was a roll call. Of the 80 children, about 20 did not know their names.

I will never forget the voice of a little boy of four who kept repeating over and over in an endless monotone, "Mommy, I'm afraid, Mommy, I'm afraid" . . .[23]

Convoy 20 left Drancy on August 17, 1942, and reached Auschwitz on August 19. All the children were gassed immediately upon their arrival.

By the end of August, the fact that terrible human suffering was taking place with the collaboration of the French government was a secret to no one, yet many people, perhaps most, were unaware of the extent of Vichy complicity. There was still that other face of France to be reckoned with, the France that had placed justice over patriotism at the time of the Dreyfus affair, for example.

No group was more eager to believe in the continued existence of that other France than the old, highly assimilated French Jewish community, in spite of breathtaking evidence that the values they counted upon for their safety were no longer dominant. They clung to their belief in French democratic traditions like shipwrecked passengers on a sinking raft, and none more so than Victor Basch, an admirable poet, philosopher and linguist who lived in a world of ideas until he was awakened to politics by the Dreyfus affair and compelled by his own conscience to take on the leadership of the League for the Rights of Man. In his memoirs, Raymond Aron recalls a meeting of the French Philosophical Society at the Sorbonne during the late 1930s, during which he suggested that democracy was, in fact, a fragile and vulnerable entity, that twentieth-century revolutions had tended to give more authority to the state than the regimes they replaced and that the future of mankind was, at the very least, uncertain. Basch felt frightened by the disinterested rationality of what he was hearing. What mattered most was the *principles* men must believe in. His large frame trembled as he rose to speak. "I have listened to you with great interest and all the more so since I disagree with everything you have said," he replied. "I must say that your pessimism lacks spirit, and that as far as I am concerned, the democracies have always triumphed and will always triumph. Today we are in a valley; there has been a regression. Well, we will climb to the summit of the mountain again. But in order to do so we must keep the democratic faith and not destroy it by arguments such as those you have just put forward . . ."[24] Victor Basch's murder by the French *Milice* would deliver a final twist of irony to his convictions.

Like Victor Basch, the Jewish leadership seemed unable to adapt its responses to the new realities. "All the Jews before the war were convinced humanists," said Richard Wertenschlag, chief rabbi of the Lyons Jewish community.[25] They were incapable of imagining that human beings could commit organized murder on the scale of the Third Reich. They believed entirely in "civilization," and especially in their French citizenship. *Patrie* and nationality were their new religion. Of course, they had had the Dreyfus affair, but since they had demonstrated their patriotism so clearly during World War I, they believed that the subsequent anti-Semitism of Action Française, for example, was a minority point of view. If they heard rumors of "death camps" they put the whole thing down to counterpropaganda.

The ignorance of the community was so total, said Rabbi Wertenschlag, that during the occupation, when his own family had fled from Alsace to Lyons, his grandfather said to his father: "In the final analysis you may as well go to the work camps. At least you'll be safe there."

At the end of July 1941, Jacob Kaplan, the deputy of Grand Rabbi Weill, addressed a pathetic letter to Xavier Vallat, head of the General Commission for Jewish Affairs and a fanatical anti-Semite. Kaplan appealed to reason; he examined the Bible to "prove" that the defamation of Judaism was "illogical" for a Christian; then he delivered what he surely thought of as his *coup de grâce* by informing Vallat that to attack the Jewish religion was to attack the very founders of Christianity itself. In support of his arguments, Kaplan quoted from Pascal, Montesquieu, Rousseau and Pope Pius XI, among others. Furthermore, he continued, did Vallat not understand that Jews had served France in both wars and died for their country on the field of battle? Kaplan was doubtless convinced that when Vallat had duly considered his arguments, anti-Semitism would be seen as preposterous and dropped as a political program.

Kaplan received a reply that may have put things into perspective. ". . . Let me simply point out that in the government's attitude there is no anti-Semitism, simply the application of reasons of state," wrote Vallat's deputy.[26]

In August 1942, the Central Consistory, the official representative of French Jewry, wrote a letter of protest to Vichy. They protested the abrogation of the traditional right of asylum that had long distinguished France, the France *they* believed in. They described the inhuman way deportees were treated — "They were heaped into freight cars, men, women, children, the elderly, the sick, all together without any provisions . . ." — and they spelled out what they believed to be the fate of those who were being deported by reminding Marshal Pétain of Hitler's open message that he intended to exterminate the Jews. They also added: "It has been established that several hundreds of thousands of Jews have been massacred in eastern Europe or have perished there after atrocious suffering due to ill treatment," and suggested that the mandarins of Vichy must be well aware that the categories of people they were delivering to the Nazis could not be required for "work camps."[27] This protest was followed in September by a declaration from Chief Rabbi Hirschler, which appealed once again to liberal values that were not part of the intellectual superstructure of Vichy France. "Whatever our suffering, none among us would have dared imagine that France would agree to commit actions that in ancient times more primitive peoples refused to engage in . . . As French men and women, we are humiliated. Because we continue to love our country, we fear the judgment of civilized people and the judgment of our own children . . ." he warned prophetically.[28]

In July 1942, following the roundups of the Vélodrome d'Hiver, some important churchmen finally came to the defense of the Jews. The Christian protest began with a letter to Pétain from the cardinals and bishops of France under the signature of Cardinal Suhard, Archbishop of Paris. And when the roundups in the unoccupied zone took place the following month, Cardinal Gerlier of Lyons sent a similar letter to the Marshal, the man he had earlier welcomed to his city by declaring that Pétain had been sent by God and that all France was behind him. The following day, the leader of the Protestant church in France, Pastor Marc Boegner, also wrote an impassioned letter of protest. "No defeat can oblige France to sully her own honor. I beg you to take the necessary steps to prevent France from inflicting a moral defeat of incalculable dimension upon herself,"[29] he urged, also appealing to a set of values that were foreign to the Vichy regime. But his arguments left the Marshal cold. Was Pétain not already defending the "honor" of France by cooperating with the Germans in order to lighten the burden of the occupation? Was not France the country of the *French*? Was it not necessary to excise the Jew, the godless communist and the Freemason with a surgeon's scalpel, as Xavier Vallat liked to put it, in order to remove the diseased part and render the nation whole again?

The Catholic church had been a bedrock of integrist, nationalist ideology since the time of the Revolution, and it was certainly one of the cornerstones of Vichy itself; but now it was actually defending foreigners, and Jews to boot. This was an important shift of direction and a serious blow to the Marshal himself.

Cardinal Gerlier then did an unprecedented thing: he personally rescued eighty-four children who were passing through Lyons en route to Drancy and put them under the protection of the church. And from pulpits across unoccupied France, Catholics and Protestants were urged to help persecuted Jews in any way they could.

The buildup of adverse public opinion had an effect on the deportations. Some roundups were cancelled, and after the end of September there were fewer people in the convoys that left Drancy for Auschwitz. Indeed, there were so few bodies in the convoy of September 30 that the twenty-two-year-old ss officer who was in charge of Drancy, Ernst Heinrichsohn, threw in the noted jurist and former senator, Pierre Masse, who had been arrested along with other Jewish notables in the spring of 1941.

Philippe Pétain was a rather feeble old man whose prestige was enormous, but the main administration of his government was carried out by Pierre Laval. Laval, Bousquet and the latter's deputy in occupied territory, Jean Leguay, were not fanatical anti-Semites like some others in their entourage. They were, on the contrary, pragmatic politicians and opportunists. They were also patriots of the extreme nationalist school, and in collaborating with the Germans — indeed, in going even further than was required, as Laval did in offering up children for deportation, and as Pétain did in passing his own, indigenous anti-Jewish laws—they believed that they were serving the interests of their country. Every ounce of independence they could wrest away from the Nazis meant more autonomy for "France," more power for the French police—and more authority for themselves, of course. Since, according to this mind-set, Jews did not belong to the nation, no harm was being done to the nation. And nothing, but nothing, was more important than the nation—that had been clear enough at the time of the Dreyfus affair—especially in this moment of defeat, and especially when they were convinced that the enemy (with whom they shared a considerable number of beliefs) was going to win the war.

Like "communism," "patriotism" was an all-purpose word. The patriot wanted to protect his country, and in that the antidemocratic Right, the democrats of the Center and Left and the communists could find common cause. More narrowly, in order to protect the "nation" (seen as a spiritual and psychological entity) against communists, non-Christians and foreigners, the "patriot" might very well collaborate with the invader. Indeed, in this particular scenario, the German occupier could actually be seen as the supreme French patriot. This was, in fact, the essence of Pierre Laval's public wish for a German victory.

There is no extant document to suggest that any of the politicians or administrators of Vichy ever questioned the implications of their collaboration when it came to the Jews. The men of Vichy were persecutors, to be sure, but they were not murderers. They were politicians and bureaucrats who chose not to examine any of the repercussions of their policies. Where *were* these men, women and children going in cattle cars that were sealed shut by French police? That was a question they did not bother—or dare—to ask. Once the wheels were in motion, the bureaucracy took precedence, as it did for the Nazis themselves. The exigencies of the numbers game smothered whatever vestige of the old morality remained to trouble the conscience. Persecution of the Jews was also now enshrined in French law. And these were law-abiding men.

The tally remains as a grim reminder of the politics of opportunism. During the summer of 1942, when Vichy and the French police cooperated fully with the Nazis, 3,000 Jews left Drancy for Auschwitz every week. By the time the war ended, just short of 76,000 people had been deported. Of these, 3,000 survived.

The same mentality that was willing to condemn an innocent Alfred Dreyfus for the "honor" of the army, and consequently the "honor" of the nation, resurfaced during the years of Vichy when democracy no longer seemed possible or even desirable. "National interest" was reason enough to pass legislation that would provide a legal basis for the enacting of indignities. For a short time it even seemed as though the other face of the nation, republican France, had been obliterated. A mistake, of course. But it is not without interest that forty years after the end of the war, one out of every three French people questioned in a poll believed that Marshal Philippe Pétain ought to have been acquitted when he was tried before the nation in July 1945.[30]

November 11, 1942, was, of course, a red-letter day for the German occupiers, the day they swept over the Demarcation Line to occupy the whole of France. Vichy's armistice army was disbanded, and whatever autonomy the regime may have enjoyed came to an end. Collaboration intensified, but so did armed resistance. *Les deux France* were at war with each other once again, and this time they carried weapons.

Into the newly occupied heartland of Lyons strode a confident Klaus Barbie. He came to tame the Resistance and "deliver" the Jews. A hundred years of German history and the whole of his own lifetime had prepared him for this moment. And he would use the divisions within France to accomplish his task.

· 4 ·

KLAUS BARBIE IN LYONS

For two thousand years, the prosperous city of Lyons had proudly dominated the south of France. Founded in 27 B.C. by the Roman legions, Lugdunum, as it was called, soon became the capital of Roman-occupied Gaul. And for a good reason. The city was constructed at the junction of two important waterways, the Rhône and the Saône rivers; and, as the years passed, the settlement became the focal point for travel and transportation north into France, south into Italy and east into both Switzerland and Germany. In the sixteenth century, the burgeoning silk industry made Lyons more famous and more wealthy still, and later on other textiles further enriched its stolidly bourgeois population. Indeed, Lyons, was so conservative that, in 1793, the post-revolutionary National Convention formally complained about the brazen and persistent royalism of its citizens.

In June 1940, as the *Blitzkrieg* pushed its way into France, about one million people lived in and around Lyons; but within days of the armistice, refugees from the occupied zone began to pour into the city, swelling its population. In the main, two groups of people found their way to Lyons: thousands of Jews fleeing the Nazis; and a mushrooming nucleus of *résistants* who sought the anonymity of a large city. Lyons was an ideal center from which to resist both the Nazis and Vichy France. It was the biggest urban conglomeration in the country after Paris and, even more important, it was very old. That meant a network of medieval streets and passages to hide in, if and when hiding became necessary.

By the time the German army swept across the southern zone in the autumn of 1942, Lyons had already become the center of Jewish refuge in France. The Resistance, too, had become a serious force to be reckoned with, not least because the communists had joined it after the German invasion of the Soviet Union in June 1941. The communists were tightly organized, disciplined and ruthless in their actions. They were also used to clandestine living, having learned the hard way during the Spanish Civil War.

When he entered his new fiefdom on November 11, 1942, the Gestapo chief, Lieutenant Klaus Barbie, had two important assignments. The first and foremost was to wage war against the Resistance. The second was to render his territory *Judenrein*. "I came to Lyons to kill," Barbie recollected in tranquility in 1972. "To kill and to fight the Resistance. That was a very strict order."

It was afternoon in Lyons, on the anniversary of the day World War I had ended, and the Lyonnais were in their churches and at the municipal war memorials remembering their dead and celebrating their last great victory over Germany. Suddenly, with indescribable irony, the new German army materialized before their eyes, accompanied by the redoubtable ss police. The occupation of the city was completely uneventful for the Wehrmacht; the Armistice Army of Vichy and the French police put up no resistance whatsoever.

There were eighty ss men in the Lyons regiment that day. Of these, thirty were dispatched to the surrounding area and fifty, including Klaus Barbie, remained in the city. The urban contingent immediately occupied the elegant Hotel Terminus, located within a stone's throw of the Perrache railway station and close to the major prisons of the city. The location of the new headquarters was ideal: Jews and *résistants* could be deported by train without much interim traveling. And prisoners being brought in daily for the famous Gestapo "interrogations" were also close at hand.

The elegance of the Hotel Terminus testified to the fact that in happier days it had catered for a better class of guests. The main lobby boasted marble floors as well as beautifully sculpted wood paneling, mirrored columns and frescoes depicting idealized scenes of life in Lyons and the Rhône Valley. Mirrored doors with knobs sculpted in heavy brass opened into paneled corridors. Large brass chandeliers illumined high-ceilinged banquet halls and reception rooms. The German Security Police both lived and worked in rooms that had welcomed dignitaries and European royalty passing through Lyons. It was not an uncomfortable base from which to wage war.

Police activities were divided into six sections. Section I looked after the management of seized property; Section II took care of internal legal affairs; Section III looked after "economic information" concerning the French economy. Section IV was the Gestapo proper and Klaus Barbie's domain. It was by far the largest and most powerful sector and was further divided into five sub-sections that dealt with the Resistance and communists, sabotage (primarily of national railway lines), Jews, Freemasons, counterintelligence and archives. Section V tried to keep an eye on the black market and supposedly investigated crimes committed by the German military personnel. Section VI presided over the collaboration, counterespionage and infiltration of enemy organizations, in particular the Resistance. (When the flood of denunciations became unmanageable, a new Information Office was created and presided over by a French collaborator who demanded he be called "*Milneuf*," his SS registration number.)

Barbie was especially interested in attacking the Resistance and spent most of his time in that pursuit. The other sectors of his jurisdiction were controlled by subordinate officers in his service, but the ultimate responsibility was his. (Forty years later, the question of who was responsible for the Jewish section would become important for Barbie's defense.)

Barbie found a natural ally in his SD commander in chief, Dr. Werner Knab, a thirty-four-year-old Munich lawyer who arrived to take over police operations in Lyons during the summer of 1943. Knab had solid experience in brutality. He came to Lyons directly from Kiev in the Ukraine where he had been a leader of the *Einsatzgruppe* C death squad and participated in the first mass murders of Jews. His skill and dedication to the job had earned him a promotion to colonel. Barbie and Knab understood each other perfectly; and Knab left his subordinate to run Section IV with complete independence. As a result, Barbie exercised unlimited power. His domain extended for thousands of square miles, north into the Jura mountains, east to the Swiss border and south along the Rhône River into the Hautes-Alpes. When Italy gave up its parcel of French territory and withdrew from the war, Barbie acquired Grenoble and the surrounding region. Indeed, Barbie was so fanatical about destroying his enemies that he regularly found himself in conflict with the Gestapo commander for the Dijon area, who complained that Barbie was encroaching on his territory.

The French Resistance began primarily as a state of mind on June 17, 1940, as Marshal Philippe Pétain spoke to the nation from Bordeaux. Pétain's talk of an armistice "with honor" struck many in his radio audience as a terrible and humiliating contradiction in terms.

The following day, General de Gaulle, who was in London, also appealed to the nation, through the services of the BBC. In *his* address, de Gaulle pronounced the word *résistance* for the first time. And by the time he had finished speaking, the battle lines were drawn.

Among the millions of people listening anxiously to Marshal Pétain on June 17, 1940, was Captain Henri Frenay, a career officer with the Forty-Third Army Corps, whose unit had been ordered to defend the Maginot Line and was now cut off from France by the invading German forces. Frenay was horrified and confused, for was not Pétain the nation's most heroic soldier? Frenay thought heroism and capitulation were mutually exclusive, or ought to be, and he drew up a personal manifesto in which he wrote rather grandly, "Our struggle is by no means over. It is first and foremost the struggle of the human spirit against barbarism and paganism while we prepare for the day of our armed liberation."

Frenay was taken prisoner, then escaped from a POW camp to rejoin the Armistice Army of Vichy. In October 1940, however, he was shaken once again by the news that Pétain had met with Hitler and decided that collaboration was the best solution for France. Frenay resigned his commission and moved to Lyons where he founded a resistance tract called *Petites Ailes*. By the following May the paper, now called *Combat*, had a circulation of 3,000 and featured writers of the stature of Albert Camus; and by the end of 1941, an authentic resistance movement called Combat had emerged.

The second major resistance movement to appear in Lyons was Libération Sud, led in the main by a charismatic romantic called Emmanuel d'Astier de la Vigerie. Like many Frenchmen, d'Astier de la Vigerie had flirted with diverse ideological commitments. His family was Old France and royalist, and one of his brothers was a general. He himself had been a member of Charles Maurras's Action Française before the war, and had been overtly antidemocratic. D'Astier de la Vigerie was also a journalist, and during the Spanish Civil War he dashed off to cover events in Spain, where he sympathized overtly with the communists.

Like Frenay, d'Astier de la Vigerie refused to accept the defeat of France. Together with a small group of like-minded individuals, he also put out a resistance tract that eventually became the basis for a movement. The political orientation of Libération was, however, different from that of Combat. Whereas Combat was distinctly to the right, Libération was on the socialist left of the spectrum.

One of the founders of Libération Sud was Lucie Aubrac, an extraordinary and courageous woman. She was born into a family of vineyard cultivators in Burgundy, a family without pretensions of any sort. But Lucie wanted an education, and in 1929, at the age of sixteen, she went to Paris to study history at the Sorbonne. For a while she belonged to the Young Communists ("At the time they seemed to represent poor people, needy people, people who weren't afraid to fight for their rights"), but her affiliation ended with graduation and a doctorate in history.

Lucie Aubrac was hired as a professor at the University of Strasbourg in Alsace, a part of France where everyone was constantly aware of impending danger on the other side of the Rhine. Before war broke out she watched Jews and political refugees stream across the border. And she fell in love—with an engineer called Raymond Samuel, a Jew from an old French family. When war broke out, Lucie and Raymond, now married, moved to Lyons, where Lucie taught history in a local high school.

It was as a history teacher that Lucie Aubrac first felt compelled to resist the Germans and the Vichy regime. The impetus came from a Nazi exhibition, called "The Jew," that was traveling through France. As a history teacher she was appalled by the distortion and the racism. "The commitment came little by little. We had no information. To listen to the radio one had to have electricity and there usually wasn't any. The newspapers were all censored by Vichy. What could be worse for a historian who must teach young people than not to have information? That is why the first act of resistance for many of the French was to procure and diffuse the news. There were other small shocks as well. When you run through roll call in your class and the little girl whose name is Lévy is afraid to reply. And the next day in roll call someone says: 'Oh, she's gone. She's with her parents and they're all gone.' Or when your Jewish colleague is fired . . ."

Once she and her friends had succeeded in tuning into the BBC news, the next obvious step was to inform others. And with that step the newspapers were born—and the movements of direct action that followed in their wake.

Action can take many forms. Lucie had given birth to a baby boy whom she was nursing. One day a Lyons doctor brought her an infant girl of three months whose Jewish parents had been arrested. The baby had been alone in her parents' apartment for two days before neighbors realized she was there. She needed to be fed. Lucie Aubrac nursed her for several weeks until the child was taken by a family and smuggled to safety in Switzerland.

"It was a time of terrible shame," she recalled. "France had been a haven for political refugees. It was shocking to see Vichy arrest the Spanish republicans, the German Jews, the Austrian Jews, the Polish Jews."

But there was, in effect, a single event that hardened her resolve and transformed her dismay into something much more deadly. A train of prisoners was leaving Lyons, and Aubrac and several friends wanted to see what was actually happening. Friendly railway workers hid them in a boxcar from which they could spy on another track in the Lyons station that was hidden from general view. A convoy of Jews was being loaded.

"I saw a former student of mine. Her name was Jeannine Cremieux. She had married and she was holding a baby on one arm. With her other hand she was carrying a package of her belongings.

"When she put her package down to grab on to a railing and pull herself up the steps into the train, a German who was standing behind her kicked her in the behind. She and the baby both fell. The baby rolled on the track, and its clothes reddened with blood. That day I wanted to kill. Do you understand? I saw that with my own eyes, that horror, and even now when I speak of it I feel distraught.

"Jeannine picked up the baby and her package and got into the train. She was gassed when she arrived in Auschwitz. After the war I went back to the school and her name was on the wall in the list of students who never returned.

"When you see a thing like that you cannot *not* join the resistance. After you feel that kind of hatred, anything is possible."

During the course of the Occupation, Lucie Aubrac would come face to face with Klaus Barbie. And under the nose of the Gestapo she would effect one of the most daring rescue operations of the entire war.

The third major resistance movement to take up residence in Lyons was the Franc-Tireur under the leadership of Jean-Pierre Lévy. Lévy came from an old family of Alsatian Jews. Until the war he had been essentially apolitical, but the defeat shocked his profound sense of *patrie*. The fact that he was also a Jew made resistance seem an even more urgent necessity.

Lévy, an engineer, had been a lieutenant in the artillery. In September 1940 he found his way to Lyons where, like the other future leaders, he founded a paper, *Le Franc-Tireur*, which eventually evolved into a full-fledged movement. Politically, Franc-Tireur was centrist.

In today's terms, many of the members of the French Resistance were scarcely more than children. These were young men and women who were often not yet out of their teens. Most had no experience with guns. Sabotage was as remote as the 1914–18 war, something their parents may have talked about, endlessly and boringly.

Not surprisingly (given the age of the *résistants*) their initial activities were essentially childish. They scribbled anti-Nazi and anti-Vichy graffiti on walls and pasted stickers on windows and in telephone books. They talked endlessly in an attempt to define what had happened to them, what had happened to France, and how they ought to proceed. But it was the clandestine papers that finally focused their disparate efforts. Production was difficult. There was no shortage of editorial material, of course — everyone was a would-be writer. The difficulties were of a physical order. First they had to find the paper, then a roneotype machine with which to print. Distribution of a clandestine paper was both difficult and dangerous; and in the long run it was these distribution networks that were the basis for the major resistance movements of France.

Three key events changed the internal resistance in France from an uprising of angry, adventurous kids pasting stickers on windows to a more or less cooperative association of serious fighters. The first was the brutal collapse of the Hitler-Stalin pact with the German invasion of the Soviet Union on June 22, 1941, an event that brought the communists into the Resistance. After the communists joined, the Resistance became more militant, more aggressive and infinitely more deadly. The second and the third events were directly traceable to the Nazis themselves. The invasion of the unoccupied zone on November 11, 1942, brought the dissolution of the Armistice Army of Vichy in its wake. This army had been an absurd Gilbert-and-Sullivan-style charade, but it had provided a role for the men in its ranks. When the Nazis occupied the southern zone, thousands of ex-soldiers simply moved over to the Resistance. But the final straw came from the leaders of Vichy themselves. On February 15, 1943, Pierre Laval announced a new, compulsory program of work in Germany. Called the STO (Service de Travail Obligatoire), the legislation called for a period of forced labor in the German Reich for all French males who had reached the age of military service in 1940, 1941, and 1942. In reality, Laval's hand had been forced by Hitler, but the result was the opposite of whatever Vichy may have hoped for. Overnight, thousands of young men who felt no desire to labor for someone else's *Vaterland* went into hiding. They hid in the mountains and forests. They learned how to carry guns and steal food for a living. They were called the Maquis, and they swelled the ranks of the Resistance into an army.

By the autumn of 1942, the war had started to go sour for Nazi Germany. There were substantial losses on the eastern front, and at home the civilian population was suffering from bombings and hunger. More manpower was needed to fuel the war effort, and what better place to look for replacements than the cooperative government of Vichy France?

Pierre Laval, who was by now the de facto leader of Vichy, was irrevocably caught in the web of collaboration. The promised New European Order continued to dangle temptingly before him (until the end he believed that France would assuredly play an important leadership role in the new society), but the price was the proverbial pound of flesh. This time, the Germans demanded 250,000 men. Furthermore, they insisted they be on the job by the middle of March 1943. Laval was obliged to create new legislation to enforce the departures. And no social class was exempt from the obligatory service.

Parents and siblings were made responsible for their relatives, and fines of up to 100,000 francs were imposed on anyone who helped a draft dodger. The Vichy government and the Nazis (who were only too happy to help) conducted surprise roundups in cafés and restaurants, arresting hundreds of men, who were then dispatched to prison camps. Identity cards indicating one's place of employment became necessary in order to obtain food.

Thousands did, indeed, find themselves packed off to Germany, but the spirit of resistance was hardening. Women lay across the railway tracks to prevent trains from leaving and allow the men to escape. Young men left shouting insults — "*Laval, assassin*" — or defiance — "*Vive de Gaulle.*" They sang "*La Marseillaise*" at the top of their lungs. Sometimes they sang the "*Internationale.*" There were also small

Klaus Barbie as a young SS officer. (*photo Sygma, Paris*)

The aged Marshal Pétain, chief of state of the collaborationist government of Vichy France, with President Pierre Laval. After the Liberation Pétain was condemned to death, but his sentence was commuted. Laval was also condemned and was subsequently executed. (*photo Keystone Canada*)

Philippe Henriot was minister of propaganda for the Vichy government, and his open admiration for Hitler is apparent in his dress and podium decorations. One of Henriot's favorite pronouncements was, "Germany is defending Christian civilization." (*photo Keystone Canada*)

A typical 1940s anti-Semitic propaganda poster that combined several popular themes. Here the Allies (Great Britain and the United States) and Soviet communism are being manipulated behind the scenes by "the Jew." A variation on this theme recurred in the 1980s (though not specifically in France) and became a link to the Klaus Barbie affair. (*photo Tallandier, Paris*)

A roundup of Jews in Paris conducted by French, and not German, police. (*photo Tallandier, Paris*)

Victor Fajnzylber sent a letter to the Vichy government explaining that he was a patriotic veteran who had recently lost his leg as a result of war wounds. He was exempted from wearing the yellow star, but not from being deported to Auschwitz, where he perished along with his wife. Both children escaped deportation and survived. (*photo Centre de Documentation Juive Contemporaine, Paris*)

A cell in which Resistance fighters were tortured by the Gestapo. Thick walls prevented the prisoners' cries from being heard from the street. (*photo Tallandier, Paris*)

A young *résistant* being tortured. This
photograph was found after the Liberation in a
room used for torture by the Gestapo. (*photo
Tallandier, Paris*)

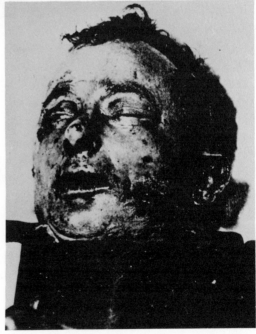

...inal outcome. (*photo Tallandier, Paris*)

Resistance fighters Lucie and Raymond Aubrac in 1943. Lucie Aubrac conducted one of the most daring operations of the war by rescuing her husband and several others from the seemingly impregnable prison of Montluc in Lyons. (*photo courtesy of Monsieur and Madame Aubrac*)

Fort Montluc in Lyons, where Klaus Barbie imprisoned *résistants* and Jews. Montluc had no plumbing and ventilation was so poor prisoners complained of suffocation. Summary executions took place dail in the courtyard. (*photo Tallandier, Paris*)

Jean Moulin, France's most famous Resistance hero, who was betrayed to Klaus Barbie in June, 1943. The fact that Moulin's death was not included among the charges brought against Barbie is a source of deep controversy in France. (*photo Keystone Canada*)

René Hardy was tried and acquitted twice for having betrayed Jean Moulin. The ongoing controversy over his innocence or guilt abated only slightly over forty years and was revived in the months leading up to the Barbie trial by Barbie's defense lawyer, among others. (*photo Keystone Canada*)

A 1972 demonstration before the Bolivian embassy in Paris demanding the extradition of Klaus Barbie, alias Altmann. (*photo Keystone Canada*)

acts of love that have lived for almost half a century. As the train pulled out of the Lyons station in March 1943, the mother of one young man pressed a bouquet of hand-picked wild flowers into her son's hand. The boy kept the dried flowers beside him during twenty-eight months of forced exile. When he returned home he divided the bouquet into two parts. Years later he laid one part on his mother's grave. "The other part will accompany me when my time comes," he wrote.[1]

All the resistance movements picked up deserters from the STO program, but the communist resistance was the most adept. Its clandestine paper, *L'Humanité*, gave specific tactical instructions on how to avoid the "deportation," as STO was called, by inciting public incidents that would arouse mass anger against the French police who were responsible for overseeing the program. *L'Humanité* informed its growing readership of demonstrations against the departures and of impending strikes and other bold expressions of rebellion. It also called for the immediate creation of an armed resistance.

As a result, the Francs-Tireurs et Partisans (FTP), the communist sector of the resistance, picked up thousands of new "soldiers."

The stronger the resistance grew, the more oppressive were the measures legislated by the Vichy government — ironically, all in the name of establishing "order." Soon the country was torn asunder as the two Frances battled each other in the most serious outbreak of mutual hatred since the Dreyfus affair — indeed, the most devastating outbreak the nation had ever seen. An authentic civil war broke out in 1943. And the principal beneficiaries were the Nazi occupiers.

"We are the standard-bearers in the struggle for a world free from oppression."

This clarion call in the name of freedom came not from the resistance or any of the leaders of the allied forces (who might very well have phrased identical words), but from Joseph Goebbels, minister of propaganda for the German Reich. The "oppressors" in the Nazi world view were, of course, Jews, communists, Freemasons and all the allied enemies of Germany.

The Nazi definition of "oppression" found an immediate echo in France, that is, in the collective response of the traditional antidemocratic Right that had rejected the Revolution, destroyed the Commune, defended the army against Dreyfus, attacked the Front Populaire of Léon Blum, rejected "foreigners," welcomed the defeat of

1940, and ecstatically embraced the National Revolution of Marshal Pétain with its emphasis on the conservative values of *famille*, *travail*, *patrie*. "Anticommunism" soon evolved into a buzzword that came to include everything considered undesirable. Jews were "communists" and communists were "Jews." Gaullists and Freemasons were also "communists." By 1943, "patriotism" meant the suppression of everyone who disagreed.

Millions of French men and women held these views, in part or in their totality, and in context, the presumably "shocking" vision of Frenchmen wearing Waffen-ss uniforms, swearing allegiance to Hitler and dashing off to die for their *French* "idealistic" beliefs was not so surprising after all. By the later years of the war, the Nazi occupier had, indeed, become the supreme French patriot.

That is why Klaus Barbie had so much help. Anticommunism was the glue that bound collaboration and the Gestapo together, in pursuit of a common goal. The Nazis, as Nazis, may have been intrinsically more interested in the Final Solution, but it was the struggle against "bolshevism" that assured them the indispensable collaboration of the French. In any case, "bolshevism" was deliberately construed to include the Jews.

Prime Minister Pierre Laval brought pro-Nazi French collaborationism into the mainstream of Vichy politics on June 22, 1942, with his famous radio broadcast. "I wish for the victory of Germany, for without [that victory] communism will take over Europe," he informed millions of listeners. Similarly, in July 1942, Secretary of State Jacques Benoist-Méchin could reassure French volunteers suffering on the eastern front that they were fighting "alongside soldiers from seven other nations who are struggling like you for the independence of their country."[2] "Independence" in this context did not mean freedom from the Wehrmacht and the ss that were occupying France, but freedom from the perceived menace of international communism. Similarly, Philippe Henriot, minister of propaganda for Vichy, was able to claim that "Germany is defending Christian civilization." And still in the same vein, Marcel Déat, one of the hard-line Paris collaborationists, could reduce the entire war to the dimensions of French "patriotism" by concluding that "The Anglo-American alliance is no more than a Front Populaire on a world scale." In other words, the Allies were also "communists."

Right-wing France was represented in the Resistance by individuals whose sense of nationalism continued to include the traditional hatred of Germany, but for most people on the Right, the ideological factors that eventually pushed them into collaboration were a hatred of democracy and communism and, to a lesser degree, anti-Semitism (lesser because there were plenty of anti-Semites in the Resistance, but fewer antidemocrats).[3] A collaborator called Jean Bassompierre put it best. "I joined the collaboration because I was always anticommunist and because I wanted to defend France and the old continent against the new Asian barbarians," he explained. As such he was prepared, in his words, "to overcome my scruples" and "join the ranks of the new crusaders."[4] The religious metaphor was important to the hard-line collaborators. It appealed, of course, to conservative Catholics, to that large majority among the faithful that was prepared on principle to accept any idea presumably sponsored by the church. But to understand the real meaning of this "new crusade" one needed to look not to France but across the Rhine; one needed to have listened to the exhortations of Adolf Hilter at Nuremberg in the early 1930s and to have understood the significance of his new "holy order." "By defending myself against the Jew I am fighting for the work of God," he wrote.[5] In Nazi France as in Nazi Germany, the God-inspired crusaders were after blood.

Contrary to postwar mythology, according to which at varying times every living French man and woman was either a *résistant* or (in recent years) a *collabo*, the truth was far more banal. About 1 percent of the French fought in the active Resistance from the beginning. By the autumn of 1943 when reaction to the STO legislation had set in, the numbers climbed to about 2 percent. But as the war ended and it became evident that the Allies were actually approaching, hundreds of thousands of "eleventh-hour" *résistants* materialized. They waved flags and shouted deliriously for de Gaulle. Some courageously battled the Germans in the streets of Paris, where many lost their lives, sometimes from inexperience. Others — dyed-in-the-wool Pétainists — woke up one morning having magically experienced an overnight conversion to Gaullism. The bulk of the population had decided to wait and see which way the battle would go. When the tide turned against Germany, they shrewdly took up position on the winning side.

At the other extreme, about 1 percent of the population was engaged in active collaboration.[6] These were the ideologues, the people who killed their fellow countrymen, wore SS uniforms, and marched off to the eastern front to fight bolshevism (where, in fact, they were badly treated by the German ss). These were the people who wrote between three and five million letters denouncing their neighbors for prestige and profit, signing themselves "A patriot serving his country," or, in another case, "A good Frenchman, a good Catholic and a war veteran."[7] These were the people who sought positions of political power at a local or national level under Nazi tutelage.

It would be a mistake, however, to write off the collaboration as a tiny movement of crackpots. The collaboration was not the offshoot of a marginal voice in France. On the contrary, it was the extreme expression of attitudes that were deeply rooted in the French psyche. Most important, it was official state policy.

The collaboration was an idea — "ideal" its devotees would have said; but once the "ideal" had made inroads into the imagination of a believer, once he was decidedly interested, even hooked, a new process took over. For the majority of French men and women in 1940, collaboration meant little more than a policy of cooperation with the occupier; but little by little it came to signify a series of commitments that were infinitely more compromising. In the end, the hard-liner who had initiated or merely yielded to the increasingly militant demands of the collaboration could see only terror over the horizon and the outlines of his own personal demise. In the national frenzy that followed the Liberation, the most visible among them were brutally destroyed.

The name Joseph Darnand is synonymous in France with *La Milice* (the Militia) one of the ugliest creations of the official state collaboration; and Darnand's personal history is in itself an interesting microcosm of the era. Like so many hard-line collaborators he was a veteran of the 1914–18 war, indeed, a hero of that war. He was anti-German, antidemocratic, anti-Semitic, anticommunist and patriotic: the classic profile of traditional rightist France.

After the war Darnard joined Action Française, and in 1928 he was named regional chief (Provence) for the Camelots du roi, the militant arm of the Action Française organization. After the defeat of 1940, Darnand made his philosophical position perfectly clear. "We have suffered catastrophe in silence for long enough. Now the true French patriots must replace the *Métèques* [half-breeds], the Jews and the foreigners. We must chase out these false Frenchmen who have led the country into ruin . . . exploited us and destroyed us."

In February 1942, with the support of the government, Darnand created a new organization called the Service d'Ordre Légionnaire. SOL, as it was called, was a major step forward for the pro-Nazi collaboration. In their khaki uniforms and berets, its members resembled Hitler's Brownshirts, and the essence of their doctrine was fascist. They were "against bolshevism and for nationalism; against disruptive Gaullism and for French unity; against the Jewish leprosy and for French purity; against pagan Freemasonry and for a Christian civilization; against laxness and for the punishment of crimes."

Their company song left nothing to the imagination.

SOL, make France pure,
Bolsheviks, Freemasons, Israel, all rotting manure,
All will be vomited, you'll soon see,
Only then will France be free.[9]

On January 31, 1943, SOL was officially transformed into *La Milice*, on orders from Pierre Laval and the Marshal himself. The *Milice* was instructed to "fight against communism" and, ominously, to "maintain order." By the autumn of that year, about 10,000 men and women were enrolled as activists within its ranks.

There were real advantages to belonging to the *Milice* at a time when food and other supplies were at a premium. There were, for instance, significant cash gifts for denunciations. There was also the opportunity to pillage seized property. The *Milice* attracted members from various fascist groups as well as ordinary people from the working and lower middle classes. It also recruited common criminals into its ranks.

Although the *Milice* was an adjunct of the French government and officially independent, it operated in close conjunction with the Gestapo; and the methods its members (*miliciens*) employed in the "preservation of order" were every bit as deadly as those of their ss brethren. Torture, premeditated murder and actions of the most ghoulish sort were commonplace as the fratricidal war among the French escalated in intensity during 1943 and 1944. When Klaus Barbie said forty years later that he could not have done his job without the able services of his French colleagues, he was speaking the truth.

Although the membership was lower middle class and working class, the leadership of the *Milice* included several of the oldest names in the French nobility. One hundred and fifty of these men went through an extensive executive-training course that was held in the chateau

Saint-Martin-d'Uriage near Grenoble. Later, a school for training female leaders of the movement was created near Lyons.

The first director of the d'Uriage school was not a Frenchman at all. De la Noue du Vair was an Acadian. He was a Ph.D. in Thomist philosophy, a royalist and a disciple of Charles Maurras and Action Française. Although his family had lived for centuries in North America, they never forgot their heritage as great feudal lords. Du Vair's grandfather had returned to defend his ancestral home during the war of 1870 and had volunteered to fight for France during World War I. In 1939 at the age of thirty-five, du Vair also felt the call of duty. If the *Milice* was for God and against communism, that was enough for him.

The family coat of arms flew from the castle steeple along with an assortment of Vichy ensigns. Inside, the tone was chivalrous, as befitted the domain of a feudal lord. This was not the place to speak of murder or torture or extortion. On the contrary, here the day began with Mass followed by a program of study of those nineteenth-century political doctrines in which right-wing ideology was rooted. The students examined the writings of Maurras and Proudhon, among others, with special emphasis on the racist theories of Gobineau. They learned about propaganda by studying the methods used by the communists. They were trained for military action with special attention paid to street fighting. According to historian Jacques Delperrie de Bayac, the program at d'Uriage aimed specifically at developing an army that could wage a civil war. The men at d'Uriage were not being trained to fight the Germans who were occupying their country. They were being prepared to kill their fellow Frenchmen.

It was the decade of the 1940s, but for du Vair the era might have been 1490. Ensconced in his feudal castle, he dreamed and plotted. Among other things, he believed that Canada would return to the French motherland because French Canadians had more children than English Canadians. He also initiated a correspondence with the Count of Paris and developed a bizarre scheme to reinstate him as king of France — in the midst of the Occupation.

Vichy was already suspicious of du Vair. He was just a touch too popular among *Milice* recruits for their liking. And besides, as an Acadian, he didn't have the right *French* credentials. So when government notables got wind of his plans, they were delighted to have found a pretext to get rid of him. Du Vair actually tried to mobilize an army of *miliciens* to storm Vichy and put the king back on his rightful throne, but when he failed to rouse enough enthusiasm he barricaded his fortress in medieval style and attempted a defense. Joseph Darnand himself marched on Saint-Martin-d'Uriage and set up camp in the town at the base of the castle, but eventually a traitor within opened the doors and du Vair was arrested. He escaped to Germany (where he was killed in a bombing attack in 1944), but several of his disciples remained loyal. One was Joseph Lecussan, a man of extraordinary brutality, who became chief of the Lyons *Milice*. Another protégé of du Vair, Count Jacques Duge de Bernonville, subsequently worked closely with Klaus Barbie and found refuge after the war in Quebec where he was protected by the mayor of Montreal, Camillien Houde, several federal MPs from Quebec and members of the Quebec National Assembly, as well as church officials and the Montreal Saint Jean Baptiste Society. (Quebec MPP René Chalont described de Bernonville as "a great Roman Catholic, a great Frenchman, and a war hero.") In 1951, faced with an extradition demand from France and certain deportation from Canada, de Bernonville fled to Brazil where he was murdered in 1972, the same year Klaus Altmann was revealed to be Klaus Barbie. (It is also worth noting that, just before he was murdered, de Bernonville had announced that he was planning to publish his memoirs of life in Lyons.)

A third protégé of du Vair was Paul Touvier, whose checkered postwar career would become a scandal in the early 1970s and an issue in the Klaus Barbie affair ten years later. In a group of violent men, Paul Touvier, head of the second section of the *Milice* in Lyons, outdid most of them in violence. He shot Jews and threw grenades into synagogues filled with worshippers. On one occasion he did not hesitate to rape the wife and daughter of a Jewish man in return for sparing all their lives. Afterward he boasted of his generosity. The man, his wife and his daughter, now in Israel, did not speak of their horrifying trade-off for forty-one years.

But Touvier was also greedy. His looting and pillaging was so uncontrolled that other *miliciens* became jealous, and bitter rivalries resulted. By the end of the war, he had collected a sizable "treasury," as it was called, and he is reputed to have used it to save himself. Rumors abounded. It was said that he bought certain members of the Resistance who promised to let him escape. It was said that as the Allies approached he freed prisoners, before the Gestapo could destroy them, in return for the same privilege. It was said that he was protected by powerful elements within the Catholic church. (This was later revealed to be true, a compromising fact that would eventually become a part of the Barbie defense strategy.)

In January 1944, one of the most horrifying institutions of the entire apparatus of collaboration was legislated into existence: the special courts-martial of the *Milice*. All due process was suspended. Indeed, if Joseph Darnand decided that a prisoner was to appear before a court-martial, the death sentence was typed up in local police headquarters in advance. The coffin and the firing squad were present in the courtyard of the prison before the trial even took place. The three *Milice*-appointed judges (chosen personally by Darnand) met within the walls of the prison and discussed the case among themselves. The "terrorist" was then brought before them to hear their inevitable conclusion. No evidence was admitted; no extenuating circumstances were allowed; no lawyer was present. The only sentence was death — which was carried out immediately in the courtyard of the prison.

Each condemned man was given pencil and paper to write a last letter to a loved one, but in Lyons the local chief of police routinely destroyed these letters so there would be no evidence of the court-martial proceedings. In the same spirit, the judges remained anonymous. They never signed their names, and they hid their faces in their collars whenever they entered or left the prison.[10]

Robbing, torturing and killing their fellow countrymen alongside the *Milice* was the Parti Populaire Française (PPF), a working-class, pro-Nazi fascist party founded in 1936 by Jacques Doriot (an ex-communist) during the final spasms of the Third Republic. The ideology of the PPF was the usual: anticommunist, anti-Semitic, anti-Freemason, anti-Gaullist, antidemocratic. The PPF in Lyons worked so closely with Barbie that in early 1944 it was officially integrated into Section IV and given its own offices in Gestapo headquarters on avenue Berthelot. (The Gestapo had had to move when torture facilities at the Hotel Terminus proved inadequate.)

The most notorious and feared collaborator in Lyons was Francis André of the PPF, known as *"Gueule tordue"* or "Twisted Mug" because of a paralyzed muscle that had distorted his face. Like Jacques Doriot, André was a born ideologue. In 1933 he joined the French Communist party, but abandoned the Left to join Doriot's ultraright PPF in 1937. From then until the outbreak of war, he was involved in many of the violent confrontations of the Left and the Right that marked

France in the 1930s. His specialty was organizing strike-breaking activities.

After the defeat of France, André joined the Légion des volontaires contre le bolshévisme in 1941 and went to fight alongside the Germans on the Russian front. He gave up and returned to France when he noted that the French volunteers were being assigned to the rear of the German units to act as buffers against attacks by Soviet partisans.

Back in Lyons, new opportunities opened up. The arrival of the Gestapo provided a well-organized superstructure to which he could attach himself and the PPF. And when the STO program created a full-scale resistance, André shifted into high gear.

Under orders from Jacques Doriot, he created the Mouvement national anti-terroriste (MNAT), comprising a force of 200 activists drawn from the region of the Rhône Valley. Their targets were communists and Jews. Barbie offered André a salary of 200,000 francs a month, but André turned it down in favor of an arrangement with SS chief Karl Oberg, in which any loot acquired during PPF operations against the Resistance was shared with the Germans. Booty from anti-Jewish operations was shared with PPF headquarters in Paris.

Not surprisingly, André and his men of the MNAT were particularly interested in attacking Jews. In April 1944, in a typical operation, his team sniffed out a Jewish furrier called Rossner. They arrived at Rossner's door in a surprise attack and found the room where the furrier had tried to hide his merchandise. In a flurry they grabbed the skins, a few coats and some money that had been hidden, shot Rossner point blank and delivered his wife to the Gestapo. Mrs. Rossner was sent to Fort Montluc, to Drancy, then to Auschwitz. She never returned.

At a time when terror was a daily staple in a city torn by fratricidal guerrilla warfare, the personal brutality of Gestapo chief Klaus Barbie was legendary. Barbie's victims were always a little surprised to discover that he was a rather short, stocky man — if his reputation was anything to go by, he should have been a colossus. He had dark hair and piercing blue eyes that he used to advantage during interrogations. Forty years later, his victims remembered his eyes. And he always wore a white scarf draped elegantly around his neck. The other memorable thing about Barbie was his arrogance. The way he moved his body, the way he carried a personal whip that seemed to acquire a dreaded personality of its own, the way his 9 mm American pistol hung casually from a slightly slackened belt. And the way he played the power game. That game consisted of humiliating his victims as well as destroying their bodies. Their suffering meant nothing to him. He made that perfectly clear by fondling his French secretary while he conducted a torture session. He kicked heads, injected acid into human bladders and hung almost lifeless people upside down from ceiling hooks while he took a break from business to play a little love song on the piano. "*Parlez-moi d'amour*" was one of his favorites. Women were always tortured naked, to the deep enjoyment of their torturers. Barbie kept two German shepherd dogs. One was trained to lunge and bite. The other was trained to mount naked women who had first been ordered on their hands and knees, a humiliation that could cut deeper than the whip, than having one's fingernails pulled out, or one's nipples burned with cigarettes. He threatened the lives of his victims' families, sometimes presenting them in person, or pretending they were just downstairs about to be tortured. He led his victims to understand he was just about to shoot them. Barbie taunted the Resistance by traveling around Lyons alone, without protection. He ate in his favorite restaurants, Le Moulin à Vent, Les Glaces, or Le Lapin Blanc. No one ever shot at him. Were they afraid they might miss?

Barbie was so good at his job that on September 18, 1943, he was personally cited by Himmler, and on November 9, 1943, he was awarded the Iron Cross, First Class, with sword.

The Ecole de Santé Militaire, a former Army, medical school, was a stolid building made of brown-gray stone on avenue Berthelot. It had deep basements where prisoners could be kept while awaiting their interrogation sessions. The thick walls also prevented the prisoners' cries from being heard from the street. The four outside walls of the Ecole enclosed a large courtyard, which was ideal for loading and unloading prisoners who were being taken back and forth from prison.

Special offices in the Ecole de Santé were set aside to receive the denunciations that "rained" on the Gestapo, according to Barbie. To denounce a neighbor or a business rival might be the equivalent of a death sentence, but once a reward was offered per head, the Gestapo could barely handle the influx. Every week a little old priest trekked in from Grenoble with his list of Jews and "communists" clutched in his hand. A few wives denounced their husbands; and a lot of people settled old scores.

Barbie used the denunciations to recruit collaborators. "The informer had to give me exact data about himself. In this way I could get to know him and persuade him to cooperate further," he acknowledged in a self-serving interview with Brazilian journalist Edwaldo Dantas Ferreira in 1972. "We also tested the authenticity of these French collaborators. When there was a face-to-face battle with the guerrillas we insisted that they dress in German uniform. That way their position was clear to everyone." In retrospect, Barbie was pleased with what he called "the French personnel of my command." "They were faithful and [they] felt close to Germany. We were in a common struggle against communism and we were willing to risk everything to achieve our goals," he recalled.

Interrogations were carried out on the fourth floor of the Ecole de Santé by Barbie and his associates and by Francis André and *his* associates in rooms that had been specially furnished with a gas heater, pokers (that were heated), an examining table with leg and arm straps, and the notorious baths. The baths are what the survivors of Barbie's interrogations remember with most horror. Victims were undressed and their wrists were tied to their ankles like trussed pigs. A pole was then pushed under their arms and they were immersed in the water, head first. The pole rested across the tub.

The victim was doused alternately with boiling water and ice water, and his head held under until he was an inch from death. All the while the same series of questions was asked. "Who is the leader of your network?" "What are the names and addresses of your colleagues?" "When and where will the next meeting be held?"

Jean Gay still trembles as he describes the bath treatment he underwent forty years ago. He was arrested by the Gestapo in Lyons on March 7, 1944. Someone had denounced him as a *résistant* in the Combat network. For several hours during two consecutive days he was submerged in the freezing then boiling water, but the one memory he cannot bring to consciousness without a renewal of psychic pain concerns his children. During the torture session, Barbie told Gay his two sons were downstairs and that they would be tortured in front of him unless he provided the information Barbie wanted. The choice was unbearable. Gay tried to kill himself by jumping out of an open window. When he regained consciousness, he was in the infirmary at Montluc prison. The next day he was deported to a prison camp.

Prisoners waiting their turn in the basement of the Ecole de Santé were treated to the spectacle of those who had preceded them to the fourth floor. This, too, was part of the torture. When you saw your friends return a mass of bleeding, torn flesh and when you saw eyes torn from sockets and fingers and toes hacked off with kitchen knives, you might be more likely to crack in advance. Especially if you were also offered, in return for information, regular access to food for yourself and your family, protection and money. What the Gestapo really wanted was to add to their pool of regular informers. The best possible outcome of a session from Barbie's point of view was to "turn" a *résistant*, to send him back to his comrades as a Gestapo spy after a token stay in prison to camouflage the new reality. When this became known, cell mates in Montluc could no longer speak to each other of their agony. The man on the next straw mat might have been "turned."

Like the Ecole de Santé, Montluc suited Klaus Barbie's needs ideally. The prison had been built in the early nineteenth century and consisted of cell blocks surrounding a central courtyard. After the occupation in November 1942, the Nazis built wooden barracks along one wall of the courtyard to house Jews. Men, women and children were packed in there while awaiting deportation to Drancy, or as a ready pool of hostages should the Germans wish to execute a few people as a show of strength.

The men and women housed in the regular cells were slightly better off than the Jews, but Montluc had no plumbing, and the ventilation was so poor that prisoners sometimes complained of near suffocation. Rest of any sort was impossible. There were cockroaches, lice and vermin of all descriptions. But the common recollection of all who spent time within those walls was the nightly *parachutage*, as they called it. As soon as the lights went out, inmates were attacked by thousands of insects. "That ravenous multitude. As soon as night fell they dropped in clusters from the ceilings, the crevices in the walls, and did not return until dawn," recalled a prisoner.

When the lights went out at night, no one knew for sure whether he would live to see another day. Roll call came early. The voices of the guards resounded through the stone corridors. The air was perfectly still as prisoners held their breath, waiting to hear the dreaded consonances of their own names. For there were three kinds of calls. "Without baggage" meant the end of the road, the firing squad. "With baggage" meant deportation to a concentration camp (Mauthausen). "Police" meant a return to the fourth floor of the Ecole de Santé.

The man who heard the sound of his name, followed by "without baggage," knew the end had come. He heard the guards shout "*Los, los*" ("Hurry, hurry") and bang on the cell door. Hurriedly he pulled on his pants and tied his shoes. His friends touched him wordlessly, trying to smile. If he had had a chance to write a final letter to his mother, or wife, he now chose someone he hoped he could trust to deliver it, should the messenger himself survive. The door opened. He stepped or was yanked out. The door clanged shut again.

From inside the cell, his mates watched in silence. He fell into line with the other condemned men. "*Los, los* . . ." His cell mates pressed their faces against the steel, following him with their eyes as long as they could, shouting words of encouragement. They banged on the walls with their tin cups, or sang "*La Marseillaise*." So did the prisoners "without baggage." This death had to have some meaning.

Minutes later there was a burst of machine-gun fire in the prison courtyard. The singing and banging ended — for the day.

Occasionally, the prisoners "without baggage" were loaded into a truck and murdered somewhere out of town. Such was the case at two localities near Lyons: Bron, where mainly civilian Jews were killed, and Saint-Genis-Laval, where the victims were mostly members of the Resistance. The details of these massacres, for that is what they were, are revolting in the extreme: executioners standing on freshly killed bodies piled upon bodies, the blood of the newly dead dripping through a ceiling onto those waiting below to die, and so on.

For the most part, the dead were left to rot in the countryside, or simply dumped into the Rhône or Saône rivers. In the month of August 1944, more than a hundred cadavers were fished out of the Rhône. The lucky ones had been shot. The others had had their heads bashed in.

Between 1942 and 1944, between 7,500 and 10,000 people were incarcerated at Montluc.[11] Only one escape attempt was successful, and it was organized and carried out by Lucie Aubrac.

Raymond Aubrac[12] was arrested along with Jean Moulin at Caluire on June 21, 1943; but, during his interrogation sessions with Barbie, he continued to maintain that he was "Claude Ermelin," from Tunisia. Between sessions he was incarcerated at Montluc.

On June 23, a very proper young woman called "Guislaine de Barbantane" arrived at the Ecole de Santé and asked to speak to the officer in charge of the Caluire interrogations. Lucie Aubrac was ushered into Klaus Barbie's office. He was dressed in a light summer suit and a pink shirt, recalled Aubrac. And there was a young woman with him.

"I am a friend of one of Dr. Dugoujon's patients who was arrested at Caluire," she began. "Claude Ermelin — from Tunisia. You must let him go because he has a serious case of tuberculosis and must have special medical treatment."

Barbie began to laugh. Then he pulled out Raymond Aubrac's file and threw it on the desk. Inside was a picture of Raymond, Lucie and their small son taken on a beach during happier days. "Who's that child?" asked Barbie.

"My godson," replied Aubrac, thinking quickly. "He's a war orphan and I look after him."

"His name is Valette. The only medical treatment he needs is a last cigarette and a glass of rum," retorted Barbie.

Lucie Aubrac was sincerely frightened, but she had another ruse up her sleeve that was worth trying. She began to cry.

"I'm expecting his child. I am disgraced." Lucie was searching for a way to see Raymond.

Barbie's response was psychologically interesting. In the midst of the horror of Section IV, a vestige of prewar chivalry remained.

"Ah, mademoiselle," he said, sympathetically. "Men, men, you should never trust them."

Then he dismissed her.

Lucie Aubrac tried to see Barbie again, but he had lost interest. She approached other Gestapo officers with gifts of money and food. Would they help her see Barbie again? On October 20, she was told Barbie had agreed to meet her the next day.

During the intervening weeks, Lucie Aubrac had hatched a plot to hijack the truck carrying her husband back and forth from Montluc to the Ecole de Santé and had co-opted the help of eleven members of the secret army. The attack was planned for October 21. On that very same morning, October 21, Barbie allowed her to talk with Raymond.

"You are a bastard," she shouted at him for Barbie's benefit. "I am expecting your child and it must have a name. I don't care if they deport you or shoot you, but you must marry me first."

Raymond Aubrac realized an escape plan was being acted out. That night as the truck transporting the prisoners back to Montluc left the Ecole de Santé, a van moved inauspiciously in front of it. Lucie was inside. Another van and a car took up position in the rear. Inside the truck the prisoners were chained together in pairs. After a few minutes, the van behind moved up to pass the truck. As it drew level with the cab, three machine guns with silencers sprayed bullets at the driver, killing all three riders. The guards in the back of the truck leaped out. All of them but one were killed on the spot. A lone guard escaped, as did all fourteen prisoners.

"The most important outcome of the maneuver was the effect it had on public opinion in Lyons," recalled Madame Aubrac many years later. "It meant the Gestapo was no longer invincible. After the war many of the prisoners who were in Montluc at the time told me the knowledge that the Gestapo could be beaten, even if only once, gave them enormous hope."

Nineteen forty-three was a year of terror in Lyons — on both sides. The *Milice* under Lecussan and Touvier and the PPF under Francis André embarked on a rampage of officially sanctioned killing and torture in collaboration with the Gestapo. On January 10, 1944, Joseph Lecussan personally murdered the philosopher and former president of the League for the Rights of Man, Victor Basch, and his wife: the same naively idealistic Victor Basch who had so passionately challenged Raymond Aron's contention that democracy was a fragile, vulnerable entity.[13]

Lecussan was a fanatical anti-Semite who was heard to mutter to himself, "Dirty Jew, you're going to die," as he set out to find Basch.[14] Basch and his wife were loaded into a car at gunpoint, then driven to what Lecussan later described as "a suitable spot." There they were shot to death and their bodies left on the side of the road. Monsieur and Madame Basch were both in their eighties.

The tide of the war turned definitively, and as the Allies approached Lyons in the summer of 1944, Klaus Barbie and his French collaborators attempted to liquidate as many *résistants* and deport as many Jews as they could,[15] in an orgy of killing before the final escape across the Rhine. Back in Germany, the war now lost, Barbie was promoted once again — to ss-Hauptsturmführer (captain). The recommendation for this honor described him as an "enthusiastic ss leader" and a man "with a definite talent for intelligence work and the pursuit of crime."[16]

In the aftermath of the Occupation, the most visible of the collaborators were either lynched by the mob or tried by the courts with varying degrees of severity. Politicians and journalists got the worst of it, as did ordinary working-class men and women. The middle and upper classes largely escaped, partly because the old class divisions still operated, partly because France needed its professionals and industrialists to rebuild its economy. Pierre Laval was executed on October 15, 1945, after a trial that is now generally recognized to have been a travesty of justice. Marshal Philippe Pétain was also condemned to death, but his sentence was commuted. Francis André was executed, and Paul Touvier was protected—under circumstances that would later be excavated publicly and embarrassingly.

Joseph Darnand was also executed, but not before he addressed a revealing letter to de Gaulle in which he asked for pardon for his *miliciens*.

In their great majority, these men are authentic Frenchmen with the warlike qualities of their race. Their patriotism had led them to make the supreme sacrifice for their country. Their only error has been loyalty . . . They are almost alone in not having abandoned a lost cause.

I can assure you that even in the breast of those who wore a German uniform beats a patriotic French heart. Many of them died on the battlefields of the Russian front crying, "Vive la France." Others shouted the same cry of love as they were shot.

Right-wing, nationalist France was in defeat, but not in eclipse.

The last French trial of a Nazi or a collaborator took place in 1960,[17] and nine years later, the first public reference to the collaboration appeared. *The Sorrow and the Pity* was refused permission to be broadcast on government-controlled national television, but it did appear in the movie houses of Paris. It was a sobering documentary that frightened those who "knew" and shocked those who didn't. Parisians lined up to witness their own very recent history. And a new era of remorse and denial began.

· 5 ·

THE DEVIL AND THE SUPERSTAR:
KLAUS BARBIE AND JEAN MOULIN

In the picture that is used whenever his name is mentioned in print, Jean Moulin, hero *par excellence* of the French Resistance, looks like everyone's idea of a spy — a good-guy spy, one who's on *our* side. A hat sits jauntily on his head, the rim tipped forward ready to hide his features from the gaze of an overly curious passer-by. A dark scarf is wrapped about his neck. In an emergency it, too, could be raised to shield his face from view. A half smile plays about his mouth as he leans against an anonymous, pock-marked wall in a secret corner in an unknown city. Above all, his face is open; intelligent and open. Perhaps this openness was at the root of Jean Moulin's personal tragedy. Perhaps he was simply not suspicious enough, not careful enough to survive the terrible dangers that stalked a man of his stature in early 1943.

For there has never been any doubt that Jean Moulin was betrayed to Klaus Barbie's Gestapo on June 21, 1943, the day Moulin was arrested in the office of his friend, Dr. Dugoujon, in Caluire, a suburb of Lyons. And there has never been any doubt that the security surrounding the most important member of the Resistance, the man who personally represented General de Gaulle inside France, was amazingly lax. The only question has been, who did it? Who among his colleagues was "turned" by Klaus Barbie and reinfiltrated back into the Resistance to betray his fellows?

For forty years one man has been the prime suspect, in spite of two trials and two acquittals. Moulin lost his life in 1943; but in early 1985 René Hardy was still alive. He had spent the last forty-two years suffering, certainly, for there were many who refused to accept the judgment of the court. When Barbie was returned to France in 1983,

Hardy was once again hounded by the press, most of whom were too young to remember the events that had changed the course of Hardy's life. Before the next year was out, however, Hardy would on his own initiative assume an even more ambiguous role in the new Klaus Barbie affair.

One thing was certain. For both Barbie and René Hardy the events of June 21, 1943, refused to fade into history. The betrayal and death of Jean Moulin had assured for each of them an indestructible notoriety.

Jean Moulin first became "visible" at the age of forty with an appointment to the post of prefect (chief administrator) of the department of Eure-et-Loir, just to the south of Paris. It was 1939 and the one hundred and fiftieth anniversary of the French Revolution gave him the opportunity to make public the commitments that were central to his life. "I am the great-grandson of a revolutionary soldier and the grandson of a man who was imprisoned during the Second Empire for having proclaimed his attachment to the Republic," he said proudly at a banquet where he was the keynote speaker.[1]

He could not have known how soon he would be put to the test.

It began on June 14, 1940. The Germans had occupied Paris, and hundreds of thousands of people were streaming out of the city, through Chartres where Moulin was headquartered. Many had escaped with nothing more than the clothes on their backs. They had been separated from their families. They had no food. Moulin, as prefect of Chartres, was faced with a crisis of massive proportions. "The situation is disastrous," he wrote in his diary on June 15.

What made things worse was the presence of a sizable minority that was waiting impatiently for the German army "to bring some order into this rotten mess," as one man put it in a screaming exhortation to a hysterical crowd that had gathered in front of Moulin's offices.

At 7:00 A.M. on June 17, the Germans arrived in Chartres. Moulin was waiting in the courtyard of City Hall, along with the mayor of Chartres and the bishop's representative in the city. The German procession stopped. "Tell all your subordinates that the war is over for them," ordered their commanding officer.

Moulin's first act of resistance set him on a collision course with the Nazi occupiers that would lead, inexorably, to his death. An old lady in a small village was brutally murdered in front of her daughter when she refused to allow the Germans to occupy her house. As prefect, Moulin protested. That evening two officers came to say that their commander wanted to talk to him.

At headquarters, Moulin was told to sign a document describing a fabricated event in which Senegalese soldiers in the French army had supposedly raped and massacred women in a neighboring village. Moulin was shocked. As prefect, he knew no such event had occurred. He asked for proof. In reply he was knocked to the floor with a rifle butt across the mouth.

For hours he was beaten and kicked until he was almost unconscious. He was accused of defending "a degenerate country of Jews and niggers." Then he was thrown into a cell for the night.

The next day he was tortured for seven consecutive hours, but in his cell that night he felt he would not be able to resist much longer. "I know that today I went to the limits of my resistance, and if this continues tomorrow, I will end up signing."[2] There seemed to be only one acceptable solution: his own death. This was not a new thought. "From the start of the war, I accepted the risk of death, as did millions of other Frenchmen," he later wrote.[3]

While lying in his cell, Moulin attempted to slit his throat with a piece of broken glass, but he was still alive when the guard did his rounds. They had to take him to the hospital: Moulin wasn't just anyone; he was the prefect. Rumors of his heroism spread like a brush fire. The die was cast.

Moulin went underground in November 1940 after he was relieved of his functions by the Vichy administration. His plan was to reach General de Gaulle in London. In June 1941, Moulin met Henry Frenay in Marseilles. Frenay said the Resistance needed access to de Gaulle. They needed to convey information, and they needed material help badly. Moulin agreed to be Frenay's advocate.

De Gaulle had already heard of Moulin. He knew of his heroic refusal to sign a declaration falsely inculpating the French army. He had also seen other positive reports in Moulin's prefect file, which had been forwarded to him by pro-Gaullist spies in the Vichy administration. De Gaulle badly needed recruits with leadership ability (he was known to complain about the quality of the men surrounding him), and he was deeply interested in Moulin.

In the meantime, Moulin was developing a plan to centralize the Resistance within France in the name of de Gaulle, but under his own leadership. He arrived in England at the end of October 1941. In November he met the General. By the end of the month, Moulin had orders to return to France to organize and lead a national resistance body that would be willing to take orders from London. To have convinced de Gaulle that he was the man for the job was no small achievement, but the task ahead was truly monumental. The Resistance was made up of men and women with strong personalities, large egos and fixed ideologies, who might not take kindly to orders from "elsewhere." Moulin suggested that some guarantee of British financial aid might help.

On January 1, 1942, Moulin was successfully parachuted into southern France. He quickly met with Frenay, the most prickly of the lot. Would 250,000 francs help as an indicator of things to come? Frenay was interested, but extremely unhappy about the idea of taking orders from anyone. He was understandably jealous of Moulin. The two men fought openly on several occasions.

The Resistance was as politically diverse as the rest of French political life, and it ran the full spectrum from the communists on the extreme Left to Frenay's Combat on the Right. For more than a year, Moulin held meetings under the most dangerous circumstances. Addresses were always unknown to the participants, who were met by guides and led to the designated house. Means of communication were changed constantly. So were names and aliases. One's closest colleagues were subject to arrest, torture and the possibility of being "turned" by the Gestapo. No one really knew for sure how he would react under torture.

But on May 27, 1943, the seemingly impossible happened. In a house on the rue du Four in Paris, the CNR (National Resistance Council) came into being. Jean Moulin had succeeded in bringing together, among others, conservative army officers, communists, socialists and Gaullists. Even Henri Frenay had agreed to cooperate. The CNR made it possible for the Resistance to operate on a national scale inside France and to have a voice outside the country under the leadership of de Gaulle.

But Moulin's triumph was short-lived.

Around the end of April, Klaus Barbie had succeeded in arresting several members of Frenay's Combat, including Jean Multon, a fairly recent recruit who had risen quickly in the hierarchy. Multon knew everyone, including where they lived and where they picked up their messages. And he told all — apparently even before his "interrogation" had begun.

Multon was personally responsible for the arrest of most of the Combat leadership, including Frenay's lifelong companion, Bertie Albrecht, who died at the hands of the Nazis.

Moulin knew he was in danger. "The Gestapo and the Vichy police know who I am and what I'm doing," he wrote in a report on May 7. "My job becomes more and more delicate, but I am determined to hold on as long as possible . . ."

Klaus Barbie knew all about Moulin, but he did *not* know what Moulin looked like. He wouldn't have known even after he had arrested Moulin — not until he had been duly informed by someone operating in his service.

René Hardy was also a member of Combat. In civilian life he had been an engineer for the French national railway lines. In the Resistance his job was to sabotage trains carrying war machinery to and from Germany.

On June 7, 1943, Hardy was arrested by Klaus Barbie. Three days later he was freed. It is impossible to know for sure whether Hardy agreed to spy for Barbie. One does know, however, that Hardy did not tell his Resistance comrades about his arrest. Nor did he mention it at his first trial in January 1947.

Hardy returned to Lyons on June 12. On June 20, he arranged to meet Henri Aubry, who was second in command to Frenay in the Combat organization. Aubry arrived to find Hardy seated on a park bench beside a man who seemed deeply engrossed in reading his newspaper. That man, it turned out, was Klaus Barbie.

Moulin had set June 21 as the date for a meeting of the CNR in the southern zone. All the leaders were expected to be present, or to send a delegate. Indeed, if Klaus Barbie had been able to design a trap in which he could net his most important quarries in one fell swoop, he couldn't have planned anything better than the meeting at Caluire. It was a Gestapo dream come true, the crowning success to Barbie's central mandate in Lyons.

Frenay was in London. He was to be represented at the meeting by Aubry; and Aubry invited René Hardy.

In France, the rest of the story has entered the realm of mythology. Errors abounded. Moulin and Raymond Aubrac arrived at the home of Dr. Dugoujon three-quarters of an hour after the meeting was scheduled to begin. By a strange coincidence, the Gestapo also arrived three-quarters of an hour late. Security was almost nonexistent.

The Gestapo surrounded and entered the house, rounding up and beating both *résistants* and Dr. Dugoujon's patients, who were in the waiting room. Everyone was handcuffed and taken to the Ecole de Santé — with one exception: René Hardy managed to escape. Someone shot low as Hardy fled, wounding him very slightly. Later he was treated in the hospital. Lucie Aubrac was convinced it was Hardy who betrayed Moulin, her husband and the entire Resistance. She sent him a sweet laced with arsenic. Hardy, as canny as a fox, refused to touch it.

At the Ecole de Santé, Barbie now knew he had his prize in hand; but he wasn't sure which of the men was "Max," Moulin's alias. Moulin said his name was Jacques Martel and that he owned an art gallery in Nice. (Moulin was, indeed, an artist.) But Barbie learned his true identity soon enough.

On the evening of June 23, Moulin was brought to the basement of the Ecole de Santé with a bandage on his head and his face covered with blood. On the evening of June 24, a creature who was already half dead was returned to Montluc.

At Montluc that night a German soldier told Christian Pineau, a *résistant* and trade unionist who had been appointed prison barber, to come out and shave a prisoner. In his book, *La Simple Vérité*, Pineau later described what he saw.

Moulin was unconscious, his eyes pushed into his skull as though they had been punched through his head. A horrible blue wound scarred his temple. A rattling sound came out of his swollen lips.

Pineau asked the guard for soap and water, and while he was waiting he felt Moulin's face and hands. His skin was cold.

Suddenly Moulin opened his eyes. Pineau wasn't sure he had recognized him.

"Water," Moulin whispered.

Pineau asked the guard for water. The latter, clearly compassionate, took the shaving bowl to rinse it.

A few words in English escaped Moulin's mouth. Pineau did not understand what he was saying. Pineau held the water to Moulin's lips; Moulin sipped a few drops, then fell into unconsciousness again.

Pineau was ordered back to his cell. At last sight, Moulin was lying unconscious in the prison courtyard.

Moulin was transferred to Paris, to Gestapo headquarters on the elegant avenue Foch. He was seen there, in a coma, by Henri Aubry and General Delestraint, who were being interrogated.

The last *résistant* to see him alive was André Lassagne, in a villa in Neuilly that had been appropriated by the Gestapo. Moulin was barely alive. His skin was yellow. His breathing was shallow and irregular.

Moulin was sent to Germany and is generally believed to have died en route. Later, his remains were buried in the Père Lachaise cemetery before being transferred to the Pantheon in 1964.

René Hardy was acquitted on January 27, 1947, but charged again in 1950, when it was revealed that he had lied at his first trial. He was acquitted a second time by a small majority of four to three. The communists were particularly vicious at the time of his trials. They hated Combat because it was so overtly right-wing; they hated Frenay; they hated everyone in the organization. They were convinced Hardy had betrayed Moulin and the entire work of the Resistance.

As for Klaus Barbie, he has always maintained that Hardy was his man. Not many people are prepared to take Barbie at his word, but his evidence was corroborated in a June 29, 1943, Gestapo report written by Ernst Kaltenbrunner, which named Hardy as the informer for the Caluire arrests. But important inconsistencies swayed the court. Barbie, for example, claimed that Hardy told him that "Max" was Moulin, but it was established that Hardy did not know this. There were, apparently, too many other ways Barbie could have learned that a meeting was to take place.

In terms of public opinion, however, Hardy was never fully "acquitted."

Klaus Barbie was and is aware that his "fame" in France is forever linked to his macabre confrontation with France's hero, but according to *his* version of their encounter, the two men were fast friends sharing a few pleasant moments in the afternoon. In his 1972 interview with Edwaldo Dantas Ferreira, Barbie claimed the following:

It is always said that I tortured Moulin. This is a lie, based on fantasy.

Moulin insisted that he was Jacques Martel. He said he was an artist. So I called my secretary and asked her to bring a sharp pencil and some paper. Then I asked Moulin to draw my portrait.

Moulin picked up the pencil and paper and started to draw a few lines. Suddenly he stopped drawing and started laughing. I laughed, too. Just by looking at his first lines one could see he couldn't draw anything. We both laughed openly. Obviously he was incompetent as an artist. Even in this he was like me.

I took the portrait that he had begun and I wrote on it, "Portrait by Max." I also wrote the date . . . This was one of the papers which my wife had to burn after the war.

While Moulin and I were laughing together, something dramatic happened. I said, laughing, "You were a good mayor of Chartres, don't try to change your occupation." Immediately he stopped laughing and said, "In fact, I am Jean Moulin." . . . Then he added, "You surely don't expect me to tell you about my activities in the Resistance."

I sent him back to his cell where he was bound hand and foot. The truth is I was afraid he would try to kill himself again.

The next night I questioned him again. It was my duty . . . I was still quite impressed by him, probably because he looked a lot like me, physically. Also he was calm and firm in his manner, like me . . .

Once, near the end of June, I had to go away. I gave definite instructions to watch him carefully, but the guards were just regular soldiers, and they became careless. They left Moulin's cell for a moment, leaving him alone. This was enough for Moulin . . .

When I came back I ran to his cell, expecting the worst . . . Handcuffed, he had taken advantage of the only moment he was alone to run with all his strength and bash his head against the wall. I used all the medical resources we had available . . . I called Paris . . . and they ordered me to bring him there immediately. As soon as the doctors had finished their treatment, I put him in my car and drove to Paris . . .

Many years later I read in Paris Match *in La Paz, Bolivia, about the end of Moulin and what happened to him after I left him in Paris . . . It said the Germans had burned his body and the urn containing his ashes had been placed in . . . Père Lachaise cemetery in Paris. In 1964, the urn was transferred with honors to the Pantheon accompanied by the weeping of de Gaulle and the funeral prayer of Malraux . . .*

In 1980, during an interview with *Stern* magazine, Barbie claimed that he had personally visited the Pantheon during a trip to Paris. "I know this may seem strange, but I placed a bouquet of flowers on Moulin's tomb," he told the reporter. "Although Moulin was my enemy during the war, I esteemed him highly."

Devil and superstar, their names are linked in memory and mythology. And four decades later, the Klaus Barbie affair would revive all the old passions that surrounded their fateful encounter.

· 6 ·

THE SOLITARY PASSION
OF SERGE AND BEATE KLARSFELD

If thou didst ever thy dear father love, . . .
Revenge his foul and most unnatural murder.
— William Shakespeare, HAMLET, I, 5, 25–6.

He is a short, stocky man with a brusque, almost rude manner. He is fed up with talking to journalists and does not make eye contact. Barbie has already been apprehended. Now it is time to move on to other "operations," like the case against Jean Leguay, chief of the Vichy police in the occupied zone, who has since enjoyed a successful business career on three continents. Or Maurice Papon, general secretary of the prefecture in Bordeaux who personally signed deportation orders for 1,500 Jews before continuing a brilliant political career. Serge Klarsfeld has been successful in having both men indicted for crimes against humanity in one of the first applications of the law in France.

Klarsfeld is outraged and saddened to realize that men and women who committed terrible crimes have gone on to lead harmonious, successful lives in their own countries — in Germany and France, for example. Others have enjoyed harmonious, successful lives elsewhere — in Spain, Syria, Latin America, Canada and the United States. Their victims — bones and ashes for forty years — live only in the tortured memory of those who loved them, people whose own lives have been drastically altered by the knowledge that the most fantastic nightmare that could ever visit a child hiding from monsters under the bed came true. The night terror did not dissipate with the dawn. The psychic experience spilled into a reality too terrible to assimilate.

For how does one bear the knowledge that one's father was ripped away from his home in the still hours of a September morning in the prime of his life, shipped to an unknown destination in a sealed, airless boxcar with hundreds of others, all seized with terror, then destroyed without emotion at the journey's end? If only one could have *helped* him, even though one was only eight years old. How does one

110

bear the knowledge that this father quite literally offered himself to the Gestapo so his family, trembling behind a false wall, might escape unnoticed?

Arno Klarsfeld and his wife, Raissa, had both come to Paris to study in the 1920s, he from Rumania and she from Russia. They met in a cafe in the Latin Quarter, married and had two children. Arno went into business.

When war broke out, Arno volunteered for the French army, though he was not yet a French citizen. France was the dreamed-of refuge where the pogroms of the Czarist east might be exchanged for true civic equality. It was natural to engage in her defense.

Klarsfeld was captured and imprisoned in Germany, but escaped to rejoin his wife and children, who had fled from the occupied zone for Nice, in the Italian occupied area. There Klarsfeld joined the Resistance.

The Germans and the officials of Vichy France were infuriated by the behavior of the Italians, who released Jews already rounded up for deportation and actually guarded the main synagogue of Nice, where much clandestine activity took place. The Italians made it possible for Jews to fabricate the false identity cards on which their lives might depend. Indeed, the commanding officer of the Italian troops in Nice went so far as to threaten to arrest any French police officer who interfered.

The fragile protection crumbled on September 8, 1943, the day Italy signed a separate armistice with the Allies. The German troops did not hesitate. By September 11 they had occupied the Italian zone and begun to apply the terms of the Final Solution with a zeal calculated to make up for lost time.

Just weeks earlier, the Klarsfelds had built a false wall in the back of their hall closet. A friend had convinced them; one never knew what could happen. He was right. Just twelve days after the German occupation, the Klarsfelds were awakened at midnight by the sound of trucks revving their motors in the street below. Arno and Raissa's bedroom was suddenly flooded with the bright, white glare of a searchlight.

Quickly they made their beds and put their clothes away, to make it look as though they had not been sleeping in the house. Then they entered their shelter.

On the other side of the wall lived a family of Alsatian Jews. In silence, the Klarsfelds listened to the Gestapo knock on their neighbors' door. Trembling, the children heard the family daughter scream in pain as she was beaten by soldiers wanting to know where her older brother was. "*Au secours*," cried the father. "Help, police! We are French citizens!" The terrible irony of his plea remained engraved in the memory of young Serge.

Serge heard his father whisper to his mother. He assured her he was strong enough to survive another camp. Then he walked out to meet the ss. He told them his family was away, in the country. They believed him, did a perfunctory search, and left taking Arno with them.

Something clicked off and something else clicked on in the heart and mind of eight-year-old Serge Klarsfeld that terrible night.

"What gives me the courage to do the work I do? The very fact of the Holocaust. After what happened I don't have the right to be afraid. Besides, it would give too much pleasure to my enemies. I only fear for the children, but it is also true that when you live in a big city it is impossible to protect yourself completely. Sometimes I think of King Louis Philippe. When there was an attack and everyone flattened themselves on the floor, he remained standing, saying, 'These are the risks of the trade.' I simply refuse to be afraid."

At night he dreams that his father returns.

She is warm, attractive, stylishly dressed and devoted to her family, a woman whose courageous exploits are seeded with thoughts of whether her husband has clean socks and her daughter found the laundry ticket, a woman who will have her hair done during a pause in the action so she will look good for the television cameras. When she is not battling dragons, she is cooking.

The modest Paris apartment reflects domesticity. Red geraniums bloom on the balcony; delicious coffee smells emanate from the kitchen, and a large collie dog called Scottie clamors for attention. But behind the domesticity, which is real enough, is another most extraordinary career for which nothing in her early life had prepared her. Little Beate Kunzel was born in 1939, attended elementary school in Berlin and dutifully recited verses in honor of the Führer. The family was Protestant. Beate's father was an insurance agent who had served in the Wehrmacht on the eastern front. They were solid, ordinary, rather taciturn people who expected little from their daughter. Beate dropped out of high school to do a secretarial course.

But she was less conventional than they had, perhaps, hoped. In

1960 Beate decided to spend a year in Paris to learn a second language and see a bit of the world. There she did what many young foreigners did and still do to earn their way. She worked as an *au pair* girl, doing cleaning and babysitting in return for room and board.

Arno and Raissa Klarsfeld had met in a very Parisian way: in a neighborhood café. Beate and Serge met in an equally Parisian manner: on the platform of the Saint-Cloud Métro Station. Serge was a graduate of the Ecole des Sciences Politiques. Beate's political education was strictly nil. At age twenty-one, she had no idea whatsoever about what had taken place in her own country.

Serge's friends openly confronted Beate with the recent past of Nazi Germany, and she quite literally did not know what to reply. It was all completely new to her. She began to study the history of World War II, and Serge told her about the Holocaust. Beate was deeply shocked. Her parents had never mentioned it. Never had she heard a word during her entire school career. Her shame was overwhelming. She and Serge wanted to marry, but any children that were born would have a dual heritage. Beate felt "German" and she wanted her children to be proud of their background.

Not all the innocent children of Nazi Germany suffer, of course: some continue in private to believe an ideology that was imprinted during impressionable childhood years, while others cannot bring themselves to repudiate the essential parent-child bond that such rejection would imply. The burden of history is difficult to bear, however, and each member of the second and sometimes third generation has had to find a way to cope, psychologically with the past.

Beate Klarsfeld's parents were neither for nor against Hitler, but Beate interiorized the reflected guilt of their entire generation. Instead of minimizing responsibility by saying, "It could have happened anywhere," or planting a symbolic tree of life in Israel, Beate's unique solution was to commit herself to an extraordinary course of action, "to restoring my country's honor," as she put it. Honor and justice. When confronted by those who claimed that the past should be laid to rest and a page of history turned, her response was to disagree, to avow that the dead cannot rest and that that page of history cannot be turned as long as people who have committed monstrous crimes against humanity have not been brought to account. Anything less is tacit approval of their acts.

Everything Beate Klarsfeld would subsequently do would be "as a German who was not a Jew." "Whatever his ideology, each German has specific responsibilities stemming from the death of millions brought about by Germans," she said later. "This is not collective guilt, but a collective moral and historic responsibility. It is a terrible challenge to be German today . . ."

In 1967 while working as an employee for the Franco-German Youth Office in Paris, Beate came across archival information that would change the course of her life and that of Serge as well. She learned that German Chancellor Kurt-Georg Kiesinger had worked directly for Goebbels as deputy director of radio propaganda for foreign countries. True to her commitment to restoring honor to Germany, Beate made the information public — and was fired from her job.

That was the turning point. Only twenty-two years after the defeat of Hitler, a director of his anti-Semitic propaganda program was Chancellor of Germany. And a collaborative German-French organization had fired her for saying so. Klarsfeld was sickened, horrified. She went to a session of the Bundestag in Bonn, determined to awaken the German public conscience with a dramatic act. Kiesinger was on his feet, speaking. Klarsfeld rose to her feet in the public gallery. "Nazi, Kiesinger, resign!" she shouted.

The guards rushed to expel her from the chamber. Reporters jostled each other to photograph the unknown young woman who had dared mention the unmentionable. Klarsfeld seized the occasion. She announced that she would return and slap the Chancellor in the face. The slap would be symbolic, from the daughter to the generation of fathers that had shamed Germany. Klarsfeld promised a spectacular gesture designed to show the world that the children of criminals rejected the rehabilitation of nazism represented by the presence of Kiesinger in the Chancellery.

On November 7, 1968, Klarsfeld attended the Congress of Christian Democrats in Berlin. Sexism worked in her favor. No one suspected the pretty, conservatively dressed young woman with a pencil and stenographer's pad in hand. She reached the podium as Kiesinger was about to make a speech. "Nazi! Nazi!" she screamed as she slapped his face. Kiesinger's bodyguards drew their revolvers, but it was too late. The Congress dissolved in pandemonium.

Klarsfeld was tried and sentenced to a year in prison. She appealed and received a four-month suspended sentence.

Beate Klarsfeld dogged Kiesinger's heels throughout the 1969 election campaign, but now she was accompanied by thousands of young Germans who agreed with her and were inspired by her courage. They raised their arms in mock salute and greeted the Chancellor with derisory cries of "*Sieg Heil.*" When Kiesinger went to Brussels, Klarsfeld instigated a riot by students and young Jews.

Kiesinger was soundly defeated by former resistance fighter Willy Brandt in the elections of 1969; and one of Brandt's first acts was to amnesty Beate Klarsfeld.

The Klarsfelds are activists; and, like a whole generation of 1960s militants who believe that no event ever really "happens" unless it is publicized in a way that will mobilize public opinion, they have never hesitated to stage events that will attract media attention. In 1970 they blocked the appointment of Ernst Achenbach, a member of the West German parliament, as German representative at the European commission in Brussels. Achenbach had lobbied in parliament to prevent the continuation of war-crimes trials — and for very good reason. In researching the archives, the Klarsfelds unearthed documents proving that, as head of the Political Section of the German embassy in Paris between 1940 and 1943, he had been engaged in active persecution of French Jews; in particular, he was implicated in the deportation of two thousand Jews in retaliation for an attack against two German officers. Beate launched a "Stop Achenbach" campaign in several major European capitals. European civil servants in Brussels threatened to go on strike; and in Bonn, Achenbach's nomination was canceled.

The numerous Klarsfeld "operations" have included the precedent-setting trial of three leaders of the Nazi Gestapo in France: Kurt Lischka, head of the Nazi police in Paris from 1940 to 1943; Herbert Hagen, right-hand man to Karl Oberg, head of the ss in France; and Ernst Heinrichsohn, ss officer in charge of the Drancy deportation camp. The Klarsfelds' attack on these men spanned nine years, succeeded in plugging a loophole that had made it impossible for Germany to try war criminals who had already been condemned *in absentia* in France and culminated in convictions for all three by a court in Cologne in 1980. Until routed out by the Klarsfelds, the three had been leading tranquil lives as professional men in Germany. (Heinrichsohn was mayor of his town.) All denied guilt. "I was told [the children] were being resettled. I couldn't spend every day worrying about what was happening," explained Heinrichsohn, whose exceptional cruelty has already been documented.[1]

Serge was a Zionist whose main interest lay in Israel, not in the pursuit of war criminals. But Beate's profound need to assume personal responsibility for the honor of Germany affected him deeply. In 1970, at the age of thirty-seven, he returned to law school so that he could work full-time alongside his wife. He needed to understand the law, to know when and how to institute legal proceedings when possible.

The Klaus Barbie affair began on July 25, 1971, in the Paris archives of the Centre de documentation juive contemporaine (CDJC), where Beate Klarsfeld was working on the organization of the German secret service in France. That was the day the director of the library leaned across her desk with some documents he had just received. "This may interest you," he said.

They were photocopies of a decision taken by Public Prosecutor Rabl in Munich on June 22, 1971, regarding the case of Klaus Barbie. An investigation that had been underway for ten years had concluded that there was not enough evidence to bring charges against the former Gestapo chief.

"As I scanned the ten pages . . . I became aware of the shocking consequences of closing the case," wrote Klarsfeld in her book, *Wherever They May Be.* "Written in a dry, pedantic style, they served to rehabilitate — through Barbie — all the Nazi criminals who had operated in France. I realized that the Barbie case was a landmark and that we would have to fight relentlessly to get the Munich investigation reopened."[2]

That night she and Serge decided on a three-front strategy: to gather and distribute fully researched documentation on Barbie; to arouse public opinion in France and West Germany; and to attack the Munich court in whatever way would produce the best results.

Back at the CDJC they assembled the data, which consisted of documents signed by Barbie concerning "The Jewish Question." They found evidence that after the death of ss officer Hollert, Barbie's nominal superior in Lyons, "Barbie signed all the telegrams."[3] They found information describing Barbie's role in the arrest and torture of Jean Moulin. They found an acknowledgment of Himmler's personal gratitude to ss-Obersturmführer Barbie. They found glowing reports concerning Barbie's "enthusiasm" for his job. They found a telegram and a letter, dated February 10 and 11, 1943, both sent to Rothke in the Gestapo Bureau for Jewish Affairs in Paris, relating the arrest, through Barbie's efforts, of eighty-six UGIF[4] workers on rue Sainte-Catherine in Lyons on February 9. The Jews had been shipped to Drancy. Another list, dated August 11, 1944, contained the names of forty-two Jewish hostages shot by the Gestapo between May 28 and August 17, 1944. Barbie also reported having sent the last convoy from France directly to Auschwitz, on August 11, with 308 Jews on board. One document was already known to the authorities: a telegram dated April 6, 1944, in which Barbie noted the arrest and deportation of more than forty Jewish children who had being hidden in an orphanage in the remote mountain village of Izieu.

About this latter telegram, Prosecutor Rabl had already concluded: "The mere fact that on April 6, 1944, [Barbie] arrested forty-one children who were obviously not destined for the labor camps and had them shipped to the concentration camp at Drancy cannot be interpreted to mean that he knew the eventual destination of those children. At least, not one sure proof of this subjective interpretation of his act can be produced."[5]

Two years earlier, Dr. Artzt, the prosecutor of the Central Bureau for Research on War Crimminals, had written to the Munich prosecutor with another interpretation: "If Barbie did clear out a camp for Jewish children and had them shipped to Drancy, there is no doubt that he, as an SS chief, knew the children would be shipped to Auschwitz to be exterminated there. So in this one case, at least, Barbie was an accessory to murder."[6]

The Klarsfelds distributed their documentation to the international news agencies, but they opened their own media campaign in Lyons, believing that reaction from the city where Barbie had operated would have the greatest effect on German public opinion. On July 28, 1971, the Lyons *Progrès* published a long story entitled "German Prosecutor Drops Charges against Klaus Barbie, Chief of Lyons Gestapo and Torturer of Jean Moulin." The next day the paper ran a column of outraged letters, and the Lyons branch of the civil liberties association, LICRA, asked "all Resistance associations and all citizens of Lyons with a sense of justice to write a letter of protest to the prosecutor."

Beate wrote a deliberately provocative piece for the newspaper *Combat*.

In April 1944 even the public no longer believed the explanation about labor in the East; certainly the Gestapo chiefs in France could not have believed it. Moreover, children between the ages of three and thirteen obviously could not have gone to the East to lend a helping hand to the German economy. Even Prosecutor Rabl must concede that . . .

Is there no one who will speak for those young Frenchmen against their executioner? . . . Are there so few French citizens who grasp how relevant to the future of Europe it is that Germany has taken this attitude toward her Nazi past? When will a public demonstration in Munich take place? Will the vacation season take precedence over a time of sorrow and pity even with those who call themselves victims of Nazi atrocities?[7]

Once again LICRA came to her aid, calling for a mass demonstration in Lyons and for a delegation of Resistance and Holocaust survivors to go to Munich.

A meeting was held to put together a delegation, but, once the shouting ceased and emotions cooled, the practical question of financing arose. Everyone wanted to "make a statement," but few wanted to pay for it. Eventually, a Resistance veteran rose to his feet. "This is a German woman telling you what you ought to do," he reminded his audience. "Wake up, for heaven's sake!"

The Klarsfeld strategy was proving successful. The Munich prosecutor let it be known that if new evidence were forthcoming, he would reopen the Barbie case.

Beate and Serge knew that UGIF, the Jewish Council under the Occupation, had had a liaison office with the Gestapo, and they suspected that UGIF chief officer, Kurt Schendel, a former Berlin lawyer who had emigrated to France, might have information they could use. By an incredible stroke of luck, Schendel was still alive and listed in the Paris telephone directory.

Schendel was anxious to help. He had never met Barbie, but he was able to declare the following in an affidavit:

Over the course of a year my observations of Department IV-B, Bureau for Jewish Affairs, and the numerous talks I had with its employees, as well as with workers in the other German bureaus, completely convinced me that all of them, except the ones at the very bottom . . . knew perfectly well what fate awaited the deportees.[8]

Schendel's affidavit was important, but might still have been considered merely interpretive by the Munich prosecutor. Of greater significance was a conversation Schendel recalled as having taken place in late 1943 or early 1944 at a meeting of UGIF directors in Paris. There was much discussion of Klaus Barbie's summary executions of Jews at Montluc. "One of the delegates from the southern zone reported that ceaseless representations had been made [to Barbie] . . . to keep arrested Jews from being shot, but that Barbie had replied: 'Shot or deported, there's no difference,' " recalled Schendel.

"That remark sticks in my memory because at the time none of us could comprehend what he meant, and our anguish over the fate of the deportees became all the greater," he continued.[9] "So as far as I'm concerned, he was beyond a doubt just as aware as [the Paris Gestapo] of the ultimate fate of the Jews deported from Lyons, which had the second largest Jewish population in France." Schendel added that an SS officer called Weiszel had been assigned from Paris to several months of duty with Barbie in Lyons, and that this man had been part of the SS secret commando forces in Hungary and Salonika and had had personal experience of the mass executions of Jews in the east.[10]

From the list of children who had been deported from the orphanage at Izieu, Beate Klarsfeld found the names of three brothers: Jacques (age thirteen), Richard (age six) and Jean-Claude (age five) Benguigui. All had been deported to Auschwitz on August 13, 1944, and gassed on arrival. Their mother had survived Auschwitz and lived in Paris.

Beate met Madame Itta Benguigui and told her that the man responsible for her children's death had just been rehabilitated in Germany. She asked if Madame Benguigui felt up to going to Munich to protest. "German public opinion could not fail to be stirred by so martyred a mother," wrote Klarsfeld, always with an eye on the media.

Madame Benguigui agreed, and the two women joined the delegation from Lyons. But Klarsfeld was bitterly disappointed by the Resistance veterans. They were fearful of an international incident and "arranged" that she not be allowed to accompany their leaders into the office of Munich public prosecutor, Manfred Ludolph. In effect, they were reluctant to be identified with her tactics and her militancy.

After presenting a memorandum to the prosecutor, the delegation returned to France. But Beate Klarsfeld and Madame Benguigui stayed behind. Klarsfeld knew the French delegation had not had much effect on the prosecutor or the public. She, on the other hand, would stage something *really* dramatic.

Her ammunition was the only picture Madame Benguigui had of her children, which Klarsfeld had had enlarged, and two signs, which she and Madame Benguigui made in their hotel room. Madame Benguigui's sign read: "I am on a hunger strike for as long as the investigation of Klaus Barbie, who murdered my children, remains closed." Klarsfeld's sign read, "Prosecutor Rabl is rehabilitating war criminals."

At nine o'clock the following morning the two women were in front of the courthouse standing on grocery crates. By 5:00 P.M. there was a large crowd, including reporters and photographers. Women stroked Madame Benguigui's hair, and people brought her blankets, for it was bitterly cold. Young Germans shouted that it was a disgrace to their country that this old woman who had suffered so much had to go to such lengths for justice.

At 6:00 P.M. Prosecutor Ludolph summoned them to his office.

"What do you want?" he asked politely.

"To have the Barbie case reopened," replied Klarsfeld.

"Have you further conclusive proofs?"

"Did you read the data I sent you yesterday?"

"I haven't had time."

"Well, now is the time," suggested Klarsfeld.

When the prosecutor read Schendel's affidavit, he exclaimed, "This is the sort of thing I was talking about. If Dr. Schendel's informant — the man who actually heard what Barbie said — can be produced, and if he confirms what Barbie is reported to have said, I promise you I will reopen the case." He put his promise in writing.

The informant was Raymond Geissmann, director for the southern region of the UGIF, and he too was still alive. Geissmann remembered well. "I remember seeing Barbie 'froth at the mouth' as he vented his hatred of Jews, and his remark, 'Deported or shot, there's no difference,' was truly spoken by him. He said it in front of me, and I reported it to my colleagues in Paris," he declared in a sworn affidavit.

The investigation was reopened, but Klaus Barbie's whereabouts were unknown. Ludolph presented the Klarsfelds with two pictures, front and profile, that had been taken of Barbie in 1943, and another of a group of businessmen seated around a table in Bolivia. One of the men looked the way Barbie might look twenty-five years later and was assumed to be him. "That picture was taken in La Paz in 1968," said the prosecutor. "Since you have demonstrated how efficient you are, why don't you help me identify that man?"

Several weeks later, Ludolph asked Klarsfeld to contact a German living in Lima, Peru, who had seen the 1943 photo in a Munich paper. He thought he could identify Barbie as a La Paz businessman.

The man was Herbert John, and he was the manager of a publishing company owned by the fabulously wealthy Peruvian industrialist, Luis Banchero Rossi. On December 28, through a friend in Munich, John sent the Klarsfelds a full set of information on Barbie. His name was Klaus Altmann, c/o Fritz Schwend, at an address near Lima. Schwend was another former ss officer. He had been in charge of the Nazis' celebrated counterfeiting of English currency and had escaped to South America, in 1949, a very wealthy man. John told Klarsfeld that Schwend "worked for the CIA in Peru," and that "he had feelers everywhere."[11]

Luis Banchero Rossi had financial dealings with his close friends Klaus Barbie and Fritz Schwend, but he had intimated that he planned to publish the history of the ODESSA network as it operated in South America. On December 28, 1971, Rossi's employee John passed information about Barbie and Schwend to Beate Klarsfeld. On January 1, 1972, Rossi was found murdered.

Was it a coincidence? A Lima judge, who publicly implicated Barbie and Schwend, didn't think so. Barbie launched a lawsuit, which he later withdrew; however, a formal charge of murder was never laid against either of the two men. Barbie, on the other hand, kept a souvenir of the affair in his personal scrapbook: a newspaper picture of Luis Banchero Rossi's corpse.[12]

Barbie-Altmann had had twenty very good years since 1951, when he and his family had arrived safely in La Paz via the well-run American "rat line."[13] The rat line had been set up in 1947 to assist people who had worked for the Americans mainly in Soviet-occupied Europe and who now needed to get out. Beneficiaries were lodged in safe houses and provided with false identification documents before being shipped to a safe port, usually in South America.

Barbie fitted the bill perfectly. He had worked for the Counter-Intelligence Corps (CIC) from 1947 on. The United States was by that time fanatically anticommunist, with Senator Joe McCarthy spearheading the battle at home, and special agents operating abroad. And who more knowledgable among anticommunist agents than the Nazis, with twelve years of invaluable experience behind them? Barbie's anti-Resistance activities made him particularly valuable.

CIC recruiters knew who Barbie was, but they preferred not to ask too many questions or examine war-criminal files too closely. Alliances were fluid. Yesterday's enemies were today's comrades in arms in the larger battle against a common adversary. It was a collaboration reminiscent of Vichy France and the Nazis.

By 1947, the French had been apprised of Barbie's whereabouts, and they wanted to bring him to trial. They did, in fact, try him in his absence, once in 1952 and again in 1954, at which time he was sentenced to death *in absentia*. Barbie, however, was being protected. And the ultimate protection was the rat line.

Barbie-Altmann flourished in Bolivia. He became director of a shipping company, the Transmaritima Boliviana, which purported to build a navy for a land-locked nation. Most important, he established close connections with the rulers of the country. He is believed to have trained a secret army along ss lines, a Germano-Italian, neo-Nazi terrorist group, called the Fiancés of Death, that enacted assassinations and kidnappings and controlled Bolivia's thriving cocaine trade. Though a Nazi, he is reputed to have been associated with the sale of weapons to terrorists on the extreme left of the political spectrum.

Just as in Lyons, Barbie frequented the best restaurants and drank the finest wines. Much of the time he lived in a villa with a swimming pool. He must surely have thought he was invulnerable.

In the last days of 1971, as Klaus and Regina Barbie enjoyed the company of their host, Fritz Schwend, Beate Klarsfeld was busy verifying Barbie's pictures. She sent them to the Ethnological Institute of the University of Munich, which used anthropometry to measure various parts of the body. The institute attested that Barbie and Altmann were the same man, as did the French police using the same techniques.

The Klarsfelds decided to press for an extradition; and, as usual, they did it by convincing the press. An editorial in *L'Aurore* evoked strong pressure from *résistants* and deportees. In Lima, Altmann fiercely denied he was Barbie.

On January 21, 1972, Ludolph telephoned from Munich to say he had found substantiating proof of identity in the registry office. Beate decided to go to Lima, and LICRA raised the money.

At 7:00 A.M., on January 27, 1972, Beate Klarsfeld broadcast her message on the radio. "What good is it for French politicians to pay tribute to Jean Moulin . . . as long as the French government is not doing what is required to bring his murderer to justice?" she challenged.[14] One hour later she was on her way to the other side of the world.

Klarsfeld arrived in Lima and met the press, only to learn that Barbie had successfully escaped back into Bolivia. She followed him to La Paz, reasoning (in typical Klarsfeld style) that "the weekend would not be lost because Bolivian papers have Sunday editions." There she was met by twenty reporters and photographers, who hurried her into a small office in the airport where she showed her documents and held a press conference. She had to explain to them what the Gestapo was and give them a capsule history of the war, for Bolivians were far removed from the events of Europe forty years earlier. Their understanding was crucial, for there was no way Barbie could be extradited unless the public understood why. "By attacking in La Paz the fascism of the past, I was helping the Bolivians make a connection between what had happened under Hitler and what was happening under their government headed by Colonel Banzer," she wrote.

During a break she went to the hairdresser — carefully cultivating, as always, the unthreatening image of a prim, bourgeois *hausfrau*.

The news soon came that the French president, Georges Pompidou, had made an official request for Barbie-Altmann's extradition,[15] and Klarsfeld was immediately arrested, for "her own protection," on grounds that local Nazis were out to get her. Two days later she was released.

She tried unsuccessfully to see the Bolivian president, Colonel Hugo Banzer, who was housing his friend Barbie in a comfortable prison cell for alleged nonpayment of debts until the "dragon lady" from France had gone. On Wednesday Klarsfeld flew home.

Klaus Altmann had been revealed to the world as Klaus Barbie, but it was clear that, in Lima and La Paz, Nazis were considered political refugees. After Klarsfeld's spectacular visit, Barbie put his career in context. "I acted like any other army officer in battle, just like the Bolivian army officers fighting Che Guevara's guerrillas," he told a Bolivian reporter.

The French extradition request seemed doomed to fail. A spokesman for President Banzer stated that there would be no proceedings.

"President Banzer thinks he has enough legal evidence to consider the problem settled," he explained. Bolivia was "an inviolable asylum," added a government minister.

Two weeks later, Beate returned to La Paz intending to stage a drama of the sort she and Madame Benguigui had enacted before the Munich courthouse. This time she was accompanied by another bereft survivor of Auschwitz, Madame Halaunbrenner, whose husband and three of her five children had died at Barbie's hands. Klarsfeld had with her thirty copies of a picture of the Halaunbrenner family before it was destroyed.

Klarsfeld held a press conference in her La Paz hotel room, and Madame Halaunbrenner told her story. Beate passed pictures around. Then she was taken off to police headquarters, held there for the day and released with a warning.

On March 6, Beate bought chains and padlocks, assured two exit visas, reserved seats for an 8:00 P.M. flight out of Bolivia and went, with Madame Halaunbrenner, to the offices of Transmaritima Boliviana. At noon the two women fastened the chains around their waists and wrists and sat down on a bench. They carried two signs written in Spanish. Madame Halaunbrenner's sign had a picture of her family and the message: "Listen, Bolivians! As a mother I only claim justice. I want Barbie-Altmann, who murdered my husband and three of my children, brought to trial." Beate's read: "In the name of the millions of Nazi victims, let Barbie-Altmann be extradited."

There was an instant traffic jam. Plainclothesmen arrived, grabbed the signs and fled. Bystanders made new ones.

"What do the chains signify?" asked a reporter holding a microphone.

"They are the chains that bind Bolivia to nazism," said Klarsfeld with breathtaking courage.

That night the two women flew to Lima where they went to the hairdresser. "We wanted to look our best for the television camera that would be waiting for us at Orly," explained Klarsfeld.

"We did not have Barbie in our luggage, but for a while we had represented the eternal quest for justice," she later wrote. "In this myth of a guilty man fleeing to the ends of the earth to escape retribution, two women—one belonging to a murderous people, the other to those it had victimized—had gone to the other side of the globe to find him and demand justice."

As she entered the Orly waiting room, Beate caught sight of her husband. "Without him by my side, without his complete and tactful involvement, without his everlasting energy, what could I have accomplished?" she asked herself with excessive modesty. "Another man doubtless would have required me to cut myself off from Germany. Serge had helped me to become a real German."

Back in Bolivia, a proud Klaus Barbie added newspaper pictures of Klarsfeld and Madame Halaunbrenner wearing chains to his scrapbook, as well as the portrait picture of the intact Halaunbrenner family before he destroyed their lives.

The Barbie case was causing an uncomfortable stir in France. There were many who wanted to forget the Nazis, especially the French involvement in the collaboration. Barbie was a bad taste in the mouth. *Les deux France* were distinctly delineated again.

The Klarsfelds received praise from the one and threats from the other. On May 10, a letter bomb was delivered to their apartment. Serge found it, thought it looked suspicious and took it to the police station where it was dismantled. But their enemies did not give up. In 1979, a time bomb destroyed the family car.

The Barbie extradition request was formally in the hands of the Bolivian Supreme Court, but since most of the judges had been appointed by the right-wing military regime, there was little hope of success. But Bolivia was trapped in the spotlight of international attention and had to *appear* to be doing something about Barbie-Altmann. On March 2, 1973, Barbie was arrested — for acquiring Bolivian citizenship under a false name.

Needing to justify himself for the very first time, Barbie began to sell his "confessions" to selected journalists around the world. The story varied from interview to interview. Sometimes he claimed he had operated on the Russian front; at other times he denied he had ever been in Lyons. On one occasion he denied being able to speak French, then blurted out, in perfect Gallic cadences, that *he* was no torturer or murderer. He told of his amicable encounter with Jean Moulin. What never changed, however, was his insistence that he had no regrets, that he was only following orders, and that in war there is no such thing as "crime." There are only "acts of war."

Barbie remained in jail for seven months, under protected and comfortable conditions. (He locked his own cell from the inside, and his wife brought him excellent food daily. In the afternoon they occasionally watched movies together.) And in July 1973 the Supreme Court of Bolivia officially refused the French extradition demand. Bolivia and France had no extradition treaty, they concluded. Furthermore, Barbie was a Bolivian citizen, and Bolivia did not recognize war crimes.

The Barbie project faded from view. Short of a kidnapping or a murder, Barbie was safe. As it happens, the Klarsfelds rejected neither of these two alternatives. And they maintained close contact with leftist enemies of the Banzer regime.

In the meantime, they turned their attention to other things. In 1976, Serge went to a neo-Nazi meeting in Munich intending to draw attention to the revival of the party. "I decided to become the first Jew since the war to be publicly beaten up by Nazis," he said in an interview. "I went to a meeting of the Deutsche Volks-Union that was being held in a beer hall and I said, 'I am a Jew and I ask for the right to speak.' They all jumped on me, of course. There were reporters there and photographers, and the next day the picture was all over the papers."

With undoubted flair he had captured the public imagination as a sort of 1970s incarnation of the Lone Ranger.

In 1979, Serge flew off to Iran to protest the execution of the leader of the Tehran Jewish community, who had been shot because he was pro-Israel. Serge managed to get an interview with the chief prosecutor, whom he asked for transcripts of the trial. Amazingly, he was given copies. There he read that the man was executed for going to Israel, having lunch with Abba Eban and stating that emigration of Jews from Iran ought to be increased.

"What are you going to do with the transcripts?" asked the mullah.

"I intend to show the world how little it takes for a Jew to be shot," replied Klarsfeld.

Klarsfeld also began to publish. With painstaking research he compiled the *Memorial to the Jews Deported from France*, which lists, chronologically, the names of every Jew in every convoy that left France from March 22, 1942, until August 11, 1944. It is an exceptionally moving document, each name particularized with a date and place of birth. Wherever possible, Klarsfeld has added information about the fate of the victims.[16] He also succeeded in having material added to French school texts describing the role of Vichy police in the deportations. Until the early 1980s, most textbooks had virtually ignored the French contribution and described only the Nazis' culpability.

In May 1982, the German ambassador in Bolivia submitted a formal request for Klaus Barbie's extradition, without much hope for success. However, the coming to power of left-liberal Hernan Siles Zuazo on October 10 of that year changed the political face of the country. Siles Zuazo was perfectly clear about Barbie-Altmann: he wanted to get rid of him. There was, however, the prickly question of a legal extradition. It was unlikely that the Supreme Court, which still had the same conservative composition, would reverse its ruling. Something else would have to be arranged.

Germany's request had been essentially *pro forma*, and when it looked as though Barbie might actually be expelled from Bolivia, the government hesistated. Germany had offered to send a Lufthansa jet to transfer Barbie out of Bolivia, but it refused to take responsibility should legal difficulties arise. There was, as well, the question of Barbie's nationality. After three decades as a Bolivian, he might have lost his German citizenship, and without it, West German courts might not be able to try him. Furthermore, the timing was all wrong. The fiftieth anniversary of Hitler's coming to power had arrived, and Germany was already drowning in painful, soul-searching analysis. The past was tolerable in print, but the living past in the person of Klaus Barbie might be a little too much for a conservative government that had to face elections the following spring. The Cologne trial of 1980 had been praised internationally for its impartiality and its conclusions, but other recent trials of Nazis had proved intensely embarrassing. For example, overtly sympathetic lawyers had put forward neo-Nazi claims that the gas chambers at Maidanek had actually been laundry rooms.

In France, the socialist government of François Mitterrand had been elected in May 1981. The Klarsfelds were in close contact with Régis Debray, a former comrade of Che Guevara, and Robert Badinter, the minister of justice, whose own father had been deported by Barbie in 1943. Something had to be done about Barbie, and with the election of Siles Zuazo, the moment seemed right. France had a left-wing government dedicated to the memory of the Resistance; indeed, as far back as 1974, Mitterrand had declared himself in favor of trying war criminals who had been active in France in French courts. Bolivia had a left-wing democracy, but no one knew how long it would last. Bolivia wanted Barbie out, but without waiting for a new Supreme Court ruling on extradition, a ruling that was bound to be negative in any case.

A decision was taken. Barbie would be expelled for having fraudulently obtained Bolivian citizenship with a false name.[17] Further discussions among Bolivian, French and German representatives concluded with an agreement that Barbie would be returned to France. There is some evidence to suggest that a cash payment took place.[18]

On January 26, 1983, Barbie was arrested once again for failure to pay a thirteen-year-old debt. On Friday, February 4, under cover of darkness, he was driven to the airport of La Paz and told he was being expelled — to Germany. Barbie seemed unconcerned. Only when the plane actually landed in the French territory of Cayenne, in French Guyana, and he was officially charged, did he understand the reality of his situation. "The expulsion is illegal," he complained bitterly. Then he added, "My life is lost."

For the Klarsfelds, Barbie's return was a personal triumph. But it was Barbie's thousands of victims, especially the children, who filled Serge Klarsfeld's thoughts as he planned to represent some of their families at the trial.

Plenty of people disliked the Klarsfelds and wished they would stop stirring up the past; however, with the exception of a cynic like Barbie himself, few doubted their commitment to justice through legal means. So it was with some chagrin that their friends learned from *Life* magazine in February 1985 that in 1982 they "had asked a Bolivian to assassinate Barbie." In the same interview, Serge Klarsfeld added that he was prepared to do the same thing in Syria if it were otherwise impossible to extradite Alois Brunner who had been Adolf Eichmann's right-hand man and an important Gestapo officer in France.

As Beate explained: "The military dictatorship in Bolivia left us no hope regarding the extradition of Barbie, and a certain number of people who knew about our work had come to us wanting help. This is how we met a certain Bolivian who was opposed to the dictatorship and consequently an enemy of Klaus Barbie. After long discussions, we bought him an airplane ticket, but shortly thereafter he informed us of a possible change of regime that might lead to an extradition. With that news, the assassination plan had no further *raison d'être*."

"That was a terrible mistake," said a man who admired the

Klarsfelds. "Serge looks as though he is just after revenge when there is so much more involved."

The Klarsfelds remain enigmatic. Propelled by a desire for "justice," they blandly propose murder. Advocates of democracy and the rule of law, they blithely condone frontier vigilante tactics. They have each risked their lives to make a point. Yet at bottom they seem to share a startling softness, even an unlikely sentimentality. At bottom they want Klaus Barbie and the other Nazis and French collaborators they have accused to *apologize* for what they have done. "If Barbie had come back to France of his own accord and said he regretted what he did, said he was young at the time and that he did terrible things, that would have been enough for us," admitted Serge. "There would have been a trial, but it would have been conducted in an atmosphere of cooperation. In a sense the man himself would have been judge of the man he used to be forty years ago.

"But I'm a realist. They never change. They look younger than their age, they live much longer than those of their victims who survived, and they never have trouble sleeping at night. But something inside me is revolted by the knowledge that human beings can do such things to each other. Every time I think of those children in the home in Izieu I am sickened. We always give them the chance to express regret — and they never do.

"I would have wished the world to be different."

· 7 ·

THE KLAUS BARBIE
DEFENSE TAKES SHAPE

While the French news media mulled over the implications of Klaus Barbie's return to France, an altogether different process was set in motion elsewhere. In Germany, Switzerland and Austria, a few concerned individuals geared up for action.

Nazis on trial outside Germany are almost always defended by a coterie of German lawyers who are considered to be specialists in such affairs; Robert Servatius, for example, defended Adolf Eichmann, having previously represented Hitler's personal physician, Dr. Karl Brandt, at Nuremberg. Since the days of Nuremberg, the German defense team has also had a sympathetic collaborator in the person of a Swiss financier from Lausanne, François Genoud, a man with a proud Nazi past and a postwar history of dedication both to the "ideals" of the Third Reich and to the Arab liberation movements of the extreme Left. Genoud has managed funds for just such purposes.

When the Klaus Barbie case broke, the German lawyers moved quickly to contact Barbie's daughter, Ute Messner, who was now a woman of forty-one, married and working as a librarian in Kufstein, Austria. Klaus Barbie needed a lawyer, but according to French law only immediate family and legal counsel were allowed to talk directly to the accused. Messner needed to advise her father quickly. The lawyers were prepared to help her find a high-powered defense attorney. Genoud would help pay costs. Naturally, Ute Messner jumped at the offer. Barbie had returned to France with little more than the clothes on his back, and Messner and her husband were not wealthy. Indeed, she subsequently acknowledged in an interview with *Stern* magazine[1] and in a telephone interview with a newspaper in Lyons[2] that she had no money to pay for her father's defense.

In the case of Klaus Barbie, a German defense team would clearly not work in the best interests of the accused. Barbie was a longtime enemy of the French, and in Lyons, where emotions were running high, the added provocation of seeing him flanked by a battery of German lawyers might perhaps prejudice his case. Judges and jurors alike might find it psychologically difficult to remain neutral, especially in Lyons where memories of the Occupation could still cut a divisive swath through the population. Furthermore, the trial was originally planned for 1984, a date that would coincide with the elections to the European Parliament. The presence of Klaus Barbie in the dock was not going to sweeten Franco-German relations — everyone was well aware of that — and it seemed important not to poison those relations beyond what was absolutely unavoidable.

When Barbie arrived in Lyons on February 5, 1983, he was informed of the charges being brought against him. He was also advised of his right to appoint his own lawyer; otherwise, the Lyons law society would designate someone from its ranks to represent him. Barbie chose the second option.

It was a Saturday, but Barbie needed a lawyer right away. Minister of Justice Robert Badinter contacted the chief state attorney in Lyons who, in turn, contacted Alain de la Servette, head of the Lyons bar association. Who was going to defend Barbie?, the attorney wanted to know. "I am," replied de la Servette.

Legal-aid cases are usually handled by younger lawyers, but de la Servette said that the Klaus Barbie defense would require the attention of a more experienced man. His attitude did not please some of the younger lawyers. After all, de la Servette's experience was in civil and not in criminal law. Feeling ran so high that several lawyers wrote to a national newspaper to say that, as individuals who had been born after the war, "we see things more clearly and with more objectivity." The Barbie affair was attracting international attention. The trial might very well be the main chance in a lawyer's career.

Legal aid was remunerated, but at a very low level, and the question of outside fees quickly became an issue. In his interviews with the French press, de la Servette denied that he was receiving outside money. Indeed, he reminded a reporter who raised the question that he had defended members of the FLN (the National Liberation Front) during the French colonial war in Algeria and had similarly refused to be paid a fee by the radicals themselves, or from any fund set up for that purpose.[3] But the law did provide for the possibility of payment *if* the accused party had the means. In an interview held almost two years later, that was a point de la Servette wanted to underline.

At some time during the days following Barbie's return to Lyons, Alain de la Servette received a letter from a group of lawyers in Germany. They wrote to offer their help. (According to de la Servette, they later wrote back "to withdraw their offer.") He was also contacted by François Genoud, who came to Lyons during the week of February 7 accompanied by a Swiss banker whom de la Servette described as Genoud's "pilot fish." De la Servette also went to see Genoud in Lausanne on at least one occasion. Ute Messner arrived in Lyons to visit her father and to meet de la Servette. During these meetings, de la Servette was informed that there was plenty of money available for Barbie's defense. Almost two years after the event, he looks distinctly uncomfortable as he relays this information. He emphasizes that a fee was offered without his asking.

Alain de la Servette was the ideal man to defend Klaus Barbie. At age fifty-eight he was president of the bar association and a lawyer of impeccable reputation. Although Lyons is known as a closed city in which one is not regarded as "belonging" with fewer than three generations of stalwart Lyonnais ancestors to point to, de la Servette, though a relative newcomer, personified bourgeois respectability. And, although he was only fifteen years old in 1942, there had never been any question about what side of the Resistance/collaboration fence he had sat on during the fateful years when Klaus Barbie terrorized his city. De la Servette was known to be a small-l liberal who believed strongly that every accused person had the right to the best counsel available, and he would doubtless be sympathetic to the view that Barbie might not receive quite as fair a trial in France if defended by German lawyers as he would by French lawyers.

De la Servette was undoubtedly surprised when his announcement that he would ensure the defense of Klaus Barbie liberated a volume of suppressed emotion in Lyons and right across France. He received death threats: "I own a .22 carbine, and I am prepared to use it against you," wrote one individual who chose to remain anonymous. De la Servette was cursed by survivors of Nazi death camps who had been dispatched from Lyons by ss Captain Klaus Barbie: "There can be no forgiveness," wrote one person. "Don't forget the thousands who paid with their lives."

"It's a bit much that Barbie's daughter is allowed to visit her father," suggested another. "I tried to visit my father, but Mr. Barbie wouldn't let me near him . . ."

On another level, several women wrote to express their "love" for Barbie. One claimed to be his granddaughter and said she prayed for him daily. Another recalled their nights of love. Unrepentant fascists wrote to offer condolences and even money. Obsessive anticommunists renewed their sympathy with the Nazi struggle against bolshevism. Anti-Semites unburdened their hearts, one referring to "the Jew, Badinter," France's minister of justice. Many people wrote to Barbie himself to ask what *really* happened to Jean Moulin.

The letters that pleased de la Servette most came from across the country, from associates in the legal profession who wrote to congratulate him on having the courage to defend an unpopular client out of the belief that everyone has the right to a legal defense.

The media descended upon Lyons. When Ute Messner came to see her father, she needed a police guard at her bedroom door. Reporters parked their cars on the sidewalks. Police cars preceded and followed the car in which Messner and de la Servette drove to the prison. According to de la Servette, a quiet man who found himself at the vortex of a whirlpool, it was a zoo. "They wanted to know what color Barbie's socks were," he recalled in amazement. Then Ute Messner gave a press conference. Daddy was really a very good man, a wonderful father and grandfather, she assured everyone.

Many of the journalists were scandalized; they wanted to know how Alain de la Servette could possibly defend the very same Nazi who had tyrannized Lyons some forty years earlier. De la Servette answered them all with the same equable reply that those who knew him well had learned to expect from the man. "To defend [an accused man] is not to exonerate him," he carefully explained. He did not mention the German lawyers, or François Genoud. He said instead: "If Klaus Barbie had chosen me as his lawyer, I would have refused. I accepted because I was assigned to the task on behalf of my colleagues, and it is as president of the bar association and not as a particular lawyer that I have agreed to the task."

If de la Servette was the ideal lawyer for Barbie, so was the second string to the defense — a young Jesuit priest-turned-lawyer, Robert Boyer, who joined de la Servette on April 1, 1983. Boyer had become a national celebrity in the late 1960s after taking up the cause of a convicted child murderer whom he had met while doing his prison rounds. The man had convinced Boyer he was innocent, and Boyer had battled successfully for a retrial, in which the convicted man was found to be innocent. After this victory, Boyer studied law and received permission from the Jesuit order to open a legal practice. He became known as the defender of the wronged and the unfortunate, and the fact that he was a priest lent a moral dimension to his courtroom pleading that other lawyers might well have envied.

Klaus Barbie couldn't do better than be defended by the president of the Lyons bar association and a popular priest who was known as the lawyer for the poor, the trammeled and, most important, the victim of a serious judicial error. Boyer's reputation was such that the very mention of his association in a legal defence might well throw immediate doubts upon the genuineness of the charges brought against the accused.

The decision to appoint a priest to the Barbie defense also pointed to a battle that was shaping up between the Barbie defense and the Catholic church of Lyons. On February 10, 1983, only five days after Barbie's return to France, the Archbishop of Lyons, Albert Decourtray, issued a statement, considered provocative by many, reminding the French that on December 20, 1981, the day after Decourtray's arrival in Lyons, he had visited the sites where Jews and *résistants* had suffered during the Occupation. The Archbishop had prayed at Montluc, at the memorial at Saint-Genis-Laval, and at the Place Bellecour where Barbie's men had enacted a massacre in full view of the population. Decourtray publicly acknowledged the responsibility the Catholic church bore for the rise of anti-Semitism that had preceded the war; and he called upon all concerned in the Barbie case to uphold the level of the debate. Prophetically, he pleaded that they "not let a war criminal set the tone of the debate."

Reaction was strong. Important people telephoned from Paris to ask what was going on. Was the Archbishop "in cahoots" with the Jews? For it was true that Decourtray was deeply involved with what he called the church's "repentance" with regard to the Jews. After Pope John-Paul II visited Auschwitz on June 17, 1983, Monsignor Decourtray of Lyons and Cardinal Lustiger, the Archbishop of Paris, had made a similar pilgrimage to the death camp. Within the diocese, however, a few unrepentant Pétainists complained that the Archbishop ought to have better things to do than to divide the faithful. The angriest reaction of all came from the lawyers, some of whom thought Decourtray was interfering with the course of the law. Was it, therefore, purely by coincidence that, six weeks later, the only priest in France who did double duty as a lawyer was appointed to defend the first Nazi to be tried in the country in thirty years?

Boyer was directly appointed by de la Servette as a legal-aid lawyer. But here the plot begins to thicken, for the idea almost certainly originated elsewhere, with François Genoud, for example, and possibly with a French lawyer called Jacques Vergès, who would soon appear on the scene as the third member of a tripartite defense team. Vergès was in touch with François Genoud long before his connection with the case was made public in May 1983. He was observed dining in Lausanne with Genoud, in February, just days after Barbie's return to France and at the very time Genoud was negotiating with de la Servette.

During their encounters during the month of February, Genoud had suggested to de la Servette that Vergès join the case, but the two men did not officially begin to work together until May. In the meantime, Vergès, too, was contacted by the German specialist lawyers. They sent "friendly greetings" and "offers of help," he later acknowledged.[4]

De la Servette was unhappy about the association, but he accepted it. "I could have handled [the case] alone," he later confided. "The political aspects didn't bother me at all." But the collaboration had repercussions he hadn't counted on. The public presumed de la Servette was being paid by legal aid, but Jacques Vergès was quite naturally receiving a fee from somewhere else. People began to ask embarrassing questions. Why, for example, was de la Servette still on the case if a privately paid lawyer had come aboard?

Jacques Vergès was a high-profile, attention-grabbing, left-winger who was widely known for having defended some of the most notorious clients in the country. Indeed, he was not-so-affectionately known as "the terrorists' lawyer," and occasionally as "Maître Guillotine," since he had, so to speak, not won all his cases.

Vergès's motives for joining the Barbie defense were perfectly in line with a lifetime of political activism; on the surface, however, his appearance in this particular drama seemed confusing. What was a radical leftist doing defending a Nazi? Even in France, where some sort of political "engagement" is a sign of one's intellectual worth, this particular relationship appeared a bit peculiar. There was, however, a little-known element: for more than two decades, Jacques Vergès had inhabited a world where the extremes of neo-nazism and left-wing radicalism have often blurred.

Vergès and François Genoud were no strangers to one another. They had met in the mid-1950s during the halcyon days of the Algerian independence movement, at a time when it was first becoming evident that nostalgic Nazis like Genoud—left in limbo by the defeat of the Third Reich—and the young extremists of Arab nationalism had much to offer each other. The two men had remained in touch over the decades, sometimes collaborating professionally. The Klaus Barbie affair was only the most recent manifestation of their ongoing relationship.

With the addition of Jacques Vergès, the defense looked impressive: the head of the law society, a priest and a fearless iconoclast. Too impressive.

There was consternation in both Catholic and Jewish circles at the involvement of Robert Boyer, and the most scandalized of all was Catholic officialdom. The religious hierarchy thought that the presence of a priest on the Klaus Barbie team might be construed to mean that the church itself was defending a Nazi. Forty years after the war, it just wouldn't do to have it seem as though old Marshal Pétain had dropped into Lyons for a little visit and whispered a pro-collaboration message in the Archbishop's ear. Especially when the church had adopted an official policy of accepting responsibility for its history of anti-Semitism.

At 6:30 P.M. on April 1, 1983, Monsignor Decourtray dispatched his political éminence grise, Charles Favre, to de la Servette's office for "discussions." The situation was delicate, for Robert Boyer had had full permission from the Jesuits to exercise his profession as a lawyer.

"You do not have the right to dirty the church," said Favre, adopting a moral stance. "There is only one priest-lawyer in France, and you have captured him in the service of a Nazi. If there were two, the Jews might have taken the other, and that would be another story. But since there is only one, what you are doing is improper."

Favre quoted encyclicals and other pontifical texts. He also suggested that de la Servette didn't really understand what he was getting into. When Favre left, it was almost midnight.

The next day Favre learned that de la Servette would not capitulate. Boyer was going to stay.

Over the next two months various leaders of the Catholic church and the Jesuit order tried to negotiate directly with Boyer. But Boyer was adamant. Barbie might be scum, said Boyer, but morally he felt obliged to defend him. Things got so bad that Boyer eventually refused to see his superior altogether, saying that he had permission to practice law, and that was that.

Monsignor Decourtray and Favre appealed to Rome — to the General of the Jesuit order. They explained that this was an issue that would certainly interest the Pope himself. Given the history of the Catholic church and the official policy of "repentance" (in Archbishop Decourtray's words) that the church had adopted since the Vatican Council of 1965; and given also the fact that the Pope had just returned from a visit to Auschwitz, how would it look if one of the priests of the church was then seen to be defending a Nazi? This trial would be international in scope. How would the church explain the presence of a priest to world public opinion?

The officials in Rome agreed that the situation was catastrophic. But Boyer was right. He did, indeed, have permission to practice law. And in defense of freedom, the church couldn't afford to be authoritarian.

On June 4, a meeting of ecclesiastical legal experts was convened in Lyons to discuss the issue of Boyer's freedom versus canon law. Things did not look good. Boyer's freedom seemed to be total — unless he was defending interests that went counter to those of the church, explained the experts.

"That's it," exclaimed the Archbishop. "What Boyer is doing is directly contrary to the official penitence of the church with regard to the Jews."

On June 14, Monsignor Decourtray issued a statement making public the position of the church and embarrassing Boyer without actually demanding his resignation from the Barbie case. "The presence of a priest . . . in the preparation of the defense is serving to reinforce a powerful and worrisome trend toward the trivialization of nazism," he said. He added that the church could not be seen to be defending a man who had not recognized any of his misdeeds, and he concluded by pointing out that while the Catholic church considered the right to a legal defense an essential, democratic freedom, it did not follow that it had to be a priest of the church who assured that defense. Finally, he concluded: "It is a duty for all Christians to denounce the insanity of nazism which promoted the extermination of Jews for no reason except that they were born Jews . . . To respect and to insist that others respect the memory of these victims must be the primary concern of Christians."

During these negotiations, Alain de la Servette had been having his own problems. It was being whispered in Lyons and elsewhere that he was downplaying the Barbie affair with the approval of the Mitterrand government, no doubt because, if there was one thing everyone agreed on, it was that the trial could awaken the old hatreds that had divided France during the Occupation. In particular, it would raise again the unresolved issue of Jean Moulin's betrayal. The government was doing its best to keep a lid on that subject by excluding "war crimes" (which would involve Moulin and the Resistance) from the charges being brought against Barbie and allowing only the charge of "crimes against humanity," for which there was no statute of limitations. But having Jacques Vergès on board was something else entirely. Unlike de la Servette, who was a conventional man, Vergès feasted on the Barbie case like a lion on its prey. And he couldn't have cared less about the concerns of the Mitterrand government.

Alain de la Servette would have liked to stay on the case. It was interesting legally, and it would surely make him internationally famous. On the other hand, he was not a stupid man. He respected Jacques Vergès as a brilliant lawyer, but it was more than clear that they would not be able to work together. De la Servette was already having to take a back seat to his colleague. Vergès definitely wanted him to stay; that was part of the strategy. He even offered him money, said de la Servette, who found the gesture offensive.

Archbishop Decourtray made his statement on June 14. On June 15, de la Servette went to Saint Joseph's prison with Jacques Vergès to force Klaus Barbie to decide between them.[5] But Barbie said he was unable to decide. And Vergès had no intention of resigning from the case.

De la Servette then issued his own statement to the press.

The rumors surrounding the Klaus Barbie case have forced me to make public my decision. I accepted the defense of an accused [man] who had the right to be defended just like anyone else. I designated Robert

Boyer as my assistant. I chose him for both his human and his profes-
sional abilities, and my decision ought not to have evoked the slightest
doubt. There can be no ambiguity when a lawyer agrees to defend an
accused, whoever he is, whatever he has done, or not done . . .

I understand the reaction of the victims including those who have
[threatened] me with hatred and violence, but I regret that such con-
siderations may have clouded an understanding of our role, which is
to separate the crime from the criminal . . .

During the course of an interview this very day, Maître Vergès
has let me and Klaus Barbie know that he is ready to take on the de-
fense alone. Under such conditions the defense is assured, and I con-
sider myself relieved from the task that I shared with Maître Boyer,
although I would have been prepared to assume it to the end . . .

I hope that this difficult trial will bring honor to French Justice
with due respect for the principles I have attempted to observe.

Alain de la Servette did not mention the ongoing embarrassment
he was experiencing over the prickly question of his fees. However,
with this declaration he successfully removed himself from the increasingly ambiguous complexities of the Barbie affair. Furthermore, since
he had appointed Robert Boyer, the latter was also obliged to resign,
which he did saying he had been planning to do so all along.

It was June 15, 1983. Jacques Vergès had become Klaus Barbie's
sole legal counsel.

Vergès merely smiled myseriously when asked who was paying
his fees and his expenses for trips to faraway places like La Paz, Bolivia,
to collect evidence and interview witnesses. François Genoud, on the
other hand, was slightly less reticent. In an interview with *Stern* magazine, he said that he would "neither confirm nor deny" his involvement in the Barbie affair, adding that "Everyone has his hobbies."[6]
Among Vergès's acquaintances, however, the answer seemed evident.
"If Jacques needs money these days he has only to go to Switzerland,"
confided a friend.

It has long been known in various European circles that "a Swiss
citizen who lives in Lausanne" has managed the Nazi treasury since
the fall of the Third Reich.[7] The money, most of which was stolen
from European Jews, was deposited in numbered bank accounts
through a clandestine club of former ss officers called Die Spinne (the
Spider), the successor to the ODESSA organization. In March 1965,

Le Monde indirectly identified this individual as François Genoud.[8]
In 1969, the Centre d'information et de documentation moyen-orient
in Brussels confirmed the identification.

François Genoud personifies a hybrid of ultra-Left and neo-Nazi
extremism that first appeared on the international scene after the last
war. One might even say he created the type along with a handful of
others. His nazism came first. Genoud was born in Lausanne in 1915
into a bourgeois family that appreciated "law and order." In the early
1930s, before Hitler came to power, his parents sent him to Germany
in the hope that he would pick up some of the discipline of the emerging new regime. During his stay, Genoud was introduced to Hitler
and actually shook his hand. He read Hitler's writings and found them
"very relevant."[9] The teenager was an instant convert. François Genoud
returned to Switzerland a convinced Nazi, and he has never lost his
faith.

Back in Switzerland, Genoud made contact with Georges
Oltramare, head of the Swiss fascist party, L'Union Nationale. According to his own account, however, Genoud preferred the pro-Nazi
Front National, which he joined in 1934.[10] In 1936 he travelled to
Palestine, where he met an individual who, like himself, would eventually combine the presumably polar opposites of fascism and extreme
left-wing nationalism. Haj Amin el Hussein was the ex-Grand Mufti
of Jerusalem, and he was to become one of Genoud's links to the Arab
world.

In 1940, the military attaché at the French embassy in Berne, Switzerland, noted that Genoud was involved in disseminating anti-French
propaganda. Also around this time, Genoud was contacted by an agent
of the Abwehr for work in the German intelligence service, and during
the course of the year he disappeared from Switzerland to travel through
Germany, Czechoslovakia, Hungary and Belgium. During this period
(and immediately following the end of the war) Genoud made the ac-
quaintance of several extremely prominent Nazis, including ss General
Karl Wolff. Wolff was Himmler's personal adjutant as far back as 1933,
and in 1939 he became Himmler's liaison officer in the Führer's headquarters. In 1943, Wolff was Supreme ss and Police Leader in the Italian campaign, and it was he who negotiated surrender on April 29,
1945. He was also part of Hitler's plan (later abandoned) to kidnap
Pope Pius XII in September 1943 (after the fall of Mussolini) with a
special regiment of 2,000 men.

Wolff was a consummate Nazi. According to a document submitted to the court at Nuremburg in 1946, he had greeted "with particular joy" the information that "for two weeks now a train has been carrying every day five thousand members of the Chosen People" from Warsaw to the killing center of Treblinka.[11]

In 1984, just before his death at the age of eighty-four, Wolff gave an interview to a Swiss journalist[12] in which he spoke of how much former Nazis everywhere owed to François Genoud. After the war, while they were in prison or in hiding, Genoud acted as an intermediary, Wolff said. In particular, he was involved in bringing aid to German soldiers and officers who were being held in French prisons.

Genoud claims that he was not involved in helping Nazis escape from Europe, but only "because the occasion did not present itself."[13] On another occasion he explained himself further, this time with regard to Klaus Barbie. "I did not help Mr. Barbie escape," he declared. "It would not have been a dishonor to help National Socialists flee, but as it happens, I did not."[14]

As part of his ongoing commitment to the ideology of the Third Reich, Genoud became a publisher of important Nazi materials. He holds all posthumous rights to the writings of Hitler, Martin Bormann and the Nazi propaganda minister, Joseph Goebbels, according to a financial agreement concluded with members of all three families in 1945 and 1946. In 1952, representing himself as an agent of the Hitler family, Genoud brought charges against a Paris publishing house that had produced Bormann's account of Hitler's conversations without his permission, and won.[15] And in 1956 a court in Cologne agreed that he owned the rights to the posthumous works of Goebbels, causing a scandal among people who claimed that the royalties from such writings ought to be in the public domain to compensate Hitler's victims.

In 1973, Genoud sold the rights to the Goebbels diary (a 16,000-page manuscript with a baroque history of its own) to Albrecht Knaus, the director of Hoffmann und Campe Verlag, a Hamburg publishing house; and in 1981, Knaus, who by then had his own publishing house in Hamburg, brought out *Hitler's Political Testament* as purportedly dictated to Martin Bormann. The preface to the book explained that Genoud had acquired the document in 1946 at the time of the Nuremburg Trials. It seems that ex-ss Captain Hans Reichenberg, who had the document, went to the Nuremburg Trials to act as an adviser for the defense. There, through his former superior, General Hermann

Ramcke, he met François Genoud, a friend of Ramcke. During the course of a developing friendship, he confided to Genoud his photocopies of eighteen chapters of the book.

By 1955, Genoud's second career as adviser, researcher and banker to the cause of Arab nationalism had begun. One of the keys to that seemingly unlikely transition can be found in *Hitler's Political Testament*. In the preface, Genoud explained that he planned to have the book translated into Arabic and Swahili because, in the body of the text, Hitler invited the people of the Third World to carry on the work of the Thousand Year Reich.

In 1955, Genoud was in Tangiers, one of the ports where Nazis seeking to escape European justice took refuge. He was also frequently in Cairo, where he worked in the Egyptian intelligence service under Nasser. (Cairo under Nasser had been the center of the Pan-Arab movement since 1945.) These were important years, the years in which nazism and the developing ultra-Left began to merge: and François Genoud was at the center of events. With his friend Hans Reichenberg, who also had discovered a new outlet for his career in the Arab world, Genoud created an import-export company called Arabo-Afrika. The business was primarily a cover for the export of anti-Semitic and anti-Israeli propaganda[16] and the delivery of weapons to the Algerian FLN movement.[17] Genoud made financial investments for various friends, Reichenberg and Dr. Hjalmar Schacht, Hitler's finance minister, among them. Genoud also renewed his friendship with Karl Wolff, who had found his way to Nasser's Egypt.

Cairo in the 1950s was paradise for Nazis with nowhere to go and nowhere to apply their carefully honed talents. In the emerging world of Arab nationalism, they found a new outlet for their profound anti-Semitism and their propaganda skills.

It was in this milieu that François Genoud first met the nine leaders of the nascent Algerian insurrection. Ahmed Ben Bella, Mohammed Khider, Ait Ahmet, Mohammed Boudiaf and their colleagues had formed the provisional government of Algeria. Genoud's skills as a financier made him infinitely valuable, and before the end of the decade he had established bank accounts in Switzerland on behalf of the North African liberation armies of Morocco, Tunisia and Algeria. The system he used involved multiple signatures—just like the system that was already in use for the secret Nazi funds.[18]

François Genoud has never attempted to hide his loyalties, and they have not weakened over the decades. In 1964, his Lausanne apartment still looked like a Hitlerian museum, with Nazi flags and portraits of the Führer decorating the walls.[19] "I am a quiet and modest man," he declared to the Lausanne magazine *L'Hebdo* in March 1982.[20] "My only crime is that I have never been a turncoat and I have never repudiated my ideas." His ideas were summed up in the following statement: "Nationalism Socialism was a unique phenomenon in history, and it found solutions for the important mutations that took place in the twentieth century. The movement was able to establish the union of an [entire] people in a common ideal. At the time, tens of thousands of Europeans thought as I do. Since then I sometimes think I'm alone."[21]

Unfortunately, Genoud is not alone; however, he may be the only proud Nazi alive who vigorously denies that he is an anti-Semite. He is very clear on this point. He is merely an anti-*Zionist*. "It is the Zionists that are anti-Semitic," he explained, picking up on a theme that has been in wide circulation in the Soviet Union and extremist Arab and neo-Nazi circles since the 1950s. Indeed, François Genoud has harsh words for the Nazi system of cataloging people according to their racial origin ("That's a Zionist idea," he volunteered) because Hitler's persecution of the Jews "involuntarily provided an enormous help to Zionism." As for the Holocaust, he is careful to minimize its extent by employing neo-Nazi arguments that have been put forward by Robert Faurisson in France, James Keegstra and Ernst Zundel in Canada, and others in Britain, Germany, the United States and, more recently, Russia. "The numbers were exaggerated and the documents are false," claimed Genoud. "There were horrible occurrences on both sides; but there was never a systematic attempt to exterminate any people."

Genoud gave the *L'Hebdo* interview to defend himself against a story about his activities published in *Le Monde* and picked up by other French publications.[22] His response to the articles was predictable. "They [the journalists] are part of a Zionist coterie that is trying to get even," he explained.

The major significance of revisionist history of this sort is that it has been adopted by extremists on both the Left and the Right of the political spectrum. In 1983, Soviet anti-Zionist literature began to question the number of Jews destroyed in the Holocaust.[23] Until then that particular aspect of Holocaust revisionism had been advanced primarily by the neo-Nazi Right. The following year in Britain, *Nationalism Today*, the paper of the neo-Nazi National Front, announced that it would soon have an "anti-Zionist supplement."

Genoud's activities since the 1950s have been nothing short of baroque. In October 1956, when a plane carrying four members of the Algerian provisional government was intercepted and the leaders imprisoned in France, he became the guardian of the children of one of the men, Mohammed Boudiaf. As such he was able to maintain the liaison between the provisional government and Nasser's information services by accompanying the children on their visits to their father in prison.[24] At about the same time, Genoud claims to have rescued Belgian Nazi leader, SS General Léon Degrelle, by spiriting him across the Spanish border in the trunk of his car.[25]

When Algerian independence was proclaimed in 1962, François Genoud was rewarded for his services. He became the director of the Banque Populaire Arabe in Algiers and brought Hitler's former finance minister, Dr. Schacht, to Algiers as well. But in 1964 Genoud was arrested and charged with having transferred $15 million of FLN "war treasury" money to a Swiss bank in the name of Mohammed Khider. Khider was a former leader of the Algerian revolution who had subsequently had a falling out with the new president, Ben Bella, and been forced to take refuge in Spain. Genoud was never tried on the charges because Nasser personally interceded on his behalf. As a result, Genoud obtained permission "to visit a sick relative" back in Switzerland. Needless to say, he never returned to Algeria.

In 1958, Genoud created the Banque Commerciale Arabe in Geneva in partnership with a Syrian named Zouheir Mardam. According to a study produced in Brussels in 1969, the bank was established "to transfer money from various Arab countries with a view to financing political intervention on behalf of these countries."[26] One of the financial consultants was, of course, Dr. Schacht, who was quoted as saying that National Socialism would conquer the world without having to wage another war.[27]

For fifteen years, the Algerian government fought to regain the money through the hierarchy of the Swiss courts. Finally, in 1979, the FLN "treasure" was returned to Algeria.

The Algerian War ended in 1962, but terrorism in the cause of Arab nationalism was just beginning. In November 1969, Genoud turned up in Winterthur, Switzerland, at the trial of three Palestinian terrorists from Dr. George Habbash's Popular Front for the Liberation of Palestine (PFLP) who had blown up an El Al plane in Zurich. Genoud explained that he was an "adviser" to the defense, one of his favorite ways of describing his activities. Seated next to him was none other than Jacques Vergès. The Swiss government had refused to allow Vergès to plead and he, too, was present in an advisory capacity.

The defendants refused to answer any questions during their trial. Their act was not criminal, but political, they said.

François Genoud and Jacques Vergès first met in Algeria in the late 1950s through mutual friends in the FLN. Each man was tormented by his own demons, but the spinning out of separate, equally fantastic dreams linked their careers. Each man publicly defended political terrorism. "Everyone has a role to play," said Genoud in 1982. "Personally, I don't know how to use a weapon, but I do understand that when one is a victim of terrorism, there is no solution but counterterrorism . . ."[28] Each man would have links to the terrorist dramas that shocked the world through the decades of the 1960s and 1970s and into the 1980s.

Jacques Vergès is no ordinary lawyer for hire, although some of his acquaintances do enjoy describing him as a publicity seeker whose only real interest is the glorification of Jacques Vergès. Most people, however, see him as a man with a mission who was politicized decades ago to a position far to the left of the familiar political streams of modern France, and who continues to fight the battles of the Third World through his legal practice. It is in part this disdain for the current Mitterrand government, which he despises as pro-American, "Zionist" and composed of sellouts who opposed independence for Algeria, that inspired Vergès to take on the defense of Klaus Barbie. The Barbie affair would allow him to pry open a few closed doors — doors that contain skeletons from the Occupation and the war in Algeria that the French government might prefer to keep under lock and key. There was also the interesting fact that Barbie himself had also been involved in the merger of Left and Right. In 1979 he held a long *tête-à-tête* with representatives of a PLO delegation that had been invited to La Paz by the national leftist parties, much to the discomfort of the latter groups, who had long been demanding Altmann-Barbie's extradition to France. Barbie was also considered to have been a friend of Giangiacomo Feltrinelli, the Italian millionaire who was one of the first to call for armed guerrilla warfare in Europe (on behalf of the Palestinians) in the 1960s. (An Italian paper named Barbie as Feltrinelli's arms supplier from Bolivia.)[29]

Jacques Vergès seemed to command a healthy degree of respect. Some of his acquaintances refused to be interviewed; others insisted on remaining anonymous. But their common theory about Vergès's specific interest in Klaus Barbie was borne out by Vergès himself. Within six months of taking on the Barbie defense, he published a quickie book in which he attacked several national heroes of the French Resistance as traitors, described his courtroom "strategy of disruption," a technique with which he planned to put Barbie on the offensive and the prosecution on the defensive, and promised to drag France and its government into the dock along with his client.[30]

The initial hoopla that had accompanied Klaus Barbie's return to France was definitely turning sour.

· 8 ·

THE MAKING OF A RADICAL

Jacques Vergès and his twin brother, Paul, were born on March 5, 1925, in Thailand, when it was still the Kingdom of Siam. Their father was a French medical doctor from an old colonial family on the island of Réunion and, until his marriage to their mother, a diplomat with the French embassy. The marriage ended the elder Vergès's diplomatic career. Raymond Vergès's wife was Vietnamese; and in 1925 Frenchmen simply did not marry Asian women.

So the lives of the Vergès brothers began with a racial scandal. The hatred that accompanied the very circumstances of their birth marked them deeply, and their father as well.

Raymond Vergès gathered his family around him and crossed the Mekong River to Laos where he resumed his practice of medicine; but by 1928 he had had enough, and the family returned "home," to Réunion Island. Shortly thereafter, his young wife died of an infected abscess. The boys were three years old.

The year 1914 had marked the apogee of western colonialism, with Britain, France and the United States extending tentacles into almost every corner of the globe (Réunion Island, a tropical enclave in the Indian Ocean, had been exploited by French commercial interests since the seventeenth century); but by the mid-1920s the system was beginning to show signs of wear. The Russian Revolution of 1917, the communist and nationalist victories in China during the 1920s and 1930s and the new, radical nationalism of Kemal Ataturk in Turkey, all gave credibility to the growing political movements that were opposed to colonialism. The stage was set for the development of a new, left-wing nationalism, and during the 1930s, '40s and '50s, the politics of revolutionary Marxism influenced the thinking of thousands of men and women in the colonized world. Raymond Vergès was one of

147

them, followed by his twin sons. Jacques, in particular, was sensitive, enraged at the colonial condition, and aching for revenge.

The colonial reality, which Jacques Vergès learned to hate, was at the very core of his existence. The Vergès brothers were oriental in appearance, but they were also French and, as such, they belonged in part to a dominating minority that soon became suspect, even to themselves. It was not an easy way to begin life.

The anger took hold in childhood as a result of the violence Vergès observed around him and the ambivalence of his own racial status. Within the family, the boys were protected as much as possible, but in the 1930s and 1940s, racism was an integral part of the colonial reality. The European community was openly disdainful and exploitive of the local population. Slavery had been abolished in 1794, but forced labor remained a primary economic tool. In neighboring Madagascar, men were taken off the street to work in public utilities or for colonial enterprises. They were lodged in barracks and fed a subsistence diet. They worked ten to fourteen hours a day. When their turn of "duty" was over, they were returned, and others were picked up to replace them. Native coolies pulled French passengers who indicated their desire to stop with a quick kick on the coolie's backside. As a child, Vergès observed the brutality. "Those experiences left their mark on me," he said half a century later, in an uncharacteristically muted voice.

The years of childhood were also a time of political unrest. Marxist ideology was gaining ground among intellectuals everywhere, and the conflicts within France during the 1930s further disturbed the climate. Against enormous opposition, Raymond Vergès created a Communist party on Réunion Island and in 1946 was elected as the local deputy to the French National Assembly. During his election campaign, Jacques's brother, Paul, was charged with murdering his father's political opponent. According to *Le Monde*, the communists were attempting to disrupt the election meeting. When the organizers called the police, the younger Vergès lodged a single bullet in the candidate's heart. (Four decades later, Jacques described the subsequent guilty verdict as "political.")[1]

"There was an atmosphere of violence on the island between the colonials and the native population and among the colonials themselves," Vergès acknowledged. Without doubt, violence would continue to seem for him an unavoidable, ever-sensible solution. Particularly when tied to politics — romantic politics.

In the 1960s, Vergès provided a rare glimpse into his early suffering in a bitter eulogy written to a man he had met as a child. "Abd-El-Krim opened an avenue toward the light for all the pariahs of Africa and Asia," he wrote. "Then, in exile, he taught us firmness in misfortune and the political intransigence without which courage and intelligence are sterile . . . With his death a page of the history of the colonial revolution has turned, that of the heroic pioneer of desperate, unequal battles . . ."[2]

Jacques Vergès left Réunion Island when he was seventeen, three years before the violence of his father's electoral campaign, to begin a career in which the private pain of his early years would be projected on to a public stage in the battle against colonialism. In 1942, he joined the French Resistance to fight the German Occupation. Although the land where he lived and had his roots was dominated by the French, he now felt called upon to defend that side of his heritage. All colonialism enraged Vergès and made him suffer; and now France herself had been colonized. France was under attack.

Since it was impossible to reach France in 1942, Vergès went to England and joined the Free French under de Gaulle. It made sense. De Gaulle was the rebel nationalist commanding his troops from abroad and defying both the foreign occupier and the collaborationist government of Marshal Pétain. But Vergès had another mission on his father's behalf: to establish contact between the French Communist party and the communists of Réunion Island.

The war ended and the German occupier was gone, but whatever illusions the adolescent Jacques Vergès may have had about France were soon shattered. The timing was particularly ironic. Hitler committed suicide on April 30, 1945, ridding the world of a tyrant and ending an epoch, but one short week later an important uprising occurred in Algeria against the French themselves. The repression was instant and brutal. In the Algerian city of Constantine, the FLN counted 40,000 victims. The French administration admitted to 1,500.

"I was still in the Resistance army when that happened and I was terribly shocked," recalled Vergès. "I didn't understand how they could fight Hitler then turn around and do that. Two years later there was a similar repression in Madagascar. The Nuremberg Trials were taking place at the time. I simply could not understand how nations could hold these trials so that the sort of thing the Germans did would never happen again. It was clear to me that the victorious colonial nations were doing exactly what the Germans had done in France."

The bitterness continued. In 1946, France became engaged in what would become a futile eight-year battle to retain its colony of Indochina. The fantasy that territories attached to other continents were actually an indistinguishable part of metropolitan France was so integral to the French vision that when the resistance against Germany ended and a war against an indigenous resistance movement in Indochina began, scarcely anyone noticed the anomaly.

But Indochina, or Vietnam, was Jacques Vergès's other half, and the colonial war was a further shock to the twenty-one-year-old veteran of the heroic French Resistance. France, the country he had fought for, *his* country, was engaged in a battle against other heroic nationalists, those of his mother's homeland, of Asia, where he was born.

Thus Vergès learned to hate the "hypocrites" of the French Resistance. Four decades later, Klaus Barbie would give him a tailor-made opportunity to express a lifetime of accumulated disdain. "I was very open to the idea of defending Barbie," he acknowledged. "What I say about him now I have thought for forty years."

After the defeat of Nazi Germany, Vergès settled in Paris where he quickly became an important protégé of the Communist party. With his quick mind and radical inclinations, he was ideal material for leadership training.

Vergès quickly demonstrated his aptitude as a militant and a tactician. He took over the association of students from Réunion Island by reminding the membership that only students with scholarships had the right to vote. Since he and the other Resistance veterans were the majority of scholarship holders — and communists — they soon had control of the organization.

He transformed the Réunion organization into the militant Association for Colonial Students, a group that included his close friend, the young Pol Pot. (Pol Pot was in Paris ostensibly studying radioelectricity.) Vergès was flamboyant and provocative from the start. In February 1949, he held an "anticolonialist-day" celebration in the courtyard of the Sorbonne, which he had had decorated with Viet-Minh flags; and in November of the same year he presided over a huge public meeting for "the liberation of oppressed peoples."

The Communist party was so impressed with Jacques Vergès that in 1950 he was sent to Prague where he became director of the International Union of Students, an important youth organization. His most brilliant contribution was in the field of propaganda: the creation of the International Student Relief Fund, in 1950. The "aid" involved was minimal, consisting mainly of photocopies of speeches and other inexpensive materials. The real purpose was to contact and to politicize young people who were living in colonized countries.

Vergès traveled constantly during this period, making Third World contacts that would last a lifetime. He even "visited" France where he was simultaneously enrolled in a law program. But the psychological aspect of the Prague years may have had the most influence on his future, for his stay (which lasted until 1954) spanned the period of the notorious Prague trials. The trials, which represented one of the first public displays of "anti-Zionism" from within the Soviet orbit, centered on Rudolph Slansky, who had been general secretary of the Communist party of Czechoslovakia. Slansky was a Jew, and in 1952 he and fifteen others were charged with being spies and Zionist agents and with plotting the destruction of the communist regime. It was soon apparent, however, even to the most casual of observers, that the real issue was the old dragon of anti-Semitism, now cleverly outfitted with a new name.

"I did not sense any anti-Semitism in the Prague trials," was Vergès's extraordinary claim during a later interview. [3] Perhaps, he added, this was because he didn't speak Czech. But if Prague was for most of the world an introduction to the new face of anti-Semitism, other echoes would soon rebound from distant places. Indeed, during the future political travels of Jacques Vergès, from Prague to the PLO and beyond, anti-Zionism would emerge as a staple item on a hardening ideological menu.

Vergès had already experienced the reality of political terror, but the Prague years clearly toughened him even further. (In this he was not alone. Alexander Shelepin, one of his acquaintances from the period, went on to become the chief of the KGB.) Indeed, three decades later, Vergès defended the Stalin régime of the 1950s. "People are always talking about the Stalin terror, but there was also friendship . . . and lyricism," he rhapsodized. "And as far as the dirty jobs were concerned, you only did them if you wanted to."[4]

In 1954, Vergès returned to Paris, where he finished his law degree and was called to the bar in 1955. In 1956, he was named Secretary of the Conference, a prestigious honor that has served as a stepping stone to greatness for some of France's most famous men. He also enrolled in a new course of studies: Oriental Languages, with an emphasis on Hindi. Why Hindi? The answer seemed clear enough. If Vergès was to have any real influence in his own home territory of Réunion, he would have to learn to speak to the large Hindu majority in their own tongue.

From the start Jacques Vergès was a firebrand lawyer, a political lawyer, a lawyer of controversial causes. The Algerian war began in 1954. Vergès defended communist militants who had attempted to disrupt the departure of a trainload of draftees — and won. But the conformist policies of the Communist party quickly alienated him. The Party voted in favor of continuing the war in Algeria. Vergès neither forgave nor forgot.

The Algerian struggle touched Vergès profoundly and became the launching pad for his career. He vibrated to the same anger that seized the rebel Moslem population. Like himself, they were "marginals" — regarded as second-class citizens by the circumstances of their birth. Vergès committed himself wholly to the Algerian nationalist movement, from instinctive as well as political motives. Eventually, he changed his name to Mansour and converted to Islam. Then in 1963 he married his first revolutionary client, Djamila Bouhired, an Algerian communist and a heroine of the revolution. The conversion was a practical necessity, for Vergès already had a wife and child in France, which made him technically a bigamist. A religious ceremony would be recognized in Algeria, but not in France, where a second, civil ceremony is required.

Jacques Vergès was not the first — nor would he be the last — to link the mysteries of love with the shadowy ambiguities of revolution and violence.

In 1954, Algeria was a colony in every sense of the word and had been so since the French military conquest of 1830. France thought of Algeria as an integral part of French territory, and the fact that it just happened to be situated somewhere else on the earth's surface was of little interest to most French people. They called this policy "assimilation," and it involved incorporating millions of others into the language, culture and ethos of the metropole while deftly brushing aside centuries of religious, linguistic and cultural differences. The grandeur of France and other notions of empire were predicated on the existence of a colonial arm that reached across oceans to transport the supposedly superior qualities of French culture into unlikely places.[5]

The European community in Algeria had appropriated the best agricultural land; and wheat, tobacco, herbs and the strong, heady Algerian wines had made the fortunes of many. But over the years, the indigenous Moslem population grew progressively poorer, except for a numerically small but powerful nobility that was wooed by the French with favors, decorations and honorary titles. Electoral fraud was practiced openly by the colonial administration to control indigenous representation at the political level, and the cooperative few who were elected from this nobility duly placed their hopes for change in the policy of assimilation and equal rights. According to a recent history of the Algerian war, there was nothing at all haphazard about political procedure in Algeria. "The politics of assimilation were revealed to be a conscious effort to dismantle the traditional institutions of Moslem society by the introduction of French law . . . The politics of assimilation were, in effect, the politics of submission," wrote the authors.[6]

The French colonials of Algeria enjoyed their privileged status and were wary of any real or potential threat to their authority. On almost any issue, this community could be counted upon to adopt a deeply conservative stance. As early as 1898, Edouard Drumont of anti-Dreyfus fame had been elected in Algeria. The right-wing Croix de Feu and the pro-Nazi Parti Populaire Français were both highly regarded during the years leading up to World War II, and when it came to the defeat of 1940, the Algerian "blackfoots" (as the colonials were pejoratively called by their compatriots in metropolitan France) welcomed Marshal Pétain with open arms. Nowhere were the anti-Semitic proclamations of Vichy France received more warmly than in Algiers, Oran and Constantine. To speak of the French Resistance was a laugh; indeed, a favorite joke of the day acknowledged that to resist in Algiers was to resist against oneself.

In the mid-1930s, the socialist government of Léon Blum proposed a series of moderate reform measures that would have allowed for increased Algerian representation in parliament and enfranchised several new categories of Moslems beyond the upper strata of notables, who already enjoyed a privileged relationship with the French. But far from understanding that such reforms might co-opt or even halt the growth of indigenous nationalism, the colonial community fought back tooth and nail. They ridiculed the proposals and unleashed such a stream of invective in their newspapers that the intended reforms died on the order paper even before they were officially debated.

Watching carefully from the wings was a new generation of young Algerian nationalists. However the failure of the Blum initiatives was not the only reason for their growing militancy. A new sense of pan-Arab ethnicity was emerging that emphasized the nationalists' alienation from French values. Even worse, they felt betrayed by the French Communist party. In the early days, the PCF, following the line from Moscow, had been militantly anticolonialist and had attracted the brightest and the angriest of the young Algerians. But then abruptly, in 1935, the Party had reversed its position and begun to promote the more conventional French assimilationist line wherein the Moslem masses would be emancipated within the framework of French laws and institutions.

The Algerian nationalists rejected assimilation, and the PCF never recovered from its strategic mistake. Nationalism in Algeria began to acquire a specifically Arab content; the colonizer was the infidel who sucked the economic lifeblood from the country to enrich himself. A new vision of the Algerian "nation" emerged. It would be pure, strong and independent. It would rise, Phoenix-like, from the ashes of oppression in a Moslem, proletarian state.

On the eve of 1954, the economy of Algeria was booming — but Moslems derived little benefit from this prosperity. The European colonials numbered slightly less than one million persons and represented 10 percent of the total population. In agriculture, they made up only 2 percent of the farmers, but occupied 25 percent of all cultivated land. Arab farming was, by contrast, essentially subsistence farming. In the cities, industrialization squeezed out the untrained, poorly educated Arabs, causing massive unemployment: in 1954 it was estimated that 25 percent of employable males were jobless.

Paternalism, racism, condescension and exploitation were all part of the colonial package. And if the majority of Arabs responded with the fatalism of the powerless — in fear and in submission — it was also true that, on the eve of 1954, the number of angry militants had grown considerably. When the French were definitively defeated at Dien Bien Phu in May 1954, the nationalists thought the time was right. Inside and outside France, it seemed that the death knell of French colonial domination had sounded.

The rebels of the FLN who struck on November 1, 1954, were led by nine men. Among them were Ahmed Ben Bella, who would become the first president of an independent Algeria in 1963, and Mohammed Khider, future friend of François Genoud and Jacques Vergès.

Had Jacques Vergès written the script for his own personal radicalization, the war in Algeria could not have come at a better time. It was as though he had spent years in preparation for that particular moment in history: participating in the Resistance, observing a doomed colonial war in Indochina, heading the Association for Colonial Students and doing an apprenticeship in Prague. He had fought on behalf of the French during the German colonization, but he now applied his considerable talents to the struggle against France, the most recent colonizer. In his commitment to the Algerian insurrection, Vergès knotted together the diverse threads of his earlier life.

Ironically, the men and women on the other side of the Algerian conflict also claimed to act out of a commitment to their ideals and to France's historical past. Important political figures had achieved prominence precisely because of the role they had played in the French Resistance. They were patriots, but on the opposite side of the political fence. They represented the other face of the nation. "Overseas France" for them was just that — an integral part of metropolitan France. The men and women of the Algérie Française movement felt the centuries of French *grandeur* and *honneur* in their blood, heard the strains of "*La Marseillaise*" in their ears and refused to be written into history as the leaders who had capitulated. Many of these individuals had fought against the Germans as patriots, and in their eyes they fought as patriots to maintain their colonies in Indochina and Algeria. In all instances, they believed they were defending France.

Jacques Vergès was set on a collision course with his former comrades who now defended colonialism. He turned to guerrilla warfare — in the courts. It was time to put the "strategy of disruption" into practice.

On September 30, 1956, Djamila Bouhired was accused of having planted bombs in two crowded Algiers cafés that were popular with European young people. Her lawyer, Jacques Vergès, chose to ignore the charges as such. His strategy was, rather, to use the court-room as a platform for a public attack on the army, the French gov-ernment and the judicial system itself. Vergès may well have been the first trial lawyer of our era to use such tactics (although they have certainly been used since, in the trials of the Chicago Seven and the FLQ in Canada, to name just two). His premise was that the tradi-tional practice of law entails a certain "connivance" among the players: judge, jury, legal counsel, the press, the public and, ultimately, the accused. Thus the judicial system itself is depicted as part of the rotten apparatus of hypocrisy and oppression.

In spite of her lawyer's speeches, Djamila Bouhired was sentenced to death. She laughed.

"Don't laugh," scolded the judge. "This is serious."[7]

Bouhired's contempt for the judge who had just ordered her head chopped off was total. What justice was there, after all, in a legal sys-tem that was corrupt at its very base?

The "strategy of disruption," as he called it, worked well for Vergès and the other lawyers who subscribed to the tactic. It was essentially a no-lose deal. If a case was won on its merits, all was well. If the ac-cused was found guilty and even sentenced to death, the lawyer could ask, triumphantly, what else one could expect from such a perverse system.

In March 1958, Bouhired's sentence was commuted to life im-prisonment, and she was freed early in 1962; but her trial, and later on the highly publicized trials of the "Suitcase Carriers," a group of liberals and leftists who supported the FLN, did mark the beginnings of public awareness. Courtroom revelations about what was really going on in Algeria had a devastating effect on the French public. It became hard to hush up horrific tales of torture and assassination with a man like Jacques Vergès using the courtroom as a soapbox from which to attack the government and inform the media. And his accusations were largely correct. In response to terrorist actions on the part of the FLN, the French government had indeed assigned a division of para-chutists in Algiers to the task of destroying both the rebels and the political organization of the FLN. The underlying rationale was thought to be clear enough. The French army needed a victory after the defeat of 1940, the loss of Indochina and the humiliation it had endured dur-ing the Suez crisis of 1956. It was a question of *honneur*, a favorite word in conservative France. The army and its supporters were also convinced that the Algerian rebellion had been instigated by international communism, and this, they believed, gave them a free hand to retaliate at their pleasure.

Mutual hatreds intensified. The army flushed hidden rebels from Arab houses and not infrequently strung them up in public as a warning. Mere suspects might be summarily executed and the wounded "finished off." From time to time, prisoners were quietly destroyed on remote paths off the main thoroughfares, or thrown live from airplanes.

Some army officers refused to participate in such goings-on, and a small number protested publicly. But torture was practiced widely during the course of "interrogations." It was to be conducted "cleanly" — that is, without sadism and, most importantly, without leaving visible traces. Actual techniques of torture were fairly standard throughout Algeria: bodies were beaten, burned with cigarettes, exposed to electric shocks and plunged in the infamous "baths" made notorious, ironically and ominously, by Klaus Barbie and his fellow Nazis just a decade earlier when inflicting like indignities on members of the French Resistance.

In the aftermath of the Bouhired trial, Jacques Vergès and his friend Georges Arnaud (author of *The Wages of Fear*) put together a quickie book called *For Djamila Bouhired*, in which they described how Bouhired had been tortured while in detention. They took it to the prestigious publishing house of René Julliard. "This is a crock of shit," said Julliard, and agreed to publish if no one else was brave enough. Jérôme Lindon of Les Editions de Minuit was more forthcoming. A left-leaning liberal who sympathized with the emerging New Left, Lindon's concerns had, until then, been more literary than political. In the years ahead he would become an important publisher of anti-Algerian-war books.

The Vergès-Arnaud polemic on Djamila Bouhired was the first to focus attention on the trial of an FLN militant, and it served to rally a growing constituency of left-wing intellectuals who were actively opposed to colonialism and particularly horrified by this war because it appeared to sanction torture. Jean-Paul Sartre was the guru of this small but influential coterie of opinion makers, and his action-oriented philosophy of existentialism deeply conditioned their thinking. Sartre argued that it is not enough to spend one's life teaching in a university or writing books and articles. People must also act, for in doing man creates himself as a moral being.

The emerging network of dissent was directed by Francis Jeanson, a student-disciple of Sartre. Jeanson was a professional "intellectual" in the French tradition. He was attached to Sartre's prestigious journal, *Les Temps Modernes*, and wrote on philosophical and political issues.

Jeanson and his wife, Colette, who was also a writer, knew Algeria from the days of World War II, when they had been appalled by the attitudes of the European minority to the French Resistance. After the war, the Jeansons returned to Algeria to live among the Moslem population, to get a sense of what their life was like. They learned about the terrible inequalities, the oppression and the suffocation. And they never forgot the experience.

From 1957 to 1959, Francis Jeanson led a national network of clandestine aid to the FLN until his group was exploded by massive arrests and a subsequent trial that stood France on its ear, made a mockery of the judicial system and established Jacques Vergès as a national hero of the Left and a formidable opponent of the state. The machinery of the Jeanson network worked beautifully, and the main tasks seemed innocuous enough, at first. Safe houses were provided for FLN militants in transit, and cars with drivers were put at their disposal. False identity papers were forged, as they had been during the days of the resistance against the Germans. Jeanson also made arrangements to facilitate border crossings into Spain and Switzerland. Most important of all, however, was the transfer of monies collected in the Algerian quarters of Paris and elsewhere which, by 1958, amounted to approximately $80,000 a month. Six to eight large suitcases were needed to transport the bills over the border into Switzerland, where banking arrangements had been made by Henri Curiel, an Egyptian revolutionary who had settled in France after he was expelled from his own country in 1951. (For Curiel, affiliation with the Jeanson network marked the mid-point of a career that would carry him to the center of international terrorist operations before he was assassinated in Paris in May 1978.) Curiel made arrangements with "a Swiss banker," probably François Genoud ("Genoud helped the FLN during the war, and the FLN accepted this," said Vergès), and the money was driven directly across the border. Indeed, the system worked so well that Curiel often suggested to Jeanson that they wait a day or so before transferring funds because the value of the French franc was rising.[8]

The Jeanson network formed the nucleus of French resistance to the Algerian war, but it remained, throughout, a minority movement of intellectuals and students. The French Communist party, for example, never overtly committed its support to Jeanson's clandestine operations, and the French working class never actively joined the movement at all.

The government responded to the growth of antiwar dissent by doing the repressive things governments do, usually at their peril. Books were banned and individuals harassed. As usual, such heavy-handed tactics merely encouraged public disaffection. Finally, in September 1960, 121 of France's best-known citizens signed a declaration in favor of Algerian independence and in bold support of the Jeanson network. To the traditional French patriot who supported the war, this declaration was nothing short of traitorous, but it was difficult if not impossible to dismiss when such illustrious names as Jean-Paul Sartre, Simone de Beauvoir, Marguerite Duras, Alain Resnais and Simone Signoret were among the signatories.

The declaration was of special interest because the activities of the Jeanson network had by this time taken a more radical turn. As early as August 1958, militants had transported the war across the Mediterranean by exploding gasoline tanks in various regions of France. A few weeks later, Algerian gunmen bungled an assassination attempt on the life of Jacques Soustelle, a former governor general of Algeria and a pillar of the right-wing Algérie Française movement, as he read his morning paper in a Paris café. Significantly, a *French* accomplice stood by in a telephone booth waiting to transmit the news of his murder.

The first dissenter to be brought to trial was Georges Arnaud, who was charged with refusing to give police the address of Francis Jeanson or to reveal his sources for an antiwar document. His trial, which opened on June 17, 1960, marked the second appearance of Jacques Vergès on the national stage and a second instance of his strategy of disruption. From the opening moments, the defense controlled the proceedings. Vergès and his client, Arnaud, pointed accusing fingers at the judge and the entire judiciary. They laughed at the charges and used the courtroom as a forum for antiwar propaganda. While Arnaud dictated rousing speeches to the court stenographer, his friends on the outside mockingly sent a daily bouquet of violets to the magistrate.

Witness after witness for the defense took the stand and made exalted speeches for the record and the international press. The judge lost control. He ruled issues out of order, but they had already been spoken aloud. Before long, the original charges — the fact that Arnaud had refused to give information about Jeanson — began to look ridiculous.

The Arnaud trial was sensational, but Jacques Vergès had not yet reached the height of his fame. That moment arrived three months later, in September 1960, when the first members of the Jeanson network went on trial. Vergès was the leading member of the so-called FLN collective, a group of French and Algerian lawyers who were totally committed to the cause of their clients. Not surprisingly, Vergès's special responsibility was media relations.

The Jeanson trials would likely have been quite startling to a North American observer, for this was political theater in an absurdist mode. Six Algerians and eighteen Frenchmen sat squeezed together in the prisoners' box behind a formidable team of twenty-six pugnacious lawyers lined up in rows before the judge. The press and the public, divided into hostile camps of "Left" and "Right" came to cheer their friends and trade insults with their enemies. The lawyers, for their part, toyed with the court by playing a game of procedure. They questioned the competence of the French-Arabic interpreter and, finally, of the court itself. They "demonstrated" the righteousness of their cause and the "corruption" of the state for daring to bring charges against their clients who were, in effect, the last of the just. They provoked the judges by being ironic, insolent and derisive. It was a contest of nerve and disdain, in which Jacques Vergès came to be known as a "bulldozer," a man whose quick intelligence had been sharpened on the razor's edge of his personal rage, a man who demonstrated "a steadfast enthusiasm for bringing down the heroes of the land"[9] when it suited his purpose to do so.

The defendants in the box smoked cigarettes, told jokes and laughed uproariously. They saluted their friends in the courtroom and blew kisses back and forth. "This isn't a marketplace," chided the judge. "The charges are serious and not in the least funny." But such remonstrances only gave the defense a new opening. "You are right to recall that this trial is taking place in a tragic atmosphere and that behind the defendants a tragedy is occurring in Algeria. But when we think of this tragedy, let us remember [that it has more than one aspect]," retorted Jacques Vergès.[10]

If events inside the courtroom verged on the absurd, they also served to heat up the public debate over Algeria. First came the startling declaration of the 121 celebrities in support of the defendants and their pro-FLN activities. Eleven days later, Paul Teitgen, who had been secretary general of the police in Algiers from 1956 to 1957, admitted on the stand that he had known about the use of torture and had left his post for that reason. Three days after that bombshell, a letter from Jean-Paul Sartre was read in open court. In his letter, the renowned philosopher proclaimed his personal support for the Jeanson network and his belief that they were working toward the creation of a true democracy in France. Then he added that had he been asked to work directly for the FLN he would have agreed.[11]

Sartre's intervention produced outrage, and journalists wondered whether he might be arrested for public defiance of the law; but on October 1, 1960, the verdict was brought down, and speculation ceased. The conclusions of the court were rigorous. Only nine defendants were acquitted: fifteen others were sentenced to terms that ranged from eight months to ten years. But the Algerian resistance had made itself heard, loudly and publicly, and the antiwar message had been relayed far beyond the borders of France. Dissent mushroomed, and on November 4, 1960, General de Gaulle spoke to the nation for the first time of an "Algerian republic."

However, support for Algérie Française and the war was also on the increase. Indeed, the French right wing had not seen a revival of this magnitude since the Vichy era. Before long, opposing students at the Sorbonne were engaged in a civil war of insults and stone throwing, as angry factions faced each other on the sidewalks in front of the student restaurants chanting "*Algérie Française*" and "*Le fascisme ne passera pas*" (fascism will be stopped).

As for Jacques Vergès's "strategy of disruption," it had survived the test. "We had the proof that the defense could control the trial . . . and make it last as long as it wanted to," reflected Vergès in the aftermath. The court had been successfully humiliated, and that lesson was not lost on the young star of the antiestablishment bar. "My morality is to be opposed to morality," he explained in his book *De la stratégie judiciaire*.

Vergès's virtuoso performance on the stage of the Algerian resistance trials was recorded by his friend Georges Arnaud in a book of personal recollections entitled, simply, *My Trial*. "I must confess that for a long time I was unable to see beyond [Vergès's] ferociousness," wrote Arnaud.

It was accompanied by an unequaled intelligence, a propensity for driving his opponent into the ground, a determination to step on the old enemy, and especially on his war wounds, an unlimited torrent of outrage ready to be dumped on the noble, white-haired mothers and illustrious widows of the enemy camp . . . and all in the service of his client . . .

Eventually the moment came when I knew that he, too, had nightmares: when I understood that from the first day of her trial, he had vowed to the woman they already wanted to kill [Djamila Bouhired] a brotherly affection that became more and more exasperated and more and more desperate.[12]

Since the Liberation, there had been no constituency Jacques Vergès despised more than his former fellows in the French Resistance who had acceded to postwar government posts in the Fourth Republic, then adopted a pro-colonialist position on Algeria; men like Georges Bidault who had been a militant in the ranks of Combat, a close friend of Jean Moulin and the leader of the CNR after Moulin's death. After the Liberation, Bidault helped found the Mouvement de Rassemblement Populaire (MRP), a Catholic, democratic party, and he held responsible cabinet positions under the Fourth Republic. When it came to Algeria, however, Bidault was a tiger. The ultranationalist was an ultraconservative for reasons that were perfectly coherent from his point of view, but anathema to a man like Vergès. By 1960, Bidault had become the rallying point for various groups on the far Right.

Michel Debré was another prominent politician who had fought in the Resistance, and then had joined the Algérie Française movement when he was a senator. So was Robert Lacoste, a socialist and trade unionist who had defied the Nazis by publishing a manifesto denouncing anti-Semitism and the repression of human rights. Fifteen years later he was, unenviably, proconsul in Algeria, where his patriotic beliefs led him to defend traditional ideas of French imperial grandeur. Lacoste soon became known as one of the most repressive players on the Algerian stage. Most damning of all, in January 1957, it was he who transferred all police powers for Algiers to the French military, under General Jacques Massu. Massu was also a hero of the French Resistance. At the Liberation, he and his men had led a charge against one of the

Gestapo headquarters in Paris, then seized the Arc de Triomphe, pulled down the Nazi swastika and run up the French flag. Twelve years later, Massu's assignment in Algeria was to destroy both terrorism and the political organization of the FLN. This he accomplished with the use of torture, a practice he defended quite openly in his 1971 book, *The Real Battle of Algiers.*

Jacques Vergès's hate list of prominent turncoats also includes François Mitterrand, president of France. Mitterrand had been a prisoner of war during the Occupation, and on his return he committed himself to building a resistance network with other former prisoners. But his record in Algeria was more ambiguous. When Mendès France was choosing his cabinet in June 1954, Mitterrand asked for the job of minister of the interior (the "interior" included Algeria, of course) because he thought it was urgent that someone do something before matters exploded; but in the months that followed, his own actions were confrontationalist in the extreme. "War is the only negotiation," he declared in November 1954. "Algeria is France and France is Algeria, and France will recognize in her territory no other authority than her own . . . ."[13] "It was Mitterrand who declared that one doesn't negotiate with the rebels, one goes to war against them," Vergès has recently pointed out. In November 1954, newspapers like *L'Humanité* and *France Observateur* were already denouncing the use of torture in Algeria. It was 1958, however, before Mitterrand protested publicly against the practice.[14]

Vergès has also not forgotten that when he first defended the Algerian rebels in Algiers in 1957, François Mitterrand was minister of justice.[15]

The Algerian war raged until 1962, when a majority of French citizens agreed in a referendum that the familiar colonial world was no more and independence for Algeria was inevitable. France had lost thousands of men, and the country was deeply and dangerously divided once again along political lines. The issue of torture had been hotly debated. Reputations had been destroyed. The Fourth Republic of Pierre Mendès France had fallen, and a military coup had threatened the Fifth Republic of General de Gaulle.

When the Algerian conflict finally ended, France had been under siege and at war for almost a quarter of a century.

Between 1954 and 1962, an entire generation of young French men and women were radicalized by the Algerian conflict, as a generation of Americans would later be radicalized by the Vietnam war. A natural repugnance in the face of torture and the suggestion that to refuse the draft was, in fact, a morally responsible act appealed to vast numbers of young men who did not care to die for the sake of a war they did not believe in. It was the anti-Algerian-war movement, however, that marked the beginning of the New Left, an extraordinary social-protest movement that rocked the entire western world for a few years as the colonial wars of Indochina and Algeria faded before the colossal intervention of the United States in Vietnam.

In France, the move toward political radicalization led many idealistic, committed members of the Jeanson network into places they might never have dreamed of before the war began. In the beginning, it all seemed innocent enough. Why not agree to lend your apartment for a night or two to help out an FLN militant who was passing through? And why not drive him to this or that destination as a token of one's goodwill? The Jeanson network evolved through just this sort of camaraderie and commitment; but as the months slid into years and the war degenerated further into terror on both sides, active support for the FLN in France came to signify other tacit agreements that were, perhaps, less innocuous. When romantic, middle-class French girls slept with dashing FLN militants and sometimes bore their children, were they also in agreement with the reality that their lovers' militant activities might include premeditated murder in the streets of Paris? And how many of the intellectuals who signed the famous Declaration of the 121 were willing to justify terror on one side and not on the other?

The key idea was "engagement," a favorite word of the French intelligentsia (although intelligence in the sense of respect for facts was not necessarily considered a virtue). "Better wrong with Sartre than right with Aron," went a saying that was long popular in French left-wing circles. History may yet prove the strong-minded pragmatism of Raymond Aron a more enduring victor in the battle for the minds of French men and women, but in the heady days of the Algerian war the fact that his support for Algerian independence did not include an ideological condemnation of colonialism as such earned him the scorn of the intellectual community, including that of his old friend Jean-Paul Sartre.[16] As a consequence of their "engagement," large numbers of the young French intelligentsia had come, by the early 1960s, to accept at least the *principle* of terror in the pursuit of their political cause. It became ultrachic to support the FLN, and later to support a wider, pan-Arab terrorism that would ripen and explode on to the European stage after the humiliating defeat of the Arab world by Israel in 1967. In 1969, Jérôme Lindon, the publisher of Les Editions de Minuit, agreed to write a preface to an anti-Israeli book by Jacques Vergès in which Vergès defended international terrorism.[17] By 1970, the climate was such that the ultrafashionable writer Jean-Edern Hallier could play host to a three-day meeting with Giangiacomo Feltrinelli, the millionaire patron of European terror; Andreas Baader, of the Baader-Meinhof band; Renato Curcio, just then forming the Red Brigades; and leaders of the French proletarian Left. According to Hallier, the purpose of the meeting was "to organize European terror."[18]

Although Jacques Vergès was a hero for the antiwar protesters of the late 1950s and early 1960s, the French authorities were less impressed, and in October 1960, Vergès was charged with "attempting to undermine the security of the State" and suspended from the bar. But Vergès had the ability to marshall (or perhaps fabricate) anger for political purposes. Ten months later, he and his colleagues put the strategy of disruption into action once again, turning the tables and accusing Michel Debré, then prime minister of France, of "complicity in murder" — the murder of Algerians. For that audacity Vergès was condemned to two weeks in prison. (The sentence was increased to a month by an appeal court, but later annulled.)

By 1960, the Algerian conflict had become the prototype for would-be armed liberationist movements everywhere. In that same year, FLN leaders convened in Tripoli to discuss concrete ways of "internationalizing" their struggle and sent a delegation to China in the hope of convincing Mao Tse Tung to lend his support. Mao was sympathetic, as it turned out, and from 1960 until the end of the war in 1962, China overtly supported the FLN with propaganda and material aid. The Soviet Union also supported the FLN and even allowed itself to go on record as agreeing with the Chinese position.

When independence was finally won, Jacques Vergès returned to Algeria. He acquired Algerian citizenship, converted to Islam, changed his name to Mansour and, in 1963, married Djamila Bouhired, the woman whose cause marked his beginnings as a brilliant strategist of revolution through the courts. The couple went to China on their honeymoon, where they were cordially received by Chairman Mao himself.

Like many young communists, Vergès had been unable to accept the policy of the French Communist party toward Algeria. The fight against colonialism was Vergès's *raison d'être*, and if the Party was going to withdraw from the battle, he would withdraw from the Party. Since Prague, however, Vergès's connections had existed on an international level, and there is no indication that he gave up those links when he left the French Communist party in 1957. In September 1963, the French communist newpaper, *L'Humanité*, called him a "renegade of the French Communist party,"[19] but there was no bloodletting of the sort one might have expected had he severed his links with communism on a larger scale. "It was all very courteous, more like the ending of a relationship than a brutal rupture," recalled Vergès many years later.[20]

In reality, Vergès was now in the vanguard of the new Maoist movement.

For a brief moment, Jacques Vergès served in the Ben Bella cabinet as minister of foreign affairs with special responsibility for Africa, but he was soon involved in a dispute with the new leader that would limit his future influence in the country. He had, as he elliptically put it, "reservations about what Ben Bella was doing." Vergès was obliged to leave the government, but soon recovered and returned to a field in which he was truly expert: the production of propaganda. In May 1963, he initiated a monthly pro-Chinese review, *Révolution Africaine*, the purpose of which was "to combat revisionism within Marxism and to struggle against reformism."[21] Essentially, the journal provided a conduit for Maoist doctrine and a platform from which to attack the French Communist party whenever possible.

The first issue of *Révolution Africaine* contained an encouraging statement from Bertrand Russell. Russell had his own concerns in 1963, and he earnestly hoped that a "neutral" Algeria would "become one of the leaders in the difficult fight against nuclear war."[22] The leaders of the new Algeria and Jacques Mansour Vergès had other priorities, however. *Révolution Africaine* reported on the third Afro-Asian Solidarity Conference held in Tanganyika in February 1963. An expected clash between the Chinese and the Soviets had not occurred. Instead, there was agreement to "supply military and financial aid to freedom fighters" in still-colonized regions of Africa and Asia and an agreement to supply "training facilities" as well. The conclusion drawn by *Révolution Africaine* was that "the Chinese views . . . crystallized the most radical positions of the Third World." Vergès was crystallizing his own ideological position.

Another article attacked the nonviolent methods of black Americans and reassured readers that "black Americans have not been converted to the pacifism of Gandhi." The graphic illustrating this article was a shiny, black revolver.

A third article commemorated the assassination of Algerian militant Larbi Ben M'Hidi at the hands of French paratroopers. *Révolution Africaine* mockingly detailed the version of the death put out by the French government, according to which Ben M'Hidi had hanged himself in his cell.

Ben Bella, who was in the Soviet camp, was far from happy with the pro-Maoist tone of *Révolution Africaine*. After eighteen issues, Vergès was unceremoniously removed from his post. He left Algiers "by a route the Algerian police have never been able to discover"[23] and returned to Paris, where he established a second review, called *Révolution*.

Révolution was banned in March 1964 because an article on the remaining French colonies was considered to constitute "an open appeal to rebellion and separatism." An English-language edition was banned in Switzerland as "an organ of Chinese communist propaganda."[24]

But the Third World was on the move, and Jacques Vergès was moving with it. The battle against France was over for the moment, but the battle against Israel was just beginning. In the emerging Palestinian cause, extremists of both the Left and the Right would return to the "anti-Zionism" of the 1952 Prague trials. In the hatreds engendered by the ensuing struggle, this mixed bag of left-wing revolutionaries and Nazis left over from the Third Reich would find common cause.

Jacques Vergès has never deviated from the course he set for himself as a very young man. "There is a profound coherence in all my work," he told a reporter from *Le Monde* in 1983. In the 1980s, his path crossed that of Klaus Barbie, and he fell into step. But as usual, Jacques Vergès marched in the service of his *own* cause, one which far surpassed in importance — for Vergès, at least — the fate of an old man waiting in a solitary prison in Lyons.

· 9 ·

HOW THE MERGER
OF THE LEFT AND THE RIGHT
LED DIRECTLY TO THE
KLAUS BARBIE AFFAIR

In 1939, Amin El Hussein, the ex-Grand Mufti of Jerusalem, took refuge from the British, escaped to Germany and attached himself and his followers to the Nazi cause. Heinrich Himmler, the ss chief, was delighted. It wasn't every day that a regiment of sympathetic Moslems joined the German war movement. Himmler respected the Mufti and often complimented him on his blue eyes, which he liked to describe as "appropriately Nordic"; but it was in a written note to the Mufti that Himmler eventually struck a chord that would resound as a leit-motif for the future and survive four decades to influence the context of the Klaus Barbie affair. "The struggle against Judaism is at the very heart of the natural alliance between National Socialism and those Arab Moslems who burn with a desire for freedom," he wrote. "This alliance will endure until the final victory."[1]

In 1955, the Mufti resurfaced at the seminal conference of Bandung, Indonesia, where the idea of the Third World first took hold. Twenty-nine countries from Africa and Asia (representing more than one-half of the world's population) sent delegates to discuss common problems, with an emphasis on colonialism. Among the Arab countries, however, hatred of Israel quickly emerged as a common theme. The representative from Iraq spoke of "the force of evil," and called Zionism "one of the blackest, most somber chapters in human history." Nasser had a few choice words to say in a similar vein. But the most surprising and convincing polemic of all came from Amin El Hussein who arrived on a surprise visit as the representative of Yemen (a country he had apparently never seen) and proceeded to reveal to the

Serge Klarsfeld and his wife, Beate, have dedicated themselves to a controversial and dangerous career of tracking down war criminals who operated in France. Through their efforts Klaus Barbie was discovered living peacefully in Bolivia. The Klarsfelds have also dared to name French citizens who played a principal role in the deportations of French Jews. (*photo Daniel Franck, Paris*)

Beate Klarsfeld leading a demonstration in Germany, in 1980, regarding the trials of several top-ranking Nazis who operated in France. (*photo Daniel Franck, Paris*)

Señor Klaus Altmann, Bolivian businessman. (*photo Keystone Canada*)

PRISON MILITAIRE

he arrival of Klaus Barbie on February 5, 1983, at Fort Montluc, where he was held briefly, for mbolic reasons, before being transferred to St. Joseph's prison in Lyons. (*photo Sygma, Paris*)

Ute Messner, 41, Klaus Barbie's daughter, is a librarian in Kufstein, Austria. On March 5, 1983, she was authorized to visit her father in St. Joseph's prison. (*photo Sygma, Paris*)

Ute Messner and Barbie's first
lawyer, Alain de la Servette (*left*),
at a press conference in Lyons on
March 5, 1983. Media pressure
was so intense that Messner was
assigned a police guard at her
bedroom door. (*photo Sygma,
Paris*)

radical lawyer, Jacques Vergès
(*enter*), hurt during a demonstra-
on before the Belgian embassy in
aris in 1961. (*photo Keystone
anada*)

Maître Jacques Vergès, lawyer for Klaus Barbie, at his desk in 1983. The desk is Louis XV; the tapestry is Flemish. Vergès made his reputation during the Algerian War and is openly sympathetic to international terrorist organizations. (*photo Sygma, Paris*)

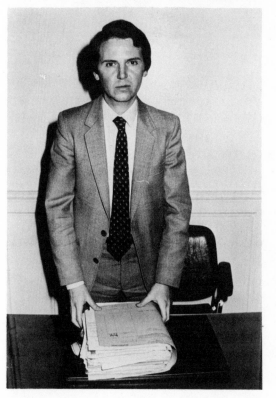

Christian Riss is the young Lyons judge who was responsible for examining the Klaus Barbie file and bringing charges against the accused. (*photo Sygma, Paris*)

Digging up a pit at Bron, near Lyons, where prisoners from Montluc were massacred by Barbie and his men on August 20, 1944. (*photo Tallandier, Paris*)

The Jewish children of the Izieu colony were ferreted out of a remote mountain area, where they were being hidden, and deported to Auschwitz. The Izieu file will be the centerpiece of the prosecution's ca against Barbie. (*photo Paulette Paillares, courtesy of Serge Klarsfeld*)

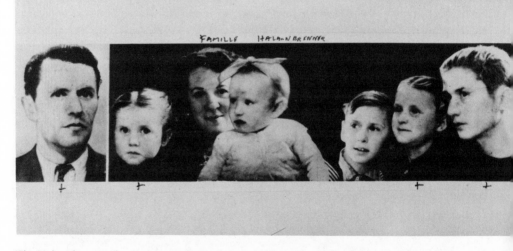

The Halaunbrenner family, three of whom were destroyed by Klaus Barbie. Madame Halaunbrenner accompanied Beate Klarsfeld to Bolivia to bring attention to the presence of Barbie in that country. After the women left, Barbie added a newspaper copy of this picture to his personal scrapbook. (*phot archives Klarsfeld*)

collected constituents that the real ambition of Israel was to annex the entire Middle East.[2]

The anti-Israel resolution was one of the very few everyone agreed upon. Israel, the conference concluded, was a base for imperialism and a threat to peace in the Middle East and the entire world.

The Bandung conference consecrated a new era in the history of anticolonialism and soon acquired a profound symbolic significance. Jacques Vergès referred to it emotionally in 1960 during the trial of the Jeanson network, while lecturing one of the judges:

What has been asked of you . . . for six years since the beginning of the war in Algeria is this: that you condemn . . . these Algerians, these men who do not speak the French language, these men whose religion is Islam, these men who thrill to belong to the fraternity of Bandung, the fraternity of the African people, all of whom are now independent . . .[3]

In retrospect, Bandung can also be seen as the first comprehensive, international opposition on the part of Third World liberation movements to Israel, Zionism and eventually to Jews outside of Israel. That same year, propaganda coming out of Cairo had already begun to blur the distinction between "Zionist" and "Jew." "Our duty is to war against the Jews for the love of God and religion . . . " read a statement that appeared not in a theological treatise, but in a local newspaper, *Al Ahram*.[4] By the time Adolf Eichmann was tried in Israel in 1961, revisionist history claiming to link Zionists and Hitler was beginning to appear on a regular basis, particularly in the Soviet Union. The "Zionist-Hitler conspiracy theory" was precisely the same "line" that François Genoud put forward in his interview with *L'Hebdo* magazine in Lausanne a full quarter of a century later. Genoud, of course, was already working in Egyptian information services when the new Left-Right anti-Zionist ideology began to take shape.

In the 1950s, radical anti-Zionist propaganda began to dip into a ready pool of traditional anti-Semitic literature that had been circulating years before both in Nazi Germany and the Soviet Union. *The Protocols of the Elders of Zion* was republished for an entirely new audience. In 1983, French historian Léon Poliakov estimated that there were more than a dozen editions of the book available in Arabic alone.

Hitler's *Mein Kampf* was also translated into Arabic, along with other mainstays of Nazi anti-Semitic literature. *Talmudic Human Sacrifices* appeared in 1962; *The Danger of World Jewry for Islam* in 1963; *Why I Hate Israel* in 1964; and *Sexual Crimes of the Jews* in 1965. In 1968, some Arab theologians began referring to "the innate nature of the Jews" and suggesting that non-Jews could acquire these nefarious characteristics "by coexisting with Jews."[5] And three of Joseph Goebbels' former associates[6] immigrated to Egypt, where their main contribution was to put together a work called *The Plot Against the Church*, in which they sought to subvert the liberal plans of Pope John XXIII to remove anti-Jewish content from the Catholic liturgy.

From time to time the seams showed in the most revealing way. For example, in September 1972, the Soviet embassy in Paris put out a bulletin containing a basically conventional attack on the policies of the Israeli government. Astonishingly, the document included part of the text of *The Protocols of the Elders of Zion*, which had been reprinted word for word, including spelling mistakes, just as it was originally reedited for the Czar. There was, however, one change: throughout the text, the word "Zionist" had been substituted for the word "Jew."

A decade later, the mix of neo-Nazi and Palestinian anti-Semitic propaganda was still in evidence. Present at the 1983 meeting of the Institute for Historical Review in Los Angeles, an association openly dedicated to rewriting the history of World War II, were well-known individuals representing themselves and/or every extremist, racist association in the world. They included the Ku Klux Klan, Robert Faurisson of France (who was one of the first to assert in the name of "free speech" that there were no gas chambers in Auschwitz), and Wallis Carto, president of the right-wing Liberty Lobby in the United States with direct connections to Palestinian businessman Issah Nakhleh, purveyor of anti-Zionist, anti-Semitic literature to the United States, among other countries.[7]

After the humiliating defeat of the Arab states by Israel in 1967, the Bandung fraternity turned its collective attention to the crisis of the Palestinian people. Negotiation seemed out of the question on both sides as mutual Israeli-Arab recriminations mushroomed. El Fatah and the PFLP of George Habbash intensified their efforts to attract financing and other aid from the non-Arab world, particularly from neo-Nazis in Europe and Latin America who had money as well as propaganda and military experience. In April 1969, a congress of the neo-

Nazi Neue Europäische Ordnung was held in Barcelona with fifty delegates from Europe and Latin America, most of them former ss officers, nostalgic Vichyists and Franco supporters. The New European Order had been a strictly Nazi-oriented outfit, but now, fifteen years later, the focus of their international meeting was the Palestinians. Yasser Arafat sent a representative from El Fatah to explain the needs of the PLO and present two requests. The first concerned the need to recruit non-Arabs for sabotage operations, fund-raising, arms supply and the mobilizing of mercenaries and foreign instructors for training camps. The second request was for money for the dissemination of anti-Zionist propaganda in Europe and South America, including a wider distribution of the *Protocols*.

The El Fatah representative convinced several former Nazis to work directly for the cause. Karl Van de Put, a Belgian who had served Germany in the Afrika Korps, offered to recruit young Europeans with military experience for El Fatah. Former Nazi officer Johann N. Schuller was already involved in arms sales to El Fatah. He had also begun to recruit former Nazi officers as instructors in El Fatah guerrilla training camps.

Even the ubiquitous ex-Grand Mufti of Jerusalem turned up in discussion. It was announced that he had recently formed a new unit of sabotage.

Palestinian leaders began advertising in the *Nationalzeitung* in Munich asking for volunteer "war correspondents" with "tank experience" to fight Zionist imperialism. By the late 1960s, satellite television was able to transmit events all over the globe, rendering the possibilities for propaganda almost limitless. "We think that killing one Jew far from the field of battle is more effective than killing a hundred Jews on the field of battle, because it attracts more attention," Dr. Habbash confided several years later in an interview with Oriana Fallaci.[8] It is worth noting that he spoke of "Jews" and not "Zionists" as the targets of terrorism. Before 1970 his PFLP had hijacked several foreign planes in full view of an international audience and blown up four, killing Jews and Gentiles alike.

Given his passionate involvement with the cause of Arab nationalism, no one was particularly surprised to see Jacques Vergès resurface in 1965 as defense lawyer for Mohammed Hajjazzi, one of the first El Fatah terrorists apprehended in Israel. Since the sensational FLN trials,

Vergès's reputation had grown considerably, and he was asked by Arafat to take on the Hajjazzi case and politicize it in his own way. In particular, the PLO leadership wanted him to hold an international press conference in which he would level accusations at Israel. Vergès agreed, with some reservations, warning the PLO that he would be expelled from Israel if he followed such instructions. The leadership insisted, nonetheless; Vergès gave his speech; and he was expelled from Israel, as expected.

One day the following year, while idly flicking through a newspaper, Vergès happened to notice that the Hajjazzi trial was about to open the next day in Israel. Never one knowingly to miss out on the action or to let an opportunity for propaganda slip by, Vergès informed two people that he was leaving immediately for Israel: a reporter from *Le Monde* and the information officer from the Israeli embassy.

"But you can't go there," shouted the information officer.

"I'll take responsibility for that," replied Vergès. "You take responsibility for arresting me."[9]

Vergès was greeted by a police officer on his arrival at Tel Aviv airport and taken to a hotel for the night before being dispatched back to Paris. His every act was political, if not childish. He ordered a meat meal with milk to insult the Israelis whom he supposed were kosher in their eating habits. He insisted on having a bottle of Evian mineral water to remind those watching him of the Evian agreement between France and Algeria.

A reporter from *Haaretz* stood under his window and called out: "A declaration, Maître Vergès."

Vergès just happened to have a declaration prepared, in which he attacked the state of Israel. He threw it out of the window.

The following morning, in the airplane, the stewardess showed him the latest issue of *Haaretz*. "And that is how Hajjazzi learned about the PLO position on his trial," Vergès later recounted.[10]

Such abrupt comings and goings compelled a spokesman for the Israeli embassy in Paris to provide an explanation. "Monsieur Vergès was more interested in progapanda than the defense of his client. In public declarations he permitted himself to deny the existence of Israel and to defame the judiciary of our country," explained a spokesman.[11] The propaganda mission, however, had been a resounding success.

In December 1968 and February 1969, PFLP terrorists hijacked

El Al planes in Athens and Zurich respectively, and at their subsequent trial in Winterthur, Switzerland, they chose Jacques Vergès as their legal counsel. Although he was once again refused permission to participate, Vergès went anyway, as an adviser. Also present as an "adviser" was François Genoud.

The possibilities for propaganda at the Winterthur trial were too important to be left to amateurs. There were international press conferences, and an anti-Zionist brochure called *The White Book* was widely circulated. The defense was paid by the Banque Commerciale Arabe, which had by then adopted the Palestinians primarily on the recommendation of Ali Hassan Salameh, otherwise known as Abu Hassan, the leader of the Black September terrorist cell that was later responsible for the murder of Israeli athletes at the 1972 Munich Olympics. Abu Hassan lived in Switzerland, where he had established an easy friendship with François Genoud.

(In 1982, Genoud publicly acknowledged his deep involvement with El Fatah.[12] In fact, he had long looked after their European operations from every point of view. He gave advice regarding the investing of huge amounts of money donated to the cause, not least from Colonel Muammar Gaddafi who contributed $50 million to the PLO after the Munich assassinations. He provided legal counsel for Fatah men who needed help in Switzerland and underwrote other costs — including at least a partial subsidizing of a multinational terrorist organization that had set up shop in Paris first under the leadership of Mohammed Boudia — who was murdered by the Israeli secret service in 1973 — then under Carlos the Jackal.[13] He was, in his own words, "an economic counselor with a special interest in the development problems of the Third World."[14] Indeed, his interest in "development problems" led him to continue his business dealings as an arms merchant specializing in sales to the Palestinians.[15])

As for Jacques Vergès, *his* contribution to the important propaganda function of the 1969 Palestinian trials in Winterthur was twofold. First he held a press conference, during which he claimed that an article in *L'Express* had accused Israel of using El Al passenger flights to transport military material at the time of the June 1967 war. The plane the writer had traveled on "contained military equipment for Mirage fighters that was loaded at Bordeaux. There were no passengers on board, with one illustrious exception: Baron Rothschild," said

Vergès, presumably quoting from the article. "There you have a reference [to Israeli activity] that does not come from a Palestinian source but from a fellow journalist," he told the reporters.

No one in the room could have been expected to remember the actual article, which had appeared two years earlier, and reporters dutifully filed their copy. But the next day, journalist Jacques Derogy, the author of the *L'Express* article that Vergès had "quoted," was more than surprised to read the Paris papers. His article had said nothing at all about military equipment on board the El Al jet. Furthermore, he had written that there were 162 passengers on board.[16]

Derogy knew Vergès personally, and he confronted him the next time they met. "Vergès said he didn't remember," recalled Derogy. "But what he said at the press conference was an absolute lie."

Vergès's second propaganda contribution was to write a book on behalf of the Palestinians, picking up on the charges he had attributed to Jacques Derogy. *For the Fedayeen* was published in 1969 by Les Editions de Minuit, with a laudatory preface by the publisher, Jérôme Lindon. Both Lindon and Vergès concluded their remarks with a highly romantic apologia for armed liberation. Indeed, ten years before the Islamic revolution in Iran, Vergès forshadowed the notion of holy combat. "There are privileged places where the heart of the Palestinian resistance beats," he wrote. "The prison Corydalos of Athens is one of them. On Christmas Eve, 1968, the Resistance confided to Mohammed Mahmoud, the teacher, and to Souleiman Maher, the student, their mission of sacrifice . . . "[17]

In the book, Vergès defended the "resistance fighters" by blaming El Al and the government of Israel for the fact that there were passengers in the plane when the terrorists destroyed it; and he characterized the killing of one of the Palestinians at the Zurich airport as a "war crime." But the central — and more sinister — message of the book lay in the warning (really a threat) it contained. "Why conduct attacks on foreign territory?" asked Vergès rhetorically. "Common sense provides the answer. El Al is everywhere. As for the neutrality of the host countries . . . [they] loan their airports for military purposes, the logistical apparatus of the Israeli camp . . .

"Countries that provide transit permits [and other privileges] to these planes have only to provide guarantees that the planes will not be used for military purposes . . . The Palestinian Resistance cannot accept secret Zionist agents in these neutral states."

Vergès had reintroduced his strategy of disruption. The accused becomes accuser; the terrorist is a hero who is sinned against; and the real aggressor is the victim. It was Israel's fault that the Palestinians killed El Al passengers, and the fault of Switzerland and Greece that terrorist actions occurred on their soil. The book also afforded a revealing glimpse into the ideology that informed Vergès's thinking. Israel is described as the "New Empire" populated by a "race of seigneurs." "Zionist" and "Jew" appear interchangeably. Talk of the Hitler death camps is "blackmail." The Eichmann trial was a "parody." Zionism is "racism" and is supported by such "international millionaires" as the "Rothschild barons." *For the Fedayeen* seemed to resurrect the worldwide Jewish conspiracy for new service in a new age.

By the late 1960s, the Palestinians were heroes in Europe, and nowhere more so than in Paris. The war in Algeria was succeeded by the U.S. war in Vietnam, and for a while thousands of young intellectuals in Europe and North America made sure they owned at least the minimal badge of political correctness — a poster of Che Guevara displayed on the dormitory wall. The world divided for a time into simplistic categories of "us" and "them," of good and evil; and perhaps nowhere more so than in France, where to follow intellectual fashion was absolutely *de rigueur*, and where divisions between the political Right and Left had existed since the days of the 1789 Revolution.

During the 1960s, Jacques Vergès was a man to contend with. He exuded fame. Success clung to him like an erotic perfume, the macho aura of a fearless tough guy who had proved he could slay giants. So on February 23, 1970, the news that he had disappeared — simply vanished into thin air — took just about everyone by surprise. On that day, Vergès attended an anticolonial rally in Paris. Speakers stood under portraits of Che Guevara, Ho Chi Minh and Lenin. (Black Panther Eldridge Cleaver was supposed to show up but didn't.) It was an important event, and *"le tout Paris"* of a left-wing persuasion was present.

After the meeting ended, Vergès announced he was going on a business trip to Spain. Then he seemed to disappear off the face of the earth. Most people thought he had been murdered (the most widely believed story was that he had been set in concrete and dropped into the Mediterranean, Mafia-style). He certainly had plenty of enemies. The French Algerians who had been forced to leave the former colony after the war ended might well have wished him dead. Ahmed Ben

Bella hadn't exactly been a friend since Vergès had veered in the direction of Chairman Mao. The Israeli secret services might have decided he should disappear; as might a rival Palestinian faction. After a few months, however, Jérôme Lindon received a postcard. It said, "I am free and in good health." There was no return address.

Speculation then began in earnest. Some people were convinced Vergès was in a Libyan terrorist training camp under the tutelage of Colonel Gaddafi; others thought he was in the Soviet Union training to be a secret agent; still others believed he was in Cambodia with his old friend Pol Pot, while the latter briefly occupied the center of the world stage. If any of his friends knew where he was, they weren't saying.

Jacques Vergès was spotted one day in late 1978, buying groceries on the rue Lepic in Montmartre. He had nothing at all to say about his eight lost years except to add mischievously to the mystery that surrounded his person. "I am a discreet man," he allowed in 1983. "I stepped through the looking glass, where I served an apprenticeship . . . "

Vergès returned to the practice of law with a vengeance, this time as counsel for Klaus Croissant, one of the lawyers for the Baader-Meinhof band. Croissant had been extradited from France at the request of the West German government on charges of having assisted a terrorist association. Croissant was convicted and imprisoned in Stuttgart from November 1977 until December 1979, and on his release he expressed a wish to return to France. Vergès took the case to the media — as usual — and in doing so explained what he considered the role of a lawyer to be. "A lawyer worthy of the name, whether he be of the Left or the Right, has the duty to help [a political prisoner] enlighten the court on the political context of his legal struggle . . . Did I do anything other than this during the Algerian war?" he asked.

But it was 1982 before the connections between the Palestinian Left and the Nazi Right resurfaced anew, and once again Jacques Vergès was a principal player in the drama. So was his old friend François Genoud. The case concerned the Paris trial of two terrorists known as the "friends of Carlos." Bruno Bréguet, a twelve-year veteran of pro-Palestinian terrorist action, and Magdalena Kopp, formerly of the Baader-Meinhof band, had been intercepted by the Paris police while carrying grenades and guns and four kilos of explosives in a borrowed car that was parked just off the Champs Elysées. Jacques Vergès was their lawyer and public apologist.

Bruno Bréguet had been on the terror circuit for more than a decade. In 1970, at the age of twenty, the young Swiss had been sent by George Habbash to plant a bomb in the Israeli port of Haifa (he was caught with dynamite on his person and jailed in Israel); but the most intriguing fact about the young left-wing revolutionary was that he became a protégé of his fellow countryman François Genoud, a Nazi. (Genoud later acknowledged his relationship with the PFLP.[18] He corrected a journalist who had written he had "no connection" by saying he had "no *particular* connection," but had "met Habbash one or two times.")

In 1970, when the original Bruno Bréguet case broke in Israel, Genoud, who was, in his own words, "very available," traveled to Bréguet's hometown of Tessin, Switzerland, to meet with the young man's family. "They were lovely people," he recalled with the mildness of a fond uncle. "I tried to help them."

Help consisted once again of "advice" and the recommendation of a young lawyer (who later became Genoud's son-in-law).

"I was quite taken by the youth of this fellow citizen who had participated in this affair a little bit like a Boy Scout. At a time when so many young people didn't care about anything at all, he set off . . . to do something 'interesting'," recalled Genoud. According to *Le Monde*,[19] Genoud paid for Bréguet's legal costs and set up a support committee on his behalf. Given his relationship as a banker to the FLN and his connections with El Fatah and the PFLP, providing such financing was perfectly consistent behavior for Genoud.

Bréguet was sentenced to fifteen years in prison in Israel, but released after seven following a vigorous publicity and lobbying campaign conducted by the Bréguet support committee. His first free act was to visit Lausanne to thank his benefactor. Genoud is vague about their subsequent relationship. "I've seen him a few times since [his release from prison]. Sometimes he sends me a postcard," he allowed.[20]

Bruno Bréguet resumed his activities. By the late 1970s he, too, was involved in assisting the PLO in Europe through the Carlos network. When the Bréguet-Kopp case came to trial in 1982, it was widely believed that François Genoud had once again paid Bréguet's legal costs with money that had, after all, been earmarked for aid to the Palestinian cause. Bréguet was a member of the PFLP, and Genoud was a longtime supporter of the same organization. Bréguet had also lived in Berlin for a period during the 1970s, where he had had easy access to the neo-Nazi groups that were dear to the heart of his benefactor.

According to writer Claire Sterling, Genoud helped finance the Carlos network in Paris in the early 1970s. Ten years later it became evident that Bruno Bréguet and Magdalena Kopp worked in the same network. In February 1982, Carlos sent a letter to the French embassy in The Hague demanding the release of Bréguet and Kopp. "You have arrested members of my organization,"[21] he wrote by way of information. Carlos gave the French government one month to accede to his request, but the letter was leaked to the press, and naturally the government refused.

There was no hard evidence to connect the events, but four days after the deadline expired a bomb exploded on the Paris-Toulouse train killing five people. The following day, the French Cultural Center in Beirut was damaged. On April 15, a French military officer and his pregnant wife were shot at point-blank range when they opened the door to their apartment in Beirut. On April 18, two bombs exploded simultaneously in Vienna, one at the Air France head office, the other in the garden of the French embassy.

When the trial opened on April 17, Jacques Vergès suggested that the explosives found in his clients' car might have been planted there by an Israeli agent. He also made his own position perfectly clear. "I do not hide the fact that I respect and esteem the two accused," he declared. Then he dropped a bombshell. There was, he claimed, an "unwritten but negotiated agreement" between France and the PLO to the effect that apprehended terrorists would be driven to the border and released as long as they had not committed any act against France itself. Robert Badinter, the minister of justice, denied the charge vehemently. "The government of France will never permit the planning and preparation of [violent] acts destined for another country," he retorted.

It was difficult to argue the case for an "unwritten agreement," but Vergès was undeniably correct in affirming that France had a history of offering asylum to political refugees of every stripe, who, traditionally, were indeed free to wage their battles as long as they didn't actually involve France or the French. But the armed liberation armies that adopted Paris as their headquarters in the late 1960s and early 1970s had added a new wrinkle to this policy. Their targets were not necessarily distant at all. Within a few years they were shooting at U.S. and Israeli military and diplomatic personnel, setting car bombs and blowing up synagogues and restaurants where Jews were known to gather. Within a short time their field of operations had expanded. Unlike the PLO, which remained primarily opposed to Israel, the Carlos network, which comprised disparate elements of the Left and the Right, saw Israel as an ally of their other enemy: U.S. imperialism and the established democratic order. "We must recognize that our revolution is a phase of world revolution. It is not limited to reconquering Palestine," explained George Habbash.[22]

The Mitterrand government couldn't protest *too* forcibly because, on assuming power in 1981, it had actually amnestied terrorists who promised on their word of honor to be very, very good. But once the Carlos letter was leaked to the press, no deal would have been possible even had the French government wanted to negotiate (and there is nothing to suggest that they did). Jacques Vergès lost the Bréguet-Kopp case, appealed and lost again; but the following year he returned to his clients in print, as part of his strategy for propagandizing the issues. The book, *Pour en finir avec Ponce Pilate* (which loosely translates as "Let's Have Done with Pontius Pilate") described Bréguet and Kopp as "courageous" and innocent victims of the state. Besides the French government, the other culprit was, of course, "the Zionists," by which Vergès meant not just Israelis but French Jews as well.

In *Pour en finir avec Ponce Pilate*, as in *For the Fedayeen*, Vergès wasted little time on the dull particularity of the charges brought against his clients. In both books, the underlying cause of the action is assumed to be a noble one, terror is justified as self-defense and the victim of the attack is characterized as being at fault. Bréguet and Kopp had become the latest means to promote Jacques Vergès's central interest —a campaign on behalf of the Palestinians and against the French government, whom he accuses of being "a protectorate" of Israel. If France were not being controlled by the "Zionists," his clients would automatically have been freed.

Vergès received a number of death threats during the Bréguet-Kopp trial. He replied by denouncing Israel and the Israeli ambassador in Paris. "If anything happens to me, I shall hold the Israeli embassy responsible,"[23] he stated in classic Catch-22 style. If nothing happened, he might claim that the Israelis had been frightened off because he was on to their tricks. If something did happen to him, well, he had already fingered the putative culprit in advance.

To conclude his book, Vergès insisted that the Bréguet-Kopp trial was wholly political. Then he quoted his own courtroom plea, followed by an explicit threat:

Judges, because blood is flowing today in Jerusalem and in the occupied territories, you are being asked to strike at those who are friends of the dead and the wounded . . . and in the name of their assassins. You are being asked to replace Easter with the Day of Atonement, the day when the priests charge scapegoats with all the sins of Israel . . . The truth is that Magdalena Kopp and Bruno Bréguet will be freed. You know it and they know it. They are soldiers imprisoned for a noble cause, the cause of dignity . . .

The rest of their army will not cease to fight and strike until they are free . . . [24]

Following the Bréguet-Kopp affair, Jacques Vergès became the lawyer for Mohand Hamami and Frederic Oriach, both members of the Paris-based multinational terror band called Direct Action, which was created in 1979. Hamami and Oriach were accused of breaking into an arsenal of arms that was under police surveillance. Oriach was also the editor of a glossy anti-Zionist, antiimperialist review called *Subversion* (a descendant of Vergès's seminal publication *Révolution*), which was described as "a political and theoretical instrument at the disposition of militant revolutionaries."[25] Furthermore, according to Italian magistrates interviewed by *Le Figaro*, Hamami was at the heart of a triple connection: Red Brigades, Direct Action and the Lebanese Armed Revolutionary Faction.

Vergès's courtroom style during the Bréguet-Kopp trial had been variously described by the French media as "curious," "strange," and, more picturesquely, "retro-bolshevist." The Hamami-Oriach trials presented the public with a defense in a similar vein. As during the Bréguet-Kopp affair, Vergès publicly denounced what he called the "Zionist lobby" in France as being the real guilty party.

Both Oriach and Vergès continued to publish (Oriach from his jail cell), each man maintaining his own connections with the world of international terror. In 1983, a new journal called *Correspondances Internationales* appeared on the scene, edited by Vergès. In the opening issue, Vergès saluted "the imprisoned comrades who have succeeded in communicating from the depths of the cells in which they have been buried by the bourgeoisie."[26] The "comrades" to whom Vergès referred were members of the Red Brigades. Indeed, the review contained a long statement by a member of the Red Brigades, Carmina Fiorillo, who was currently in prison.

Vergès was noticeably uneasy when asked to describe his relationship to *Correspondances Internationales*, particularly since he claims to be "only a lawyer" and to have "no political activity:"

"I am editor because they needed a French person to direct the publication in France. The journal itself is devoted to the activities of what some people call the 'armed resistance,' or 'urban guerrillas,' or 'terrorists.' It publishes studies concerning social problems in Europe. Perhaps you know that there are 4,000 political prisoners in Italy. When you have that many, you are no longer dealing with a problem of individual criminals. You have a political problem, a public defiance of society. Well, the journal is a place where these problems can be debated."

When asked whether the debate included opinions from people opposed to terrorism, he replied: "No, it doesn't. But no one can say that my opinions are the same as those of the journal."[27]

And what are the views of the comrades in the Red Brigades? Like Vergès himself they constantly tell us what they think, what they plan to do and what their next steps will be. When Mario Moretti, who is considered to be the brain of the Red Brigades, was arrested in Milan on April 4, 1981, he declared: "In Italy and elsewhere we will hit our targets." Those targets had been enumerated earlier the same year in his *Journal of the Red Brigades*. They included, chronologically, an attack on the judiciary, then the politicians, followed by the press and business management. Next came NATO , "the armed protection of the criminal multinationals." Moretti explained that the war would be waged "everywhere, and in collaboration with foreign revolutionaries."[28]

And it was. In October 1983, neo-Nazis in Brussels were found to be working with the Syrians. In February 1984, the Italian-based Fighting Communist Party openly claimed responsibility for the murder of General Leamon R. Hunt, chief of the multinational forces in the Sinai. And in early 1985, a rash of attacks on NATO and Jewish targets in Germany, France, Belgium, Portugal and Spain pointed to a combined effort on the part of several terrorist organizations that had been thought to be independent of each other.

Also in February 1985, Jacques Vergès turned up (predictably) as chief lawyer for three members of the Secret Armenian Liberation Army accused of a bomb attack at the Paris-Orly airport in July 1983. When his clients were found guilty, Vergès reverted to a familiar pattern. The court should not be dealing with a "political problem," he said, then continued with a clear threat of reprisals. "The friends of [the condemned] will not let them down," he warned,[29] just as he had threatened in 1983 that "the rest of their army [of Bréguet and Kopp] will not cease to fight and strike until they are free."

By 1985, the alliance of the old-style fascist Right and the new-style revolutionary Left had become more visible. The seeds of Nasser's Cairo in the 1950s and the 1969 meeting of the New European Order in Madrid were bearing fruit. In 1985, one of the left-wing Armenian terrorists defended by Jacques Vergès was found to be carrying a German passport that had been stolen by the neo-Nazi Hoffmann group[30] and distributed in a PFLP training camp in Lebanon. And in April 1985, an important double arrest in Paris netted Odfried Hepp, the last member at large of the same Hoffmann organization, in the company of a Tunisian member of the Palestine Liberation Front. (Hepp was suspected of having planned and/or participated in the anti-Semitic attack on Goldenberg's restaurant in Paris in 1982.) Hepp, however, claimed to be a member in good standing of the Palestine Liberation Front, Aboul Abas branch, with its base in Tunis.

According to Arndt Heinz Marx, associate president (until his arrest in 1984) of the neo-Nazi National Socialist Front in Frankfurt, both Hepp and Marx trained in an El Fatah camp in Lebanon from July 1980 until June 1981 with a group of fifteen German neo-Nazis. "I was a member of El Fatah, a fedayeen," said Marx. "El Fatah and the PLO are fighting for the rights of their people as we are fighting for the German people. The Palestinians and ourselves have the same enemy: International Zionism, the Jews . . . "[31]

Marx added that guerrillas training in Lebanon were not intending to attack Israel directly, but were preparing "for combat in Europe."

As for François Genoud, his connections to both nazism and the extreme Left were evident and ongoing. In June 1984, a Zurich newspaper pointedly reported that he had close ties with the Libyan embassy in Berne.[32] And his own daughter, Martine, had been married to a revolutionary who was killed in an internecine battle in Lebanon in the early 1980s.

Finally, there was the case of former general Otto Ernst Remer, a friend of Hitler and Goebbels who also has spent the postwar years in the service of his "ideals." Like François Genoud, Remer went to Cairo in the 1950s, where he was a political adviser to Nasser. Like Genoud, he is suspected of working with a "trading company"[33] that supplied the FLN with arms from Eastern Europe during the Algerian war.

Interviewed in Germany, Remer advocated an alliance between Germany and the Soviet Union against the United States. "There is a problem concerning who holds the real power in the United States. Without a doubt, the Zionists control Wall Street. That's where the evil originates, because Israel has a pro-war foreign policy. Israel is the instrument of Wall Street, and as a result, the Middle East foments war . . . "[34]

And there it was, as clear as Hitler at Nuremberg in 1934, as clear as *Mein Kampf*, as clear as the *Protocols*. For both Arndt Heinz Marx and Otto Remer, the struggle of the combined Left/Right guerrillas against the United States was, at its core, the struggle against the Jews — the Jews who controlled Wall Street, the Jews who held the *real* power in an America that used Israel as a willing handmaiden of war, the Jews who . . . controlled the world.

"The struggle against Judaism is at the very heart of the natural alliance between National Socialism and those Arab Moslems who burn with a desire for freedom," Himmler had written in a prescient little note forty years earlier. In the interim, the alliance had taken root, ripened and exploded on to the international stage with renewed vigor. And in the not-so-strange association of Klaus Barbie and Jacques Vergès, Himmler's words had merely acquired a rich new context.

· 10 ·

THROUGH THE LOOKING GLASS

"The Barbie trial is a mirror. It reflects all the ambiguities of the Occupation," said Jacques Vergès in September 1983.[1] It was an insightful remark and an idea he would return to during the months ahead, but most interesting of all was his use of the common, six-letter word "mirror."

"Mirror" appeared frequently in Jacques Vergès's conversation. About his strange disappearance between 1970 and 1978, his consistent and only comment was, "I went beyond the looking glass, where I served an apprenticeship."[2] But mirrors are mysterious things, for what looks back at us is never quite exact. Some mirrors turn reality upside down, while others twist it into strange dimensions. Lewis Carroll's Alice looked into just such a magic mirror before she walked into another universe, the world beyond the looking glass, where reality ebbed and flowed in a magical, topsy-turvy cosmos.

Mirrors (with or without the accompanying smoke) provided a clue to the deliberately mysterious, purposefully elusive, very calculating personality of Jacques Vergès. What *is* reality, after all, if you can reflect it, reverse it, stretch it, expand it, then "explain" it in words that still sound solidly familiar to the ears of the bourgeois, linear-thinking populace? Will they not begin to doubt their habitual responses? Who among them will dare to say that the emperor is wearing no clothes? Which Alice in their midst will gasp and cry, "Why, you're nothing but a pack of cards?" And if she did, would the illusion then dissolve? Jacques Vergès smiles as he performs verbal pirouettes around his opponents and holds up magic looking glasses for their edification. Not surprisingly, his favorite parlorgame is chess. Like a master player he moves his men around the board with an eye on capturing the king.

The man sitting behind the antique Louis xv desk is certainly no Che Guevara in battle fatigues. Jacques Vergès is nothing short of elegant in a gray suit with a matching argyle cashmere sweater. Perfectly tailored and perfectly self-contained. His manners are faultless in the style of French men of his generation. But there is something unmistakably distant in his eyes as he leans back to draw on a thin cigar and appraise the interviewer from behind round, rimless glasses.

No, Jacques Vergès is not in the Che school of revolution, nor is he in the Arafat mode where the revolutionary is too busy with important matters to bother to shave. Vergès, on the contrary, is an esthete. Various works of African art decorate the nooks and crannies of his Montparnasse office, and a magnificent Flemish tapestry covers one wall. A beautifully preserved sixteenth-century edition of the Code of Justinian lies open on an elevated book stand. Furthermore, Vergès is reputed to employ the finest bath oils in the battle against dry skin.

"Some people call you a 'destabilizer.' Is that a compliment?" I ask.

"Oh, yes," he laughs. "A tremendous compliment."

He puffs happily on his cigar.

What is fascinating about Jacques Vergès is his calculated use of passion. The passion for the underdogs of the Third World, the passion against the "hypocrites" of the Resistance, the passion for the unorthodox, violent solution, the passion against "Zionism" and "Zionists" ("I have Jewish friends who are anti-Semites," he offers, as if that explains something.) All these passions may once have been authentic. Now, however, even anger is a calculated response.

"I never take issue with any interpretation of my biography," he continues.

"Nothing that is written about you displeases you?"

"Not really. Perhaps it's a question of temperament. I'm just indifferent."

"What happens when you get angry?"

"I've simply made a decision. It is planned anger."[3]

What does remain a passion is the joy of anarchy, the indescribable fun involved in being "bad," in breaking the "rules" (while claiming to defend them staunchly), in making his opponents scurry about like worried chickens. The euphoria of personal power. And the thrill of danger. Crime, for example. Jacques Vergès thinks it makes the world beautiful.

"Crime is what differentiates human society from the animal world. In the beehive you don't have workers who dream of becoming queen," he explains. "Crime advances society. When I defended Algerians who had committed crimes in the streets of Paris, they were considered to be murderers and arsonists. But today I can't help noticing that when representatives of the Algerian government come to France they get the red-carpet treatment. In other words, what is considered a crime today will work to the credit of the criminal ten years later. For me this means that one must think very seriously about every crime and what it reveals about society. I devote myself entirely to this process. This is my work, although that is certainly the wrong word. It is a passion at the center of my life, and I experience it as an artist before his creation."

Oscar Wilde, perhaps, esthete and iconoclast, or Jean Genet, the novelist so admired by Sartre, who wrote, from the inside, of the esthetics of the criminal experience? As a man of the late twentieth century, Jacques Vergès sees himself more as a film director assessing his "rushes," deciding what to use and what to reject in his artistic creation.

He has his own conception of the legal process: "In any trial you have one truth opposed to another. With the same film rushes, the prosecutor will develop his case, and I will develop mine. Each side will be equally true and equally false, because they are both incomplete and partial. The prosecutor must speak in the name of society, and in that sense he is condemned to a certain lack of originality. He is obliged to stay with the most banal explanations. On the other hand, a defense lawyer defends his client in the hope of interesting the public, because the lawyer who wins over public opinion wins the case. Therefore, he must demonstrate that his client does not fit into a conventional schema. He must reveal the special aspects of the case. In this the job of the defense lawyer is infinitely more interesting and satisfying: for himself and for his client."

Vergès finds inspiration for his novel approach to the law in nineteenth-century literary sources. "If you take all the great novels that have moved you most, they are almost always about a crime," he explains. Dostoevski's *Crime and Punishment*, of course: "A young man involved in crime and struggling to cope with its significance."

Stendhal, especially *Le Rouge et le noir*: "Based on the true story of a young man who committed a murder. Stendhal doesn't deny the murder, but he describes it in such a way that all nineteenth-century youth was able to recognize itself in Julien Sorel.

"The subject of crime attracts me as it attracts all the novelists."

So every criminal, as an authentic, creative harbinger of the future, must be protected from the political state, which is, of necessity, authoritarian. The day we cease to nurture crime is the day we cease to be human. "That would be the end of history," volunteers Vergès. "We would become a race of dolphins."

With all the theorizing, romance and fundamental self-dramatization, is it surprising to learn that Jacques Vergès occasionally gets the giggles? Several years ago he called a journalist friend in the middle of the night. "Come on over," he said. "There's something going on."

The friend pulled his clothes on sleepily and made his way across Paris. Vergès opened his door wearing a yellow and black silk bathrobe and brandishing a revolver.

"What's all this about?" panted the friend in horror.

"There was some sort of a threat," related Vergès vaguely and happily. Then he happened to catch sight of himself in the hall mirror. The reflected vision of the lawyer-anarchist-revolutionary in silk, his revolver in hand, was irresistible. The two men laughed until they ached.

From the beginning, Vergès worked the Barbie case simultaneously on two levels. The first was conventional enough; he made application on behalf of his client wherever he thought it appropriate, although his demands were such that he was accused of playing the same game of procedure he had deployed to brilliant advantage during the FLN trials. He demanded, for example, that Barbie be released from prison on the grounds that his expulsion from Bolivia was "extradition in disguise" and a "legal monstrosity." The request was denied several days later by the magistrate and later by two higher appeal courts. He claimed that an important piece of evidence for the prosecution was false, a photocopy of a telegram signed by Barbie announcing the arrest of the children at Izieu and their imminent arrival at the Drancy holding camp. He lost that one, too, when the original was found in the archives of the Centre de documentation juive. But his most important and troubling legal initiative was his claim that the act of 1964 in which France ratified the international law regarding crimes against humanity could not be applied retroactively to include a Nazi criminal. He took that one through every appeal court in France and all the way to the European Court in Strasbourg, but he lost on the grounds that the Nuremberg law had been deliberately written to transcend both national and temporal boundaries.

Although he had been acting on behalf of Barbie since the spring of 1983, Vergès claimed in the autumn of 1984 that he "never had any illusions" about the success of his legal initiatives. "I took those steps mainly to put the problem before the lawyers and the public," he said. "However, it is evident that the French judiciary is less independent than it used to be . . . "

Vergès turned the Klaus Barbie case into the Klaus Barbie affair with a brilliant second-level attack aimed at disorienting his opponents. His mirror games of reversed images were deliberately confusing. Here was a man of the law who proclaimed: "My law is to oppose the law,"[4] and, "A society without crime would be a dead society."[5] Here was a hero of the left-wing Algerian resistance whose supporters had included Jean-Paul Sartre and Simone de Beauvoir, but who now seemed to have strangely close connections with the camp of the ultraconservatives, if not the neo-Nazi Right. Here was a man of action, a political *engagé* who had traveled an openly documented route from Stalin to Khrushchev to Mao and the PLO; a man who had never hesitated to enter the fray on behalf of the oppressed, but whose own demeanor and what was visible of his lifestyle were nothing short of aristocratic. He was a lawyer with an open appreciation of violence; indeed, he claimed to be one of the first, perhaps *the* first, to have called for the importation of the armed revolutionary struggle into Europe.[6]

With his magic mirror Vergès inverted accepted reality, then defended his claims in bombastic language that actually sounded logical. Was France a democratic country? Jacques Vergès wasn't sure. Was Nazi Germany necessarily more totalitarian than France itself? The answer, according to Vergès, was anything but obvious.

The trick was to surprise the opposition by turning the defendant — in this case, Klaus Barbie — into the prosecutor, and by putting the prosecution on the defensive. "The defendant reverses the roles and assumes an offensive stance. Then he opens up a second front in the area *he* chooses . . . " wrote Vergès, informing us once again about his plans and his strategy.[7] The more outrageous his claims, the more media attention he attracted. That, of course, was the name of the game.

"To acknowledge that violence is supreme is not necessarily to justify violence," wrote Vergès in 1964. "Nor is it a justification of violence to examine how it is used: for whom, by whom and against whom."

According to Vergès's theory, violence is inevitable and morally neutral. "An expeditionary force that has been trapped by a hostile population will be pushed into the use of torture, massacre and a violation of human rights and common law," he wrote in a revealing passage. "To recognize this as fact is not necessarily to approve, but to discover the root of the evil as well as its remedy; the victory of the people and the defeat of the expeditionary force. To denounce torture without referring to its political context is to believe that a colonial war can be conducted with white gloves and the U.N. Charter. This kind of dishonesty comes directly from the liberal mentality . . . "[8]

For Vergès, "politics" explains and excuses everything, for nothing is real "but thinking makes it so." "Murder," "crime" and "facts" in general exist only selectively as viewed through the filter of the mind. The murder committed by his twin brother, Paul, during their father's postwar election campaign on Réunion was "political," he said. The guilty verdict of the court was also "political." Therefore Vergès was able to conclude that his brother was "innocent."[9]

"The denunciation of Stalin's 'crimes' was also subject to a deliberate confusion," he wrote in 1964. "The critics neglected to analyse the social-political aspects of the trials . . .

"To protest against the inevitable violence of the State is vain and hypocritical. No one is innocent in political combat. To defend the existing order or to attack it will always imply human sacrifice . . . "[10]

Vergès's strategy of disruption is well known in French legal circles, where the theory of a politicized trial is admired in some quarters. His Maoist politics are also public knowledge. So it was with some interest that Vergès's colleagues and the public in general observed the new application of his strategy in the context of the Klaus Barbie defense. In accordance with his strategy of reversed images, Vergès now cast himself and his client, Barbie, as the lone, principled defenders of democracy against a transgressor state. "This trial should not be ideological in nature," announced Vergès, the ideologue *par excellence.* "It is a battle of principle in the name of democracy. So as not to concede a posthumous victory to Hitler," he added, subtly appropriating in defense of a Nazi the very phrase used by Jews when arguing the importance of Holocaust studies.

Jacques Vergès argued that the government had sold Barbie for "100 million francs and 3,000 tons of flour." He insinuated that the government was in the service of Israel and French "Zionists." He claimed that Barbie was an unfortunate victim who had been returned to France to woo the "Jewish vote."[11] But the core of his attack, his *pièce de résistance*, took him back to his own favorite subject and the original source of his public acclaim: the Algerian war.

On behalf of his client, Vergès now charged that the French had been "Nazis" in Algeria. He said they had tortured and played as dirty as any sycophant of the Third Reich, including Klaus Barbie. He accused them of conveniently amnestying themselves after the fact, then deliberately shoving the whole era into a dark corner of history, just as they had done with the ugliness of the Occupation and Vichy France and the collaboration. What right, he asked, had members of the government of France to ride on their reputations as former heroes of the French Resistance and pat themselves on the back for having brought a Nazi back for trial when many of them had fought tooth and nail against the indigenous independence movement in Algeria? He, Jacques Vergès, would see to it that the *real* issues were raised during the course of the Klaus Barbie affair.

"When I speak of Nazis today I am speaking of those politicians who were responsible for the wars in Indochina and Algeria. Their heads were full of Montaigne just as the torturers of yesterday had their heads full of Goethe and Bach . . . "

Like a dog with a bone, he never let up.

There were just enough truths and half-truths in Vergès's allegations about the Algerian war to cause tremors in high places, but the exquisitely clever distortion was to identify what went on during those sorry years with Nazis and nazism, to deliberately confuse the official state terror of Hitler's Germany with terror *denied* by the state, as the French government persisted in denying any official condonation of what took place in Algeria. Klaus Barbie wasn't even being tried on the real issue, claimed Vergès, the issue of his relationship to the French Resistance and, in particular, to Jean Moulin. Crimes against humanity? Just a sop to the "Zionists" — an admission that there were no "real" charges. "In 1952 and 1954, Barbie was tried *in absentia* for every possible crime one could hold against him. I don't understand how something that was doubtful in 1954 can become a certitude thirty years later," Vergès said in his office, neglecting to mention that until recent years the fate of French Jews during the Occupation was a taboo subject.

"The government is conducting this trial against France itself," declared Vergès. "It is the trial of the collaborators and, paradoxically, it is becoming the trial of the Resistance."

Pure "mirror talk;" for Vergès himself was already conducting a trial "against France, against the collaborators and against the Resistance." And all in the name of Klaus Barbie, who had become, through Vergès, both victim and prosecutor.

The first threat was to take the decisions of the French judiciary to the United Nations, the very body Vergès had excoriated as "liberal" and "white-gloved" in 1964. Of course, the composition and point of view of the U.N. had changed in the twenty intervening years, and a Third World sensibility might well prevail in his favor. But the central point of the exercise would be to embarrass the government by attracting adverse media attention on an international scale.

Vergès's second move was to suggest that Barbie's life was in danger while in prison and that "certain people might think that the death of Mr. Altmann [Barbie] is the only way to avoid the judicial and political impasse this trial represents."[12] The strategy was obvious: In telling the media that there was a political and judicial impasse, Vergès planted the idea in the mind of the public. He then projected responsibility for the supposed impasse on to the government and hinted that a carefully sponsored murder might be in the making. If Barbie died in the interim, he, Vergès, had already sowed a seed of doubt.

Vergès then proceeded to set the stage for an important legal test of the crimes-against-humanity law as it might relate to the events of the Algerian war. In June 1984, he announced that he was representing an Algerian family whose father had been murdered by an official of the French army in 1957. The family was laying charges against the state under the aegis of crimes against humanity. As one French paper put it, "The terrain was a minefield." If the minister of justice accepted the charge, the debate over Algeria would become public, as Vergès wished. If he refused, Vergès could point to the decision as another example of "corruption." Vergès reinforced the Algerian issue that same month by publishing an article, entitled "Crooks, Perjurers, Forgers, Thieves, Pimps and Murderers," in which he detailed some of the atrocities that had occurred during the Algerian conflict.[13]

As for the collaboration, Vergès was intent on exposing that skeleton in the closet as well. The fact of the collaboration was no secret in modern France: there had been several fictional works on the subject as well as the documentary *The Sorrow and the Pity*, and an excellent historical work by political scientist Pascal Ory.[14] But the subject remained highly controversial and, at an important psychological level, unacknowledged—particularly the role of the government-sponsored *Milice*.

Was it a coincidence? On September 19, 1984, a mysterious announcement was spotted in a tiny regional newspaper.[15] The family of Paul Touvier (former head of the Second Section of the *Milice* in Lyons) wished to thank all those who had sent messages of sympathy on the occasion of his death. There was only one problem. Nowhere was there any official evidence of Touvier's demise.

Touvier-watchers, Barbie-watchers and Vergès-watchers thought they sniffed a possible setup. Did someone want to flush Touvier out of hiding, or at the very least embarrass the Catholic hierarchy of Lyons? Touvier was definitely an embarrassment. In 1972, journalist Jacques Derogy had revealed that Touvier had benefited from ongoing ecclesiastical protection through the person of Monsignor Charles Duquaire, who had been secretary to Cardinal Gerlier. Since the war, Touvier had been hidden by various priests and nuns in different monasteries and convents. The Catholic church had collaborated with the Pétain regime; that was a fact. And there were enough priests and mother superiors who had not changed their views in the intervening four decades to offer refuge to the fugitive who had managed to escape the postwar purge of the collaboration.

In 1971, Monsignor Duquaire (who had since moved on to the secretariat of the Holy See in Rome) prevailed upon the then president of the Republic, Georges Pompidou, to pardon Touvier. Derogy revealed that Pompidou had done so late that same year.

On September 20, 1984, the day after Touvier's "death notice" appeared, Jacques Vergès sent the following telegram to Monsignor Decourtray, the Archbishop of Lyons:

Recalled to God, Monsieur Paul Touvier, chief of the French Milice *and protégé of the Lyons Episcopacy. I send you my deeply felt condolences even if for other reasons. Don't worry, Monsieur Klaus Altmann will take the rap.*

Naturally, the press received a copy.

The Archbishop was outraged. On September 21, he issued his own statement, saying his first reaction had been to throw the telegram into the garbage, but on learning that it was, indeed, authentic, he could only say that he regretted the author's idea of "justice, the law, and the role of a lawyer." Period.

Vergès's subsequent comments were revealing. He was furious at the Archbishop for having forced Jesuit priest Robert Boyer off the Barbie case. "With one hand the Church protects a Frenchman who committed terrible crimes, and with the other hand it refuses to allow a Jesuit lawyer the right to defend Barbie. So when I heard the news of Touvier's death — true or false — it seemed quite normal to me to send a telegram of condolences to the Archbishop of Lyons," he said.

But the strategy had been successful. Most newspapers ran stories about Touvier "the rat" and reminded their readers of the church's complicity. Anyone who was old enough to remember the Liberation would have recalled rumors concerning Touvier and the *Milice* "treasure," which consisted of stolen money and property. They would have recalled rumors that Touvier had bought his protection from the Catholic church in Lyons. Or that he had escaped both legal and vigilante justice because he bought important members of the Resistance. From Vergès's point of view, any talk of the collaboration could only help his client by intimidating the opposition. Barbie, at least, was not a *French* traitor.

Vergès also acknowledged that he planned to attack the Lyons Jewish community. If the pro-Zionist government of François Mitterrand wanted a trial based on crimes against humanity, well, he, Jacques Vergès, would give them all something to talk about. But he would wait until the trial itself, he said. That, of course, was when the international media would be present to record his accusations. If Vergès could embarrass both the Catholics and the Jews of Lyons, prove that *they* were equally guilty, what could anyone possibly hold against poor old Klaus Barbie?

The collaboration of the Union générale des Israelites de France (UGIF) was a known fact, like the protection of Touvier by clerics of the Catholic church. A detailed (and controversial) book had been published in 1980 based on the very first examination of UGIF archives, which had been collecting dust in the Paris Centre de documentation juive contemporaine for thirty-five years. The author, Maurice Rajsfus, had been able to confirm rumors of a direct liaison service between the Gestapo and the UGIF. That relationship was a pathetic one-way street. The Nazis confided Jewish children to the UGIF with an explicit threat: "If the children disappear from the homes you administer, we will take hostages [and] deport you."[16] In the end they deported the children anyway, and some of the UGIF directors as well. In the interim, the UGIF did everything in its power to maintain an association with the Germans, thinking that was where protection ultimately lay.

In testimony given in Lyons on September 4, 1944, a social worker from the UGIF, Irène Cahen, acknowledged that she was in constant contact with Klaus Barbie's Section IV of the Gestapo.

As of February 1944, the Gestapo would telephone me to come and take children whose parents had been arrested. They were confided to families that were paid to look after them and who were told not to let them leave and to give them only to individuals who had been designated by the UGIF. These instructions came directly from my directors in the UGIF and not from the Gestapo.

On several occasions the Jewish Resistance, which was mainly communist, foreign-born and adamantly opposed to the notables of the UGIF, raided UGIF locales to kidnap children and steal files containing names and addresses that might be appropriated by the Germans. In her testimony, Cahen recounted one such event and her subsequent response:

On July 29, 1944, the Germans gave me a child of twenty months whose parents I knew. When the Resistance came to my home to kidnap the child I first said that I didn't have it. Then I said I couldn't give it to them. I told them that if they took the child I'd be sent to Montluc. The maid called the police and they left . . . Afterward I confided the child [elsewhere] fearing the Resistance would come back.

 The directors were told what happened, and they approved my action of not handing over the child . . . I never entertained the idea of hiding any of the children. I was obliged to return them to the Gestapo . . . [17]

Rajsfus lost his parents in Auschwitz and believes he is alive today only because he refused to follow instructions he subsequently received from the UGIF in Paris telling him to report to their orphanage. His book is a relentless and strident attack on the organization. Perhaps it is closer to the truth to acknowledge that the UGIF, like so many of the Jewish councils established under the Nazis, was essentially tragic. The UGIF was administered by highly assimilated French Jews whose values were vastly different from those of the radical, left-wing refugees who had fled to their country. Ironically, a part of their motivation was not unsimilar to that of Vichy Prime Minister Pierre Laval. No Jew in France would have wished for the victory of Nazi Germany, as did Laval, but like Laval, the notables of the UGIF believed that if they refused to coordinate the Jewish community, Vichy and the Nazis would find others, non-Jews, who would do it only too well, and the misery of the Jews would be intensified.[18] Whereas, if they were in the job, they reasoned, they would be in a better position to control events. Besides, the UGIF was officially under French jurisdiction, and in 1941, when UGIF was created, what French-Jewish citizens would have dreamed that their own countrymen might do them real harm?

The saddest example of the blindness of France's assimilated Jews comes from the diary of Raymond-Raoul Lambert, who was head of the UGIF in the southern zone until he and his family were deported to Auschwitz in 1943. Lambert consoled himself during the black years by reading the works of Maurice Barrès. Barrès had flirted with several political ideologies, some quite liberal, but he had finally settled on a xenophobic nationalism that was literally predicated on anti-Semitism and the rejection of the Jews from the French community. And it was he who had spearheaded the attack of the intellectual Right on Dreyfus. Even more revealingly, Lambert placed his confidence in the head of the General Commission for Jewish Affairs, Xavier Vallat, whom he considered a personal friend. Lambert hoped that Vallat's fanatical anti-Germanness would prevail over his fanatical anti-Semitism. It didn't; and the ambiguous role of the UGIF evolved out of just such misapprehensions.

The illusion of autonomy soon became a fixed idea and a desperate rationale. So much so that, in July 1944, when Barbie's Gestapo was speeding up the rate of Jewish deportations, when there remained almost nothing of the UGIF in the southern zone, and when even UGIF workers and directors were no longer safe, Raymond Geissmann, the new director, continued to put forward the same arguments and take offense at the suggestion that the UGIF was doing more harm than good and ought to be shut down.[19]

In spite of their essentially bureaucratic approach to their job, there were individual acts of heroism among the directors and workers in the UGIF. The most obvious on the part of many was the decision to stay and work in France when they had the means and the connections to get out. But there were, as always, isolated acts of treachery on the part of desperate people seeking to save themselves and their families at any cost. Were there Jews who bought — or thought they were buying — safety with community money that did not belong to them? "Probably," said Dr. Marc Aron, head of CRIF, the central congress of French-Jewish organizations in Lyons. "When people are desperate not all of them will behave honorably."

One thing is known. In February 1985, a terrified Lyonnais Jew packed his trunk and left France until the Barbie trial was over. He had, he said, received a message through an intermediary indicating that if he was not prepared to talk about his father's activities during the Occupation, Vergès (and Barbie) would name his father as a Jewish collaborator.

But the "trial of the Resistance" remained the centerpiece of Vergès's strategy, for there was nothing closer to the heart of postwar France than the collective mythology of an all-heroic Resistance. Jean Moulin personified that heroism: François Mitterrand himself had laid a flower on Moulin's grave shortly after taking office in May 1981. And Klaus Barbie was presumed to be responsible for Moulin's death. This act more than Barbie's presumed "crimes against humanity" underscored France's enduring hatred for Barbie.

The Mitterrand government certainly believed there was a political advantage to bringing this particular Nazi to trial. Especially if they could legally exclude Barbie's relationship to the Resistance (and Moulin) from the charges and convict Barbie without having to open wounds and revive unresolved questions about Moulin's evident betrayal.

No one in the presidential palace had counted on Jacques Vergès, however. Vergès himself had not counted on such luck passing his way.

As a master tactician, Vergès grasped the opportunity to sow discord among his and Barbie's mutual enemies in the Resistance and attack the government at the same time. He could "defend" his client by ignoring the charges and focusing on something else altogether. In prying open Pandora's box, he might encourage the forces contained within to destroy each other all by themselves — and in public.

Vergès's 1983 book, *Pour en finir avec Ponce Pilate*, contained several pages on the Barbie affair, including the following bombshell: "Every effort will be made during the Barbie trial to avoid discussion of Jean Moulin, because people do not want the circumstances of his arrest and death discussed in public. Why is this so? Because Jean Moulin was not arrested in the course of a chance swoop by the Gestapo; he was handed over to the Germans by other members of the Resistance."

There was nothing new in this "revelation" since everyone "knew" Moulin had been betrayed — if not by René Hardy then by someone else. But Vergès's attack went further; he charged that Moulin was betrayed for ideological reasons, because he was a communist, or "crypto-communist," and that an entire cabal of anticommunist members of the Resistance had betrayed him in an antibolshevist plot cooked up with Barbie and the Gestapo. When Moulin eventually realized he had been betrayed by his comrades, he committed suicide by banging his head against a wall, said Vergès, quoting his client.

Like so much of what Vergès said and wrote, there were elements of truth in his charges. Everyone knew that Moulin had been betrayed, that there had been deep divisions within the Resistance and that Moulin was not universally admired. The communists had always liked to claim that Moulin was one of theirs, since they tended, generally speaking, to appropriate the Resistance for themselves. But French historians were in agreement that there existed no substantive evidence that Moulin had been a communist, although he had worked closely with the communists as he did with the other Resistance organizations. Jacques Vergès produced no new evidence to substantiate his charges, but he did sully the reputations of several people.

On November 12, 1983, Vergès made his accusations on national television before millions of viewers; and, before he had left the station, the Furies were loose again. Reaction was violent. Henri Frenay, the founder of Combat, declared "there are no words severe enough to properly describe what Maître Vergès has done." The federation of former deportees, prisoners and resistance fighters (FNDIRP) denounced "the odious and provocative character" of Maître Vergès's declarations. Max Gallo, spokesman for the government, declared that "the government will not remain passive before any attempt to stain the memory of Resistance fighters." Angry protests were directed against the Antenne 2 network for allowing Vergès to appear. It seemed that every magazine and newspaper in the country carried the Vergès story. The Barbie affair had become the Vergès affair. And Jacques Vergès was delighted.

Telephones rang in a dozen Paris apartments as former Resistance leaders conferred over what action to take. Finally they decided to do nothing. "It would have made Vergès too happy," explained their lawyer, Yves Jouffa, who also happened to be president of the League for the Rights of Man. As for Minister of Justice Robert Badinter, his press secretary remained circumspect. "We know who Jacques Vergès is and we are not answering his charges," she said.[20]

The only group to take action was the International League Against Racism and Anti-Semitism. LICRA, as the organization is called, wrote to the highest appeal court in Paris and to the head of the law society demanding that Vergès be disbarred. "A lawyer's oath seals a moral contract between himself and the judiciary," explained LICRA's lawyer, Charles Korman. "With his oath a lawyer agrees to adhere to a set of values and rules and certainly to the political system that derives from those values and rules. He can criticize them, but from the inside . . . "

The LICRA action was widely criticized from within the legal fraternity — Yves Jouffa, for example, refused to be identified with the LICRA letter, from reasons of principle, he said — but the fact that a respected organization felt obliged to take such a position told its own story. Like the media, the legal profession had its own Catch-22 dilemmas. Were there any limits to a lawyer's freedom in the defense of his client? And if so, what were they?

The LICRA initiative failed, and Jacques Vergès remained a member of the bar.

Klaus Barbie may have chuckled to himself as he watched the scenario unfold from his cell in Lyons. If he and his lawyer could convince the French public that Moulin had committed suicide, then the hatred the French felt for Barbie might be conveniently neutralized. If Barbie hadn't tortured and killed Moulin, then he was nothing more than a slightly exuberant young ss officer who had merely done his duty; one who was no different from the former Resistance hypocrites who had betrayed Moulin, then gone on to become leaders of the land and destroy civilian populations in Algeria. The strategy of disruption was working perfectly.

On May 7, 1984, Paris journalists were summoned to a mysterious press conference in the Hotel Lutetia, where they were met by a journalist called Paul Ribeaud who had once been a member of the Algérie Française movement. The occasion was the publication of René Hardy's new book, *Derniers Mots* ("Last Words") in which Hardy had apparently decided to tell the whole truth about the Jean Moulin escapade. Hardy was seventy-three years old and deathly ill. The moment of truth had arrived. Ribeaud had encouraged Hardy to get it all down, no holds barred, he said.

Ribeaud delivered a prepared speech during which he implied to the assembled media that certain members of Combat had actually been working with the Germans since the mid-1930s in the struggle against communism. Hardy had informed Combat leader Pierre de Benouville well ahead of time that Klaus Barbie knew about the meeting of the Resistance that was to take place a few days later at Caluire, he said. A reporter from *Le Nouvel Observateur* challenged the insinuations. "I never *said* that," retorted Ribeaud. But according to the group of journalists present, that was precisely what he had said. And it seemed that Hardy had included the accusation against de Benouville in his new book.

The accusation, as such, was extraordinary. Had certain anticommunist elements in the Resistance actually been working in collaboration with the Nazis since *before* the war? If so, they would naturally have wanted to get rid of commie-lovers like Moulin. Klaus Barbie would have been little more than an accessory to a plan of long standing.

There was silence in the room. What was one to do with this "news?" What new machinations were being played out forty years after the fact? Suddenly, there was a slight noise. All heads turned . . . to see Jacques Vergès enter the room.

Vergès? Of course Vergès was connected to this new wrinkle. By distracting attention from the role his client played in the Moulin drama, Vergès could hit his favorite targets once again. One might have predicted his appearance in the new chapter of the Moulin-Hardy saga.

Also at the time when the Hardy book appeared, a documentary film, called *The Bitter Truth*, was offered to the television networks. The filmmaker, an unknown by the name of Claude Bal, had either contacted or been contacted by Vergès early in 1983, just after Barbie's return to France. (Vergès claimed that Bal called him.)

The subject was the same; the betrayal of Moulin by the Resistance as part of the battle against communism; and the film "starred" none other than René Hardy and . . . Jacques Vergès. Now larger than life on the celluloid screen, Vergès had a chance to play the "rushes" game. He now claimed that Resistance heroes Lucie and Raymond Aubrac "had benefited from the complicity of one of Barbie's aides" soon after the Nazi occupation of Lyons.[21]

The networks thought they were being manipulated and refused to broadcast the documentary (there were so many private screenings in the weeks ahead that most of Paris eventually saw it anyway), but the fairy tale continued. Bal, it seemed, just happened to have received a letter from none other than Klaus Barbie, presumably written from his prison cell in La Paz before his return to France. Barbie (who signed himself Altmann) also accused Pierre de Benouville of having betrayed Moulin and spoke of a secret agreement "to struggle against communism."

The Resistance had ignored the Hardy book, but with the appearance of the Bal film, it rose to the bait. Historian and lawyer Henri Noguères gave an interview in which he stated that "a lawyer does not have the right to lie and slander any more than he has the right to commit any other crime."[22] Then he wrote an article accusing Vergès of being "a liar and a defamer"[23] and a year later published a book in which he developed his attack.[24] Lucie Aubrac went on television to defend herself and the united Resistance of forty years earlier. "There were people on the Left and on the Right in the Resistance, but everyone recognized de Gaulle as a sort of savior," she said. "All the underground papers wrote the same thing at the time: 'A united battle for France; our common destiny, de Gaulle.' " And she too wrote a book explaining what her role in the Resistance had been.[25]

René Hardy had reason, perhaps, to want to "get" the Aubracs before he died. Lucie admitted freely that she had bungled an attempt to poison him after the Caluire affair and, in spite of two trials and two acquittals, neither she nor her husband had ever accepted his innocence. For four decades they had continued to speak out against him. But still the question remained. Why was all this going on *now*?

"Hardy didn't make these things up himself," Lucie Aubrac continued during the television interview. "Someone is whispering in his ear. Vergès uses every means at his disposal to divide the Resistance and to turn Barbie into a good German soldier. It was clear to me that the purpose of the Claude Bal film was to make Klaus Barbie look innocent and the Resistance look guilty. I'm the living proof! I'm seventy-two years old and in perfect health. I could be traveling or dabbling in archeology, which has always been my passion. But instead I am obliged to answer questions from journalists. *I* have become the defendant in the case!"

Hardy followed suit by charging Lucie Aubrac with slander. Lucie and Raymond Aubrac charged Hardy and Claude Bal with slander. And in February 1985, the investigating magistrate independently charged Jacques Vergès.

Forty years later the old battles were raging again, for like so much else in modern French history, the issues had never been laid to rest. Lucie Aubrac, for one, rued the day Klaus Barbie had ever returned to France. "I was thrilled when he was first arrested at the thought that justice would be done," she said. "I thought the trial might be an important moral lesson for the younger generation. But in fact he awoke feelings that were not yet dead. If Vergès is successful in his attempts to divert attention from the charges being brought against Barbie, he will also have succeeded in trivializing the Holocaust and fascism. For this reason I am sorry I cheered Barbie's return to France."

Klaus Barbie had returned to continue his old job, so to speak. He was still torturing the Resistance.

As for Jacques Vergès, he visibly loved the action. "Other people may not enjoy what I'm doing, but I'm having a very good time," he confided in an interview. "You'll notice that *I'm* the one talking in the press, not the government. *I'm* saying Barbie was kidnapped, *I'm* saying they're applying the law retroactively, *I'm* talking about the Jean Moulin affair, *I'm* accusing people of having betrayed Moulin. At the beginning Barbie was 'the butcher of Lyons,' the this, the that. Now there's no reply at all." He smiled, immensely pleased with himself.

In the months ahead, Klaus Barbie would be reduced to a pawn in the real battle, the ongoing battle, the battle of Jacques Vergès's lifetime. Through his client, Vergès could aim new artillery at his three favorite targets; the notables who fought in the French Resistance before turning around to support the colonial war in Algeria; Israel and

202 · Unhealed Wounds

the "Zionists" (a term that appeared to include cabinet ministers of the Mitterrand government); and, finally, the legal apparatus of the state itself, which he described as being in a chronic and disreputable state of "connivance." Through Klaus Barbie, Jacques Vergès might actually succeed in discrediting the government, as the Algerian conflict discredited and finaly destroyed the ill-fated Fourth Republic of Pierre Mendès France.

What really interested him in the Barbie affair? asked a puzzled interlocuter. Jacques Vergès waxed lyrical. Why, it was the very enormity of the Nazi crimes that excited him, he replied. He paused a moment, then continued, poetically: such crimes broke new ground in human history; indeed, rhapsodized the man of the law, the Nazi crimes were like "a lookout on the Sargasso Sea announcing new lands [ahead]."[26]

And he smiled from the other side of the looking glass.

· 11 ·

THE PROSECUTION

From the beginning, the very terms of Klaus Barbie's trial were controversial. The joy that greeted his return sprang from the one major event that had made Barbie notorious: the death of Jean Moulin. So the realization, in mid-February 1983, that the charges brought against the prisoner would exclude everything that had to do with the French Resistance caused consternation, especially among Resistance veterans. Under the law it seemed that only offenses that fell under the category of "crimes against humanity" could be considered.

"Crimes against humanity" were first defined by the international military tribunal of Nuremberg in 1945 and ratified by the United Nations in 1946 as a response to the shocking nature of the Nazi genocide. The systematic, planned destruction of the Jews of Europe had no real analogue in history. The Final Solution was not a political act undertaken to win territory or other spoils of war. Nor was it enacted to punish a defeated enemy. What was new about the massacre of Jews and Gypsies was that it was not undertaken *in response* to anything at all. Victims were chosen not for anything they did or might have done, but for what they were; for an accident of birth.

Crimes against humanity were defined as "murder, extermination, slavery, deportation, or other inhuman acts committed against any civilian population before or during the war; or persecution on political, religious and racial grounds . . . whether or not in violation of the domestic law of the country where perpetrated." Such crimes were considered to be different in kind from war crimes, which were, in essence, violations of the Geneva Convention. Most important, no statute of limitations could apply. It was intended, as the late Raymond Aron put it, that "time never erase [these crimes]. That they be neither forgotten nor forgiven."[1]

The French penal code contained an important statute of limitations. A crime that had gone unpunished for ten years was automatically "prescribed" — prevented from prosecution — on grounds that the perpetrator may have reordered his life, married, started a family, or otherwise "gone straight." An eruption of the past might do more harm than good, went the reasoning.

All crimes were the same under this law. The local teenage pickpocket and the Nazi who dispatched children to their deaths were both deemed free men ten years after the deed was done. This statute of limitations opened the door to startling possibilities after World War II ended. Might tour buses bring former Gestapo officers and their families into France to visit the scene of their "operations?" Would the local population be subjected to the sight of former ss officers picnicking on the grass? It was not an impossible scenario, not impossible at all.

In December 1964, the French National Assembly debated ways of extending the criminal status of war criminals; and what they came up with was a ratification of the law of "crimes against humanity." On December 26 of that year, the international legislation enacted at Nuremberg was incorporated into the penal code of France, with a special note emphasizing that crimes against humanity were, by their very nature, not subject to a statute of limitations.

Unlike Britain, France had a legal provision for trying criminals *in absentia*. As such, Klaus Barbie had been tried twice for war crimes — specifically, crimes against the soldiers of the Resistance — and twice sentenced to death, in 1952 and in 1954. But the sentence itself was subject to prescription. In any event, capital punishment was abolished by the Mitterrand government in 1981, and under French law Barbie could not be retried on charges that had already been brought against him in his absence.

There were practical as well as legal reasons for excluding the Resistance from the charges brought against Barbie. Since only crimes against humanity were admissible, each former *résistant* would have to have his case examined on an individual basis to determine whether it fitted the definition. In general, the minister of justice was calling all acts against the Resistance war crimes, on grounds that the men and women who fought in the Resistance did so voluntarily and had, as such, been "soldiers." With hundreds of people pushing to have their cases evaluated, the trial might be delayed for years. Barbie was almost seventy. He might not last that long. But the most important reason for excluding the Resistance was never acknowledged publicly. No one (with the possible exception of the communists) wanted to open the door to that closet full of skeletons from the collaboration, for it was not inconceivable that the ruling Socialist party might find a few rattling around in its own cupboard. France was full of collaborators who had never paid their dues. Some of them had even managed to have themselves declared honored veterans of the Resistance. Barbie had threatened that he was prepared to name names, and it was important that the legal parameters of the trial limit that possibility.

But in a country where political controversy is a staple of life, the government would have to defend the very idea of unlimitable "crimes against humanity." The tradition of prescription and amnesty was deeply ingrained. As writer Raymond Bourgine put it, "Hatred is not our vocation . . . Every once in a while we agree to forget the divisions of the past so we can live in brotherhood."[2] From this point of view, British justice, in which a criminal act remains outstanding for as long as the felon has not been tried, in person, in a court of law, may be seen as little more than legal vengeance after a ten-year time span has elapsed. The essential catchwords are "grace," "forgetfulness" and "forgiveness".[3] It was on this basis that in 1958 General de Gaulle freed Karl Oberg, the supreme ss commander in France; that in 1962 all presumed war crimes from the Algerian conflict were amnestied; and that in 1971 President Georges Pompidou pardoned Lyons *Milice* chief Paul Touvier, on the persistent recommendation of Monsignor Charles Duquaire.

The law regarding crimes against humanity was correctly seen to favor the prosecution of Nazis and, as such, also to "favor" the Jews. And the Jews as a group did not necessarily agree with the Christian attitudes inherent in the tradition of presidential grace. Their attitude seemed to be closer to the British legal tradition.

The Grand Rabbi of Lyons, Richard Wertenschlag, summed it up nicely: "An overemphasis on justice can suppress mercy, but an overemphasis on mercy can destroy justice. Justice must be both transcendent and immanent, here on earth. When justice has been done and been seen to be done, *then* one can allow forgiveness. But for such to be the case, the criminal must be conscious of his crime. 'Forgiveness' would be simply inappropriate in the case of Klaus Barbie, for he continues to consider himself innocent and his victims guilty. He remains a convinced and proud Nazi."

The Barbie affair was producing dangerous mutterings about "Jewish vengeance," especially once it became clear that only charges concerning Barbie's crimes against the Jews would be admitted. And Serge Klarsfeld's admission that he had hired a hit man to take care of Barbie should legal means prove fruitless did not help matters. Whatever one thought of the Klarsfelds' tactics, there remained a real division of opinion over the very nature of "justice." Particularly when *French* men had been charged with crimes against humanity. According to Raymond Bourgine, the indictment of *milicien* Paul Touvier and Vichy officials Jean Leguay and René Bousquet opened the door to an indictment of "the whole of the Vichy government; that is, the whole of the French population during the Occupation."4 That, of course, was where the real fear lay. Those collaboration skeletons in the closet.

Even for those who accepted the category of crimes against humanity, the definition of which crimes might fall within its jurisdiction was not entirely clear. The wording of the law was general, and it could be argued that torture ought to be included whether the victim was a Resistance soldier or a Jewish civilian. Officially, of course, the situation was beyond discussion. Judge Christian Riss, the young magistrate whose job it was to prepare the government's case against Barbie, did not allow that there might be matter for controversy. "One simply cannot include acts against the Resistance," he said. But behind the scenes, many people were less sure. "I happen to agree that one cannot easily make the narrow distinction. When a Resistance fighter is tortured, I consider that a crime against humanity and not a war crime," said Yves Jouffa, the president of the League for the Rights of Man. The veterans of the Resistance were themselves adamant that those of their members who had been murdered, tortured and deported came within the new law: in particular, veterans of the communist Resistance.

The communists had a lot to gain from the trial of Klaus Barbie. They had been the most militant group within the Resistance, and they had been special targets for the antibolshevism of both the Nazis and the men of Vichy. One hundred and fifty thousand communist men and women had died during the struggle. Indeed, their role in liberating France from fascism was an important element in their postwar popularity. The Barbie trial would give the communists an opportunity to remind voters of their contribution, particularly at a time when their electoral support was declining rapidly. And it would give them one more stick with which to beat the Right. "The entire trial will be an accusation of the Right. The French right-wing was in collaboration with the Germans," said Daniel Voguet, one of the principal lawyers for the French Communist party (PCF).[5]

In July 1983, the PCF put together a powerful delegation and marched off to Lyons where they gave a press conference to the assembled media. "The importance of this trial is to show young French people the monstrous nature of nazism," said Mireille Bertrand, the leader of the delegation and a member of the Party's political bureau. "It is more than the trial of one man. It is the trial of nazism itself."

Bertrand and the other members of the delegation claimed that a trial of such pedagogical importance needed to include *all* of Klaus Barbie's crimes. "We wish to remind people of the struggle and the sacrifices of the Resistance so that such horrors may never recur," she added.

Mireille Bertrand's interest in the Barbie trial went beyond politics, for her father and her uncle were both murdered by the Lyons Gestapo. "We [communists] had been trying to get Barbie back to France for years, and when he was returned in February 1983 we congratulated ourselves that a trial would finally take place. Thousands of *résistants* died or were tortured by Barbie, or by French men and women working for Barbie. We want that reality to be taken into consideration because it is part of history," she said in an interview.[6]

Unlike some of the other resistance groups, the communists were not afraid that Barbie would name turncoats within their organization during the course of his trial. The communist Resistance in Lyons was so tightly structured that commandos knew only their immediate superior; and this was the case all the way up the line. Barbie and his fellows could torture to the point of death. The communist they were torturing probably had nothing to tell them. On the rare occasion when someone with information did capitulate under torture, the organization retaliated swiftly. No one told and lived.

In December 1984, in an attempt to broaden the legal parameters of the trial, Communist party lawyers in both Paris and Lyons brought a suit against Barbie on behalf of Max Barel, the teenage son of a communist politician whom Barbie had literally scalded to death. The gesture seemed *pro forma* because no one expected it to succeed. "I doubt whether it will be accepted, because Barel was a *résistant* and as such the crime will be considered to be prescribed," admitted Daniel Voguet. Voguet claimed that there were strong legal grounds for including the murder and torture of certain Resistance fighters within the crimes-against-humanity legislation, which rested both on an interpretation of international law and French obligations with regard to international law. Once again, however, he was not hopeful that the legal arguments would prevail. "It's not a legal problem at this stage; it's a political problem," he said. "The minister of justice and almost certainly the president of the republic himself have decided to limit this trial by excluding the Resistance. Maybe because the socialists don't have much to brag about when it comes to the Resistance," he added, laughing. "We communists do, of course. So if they succeed in eliminating the communists, the socialists will come out looking very good, especially since the trial is going to damage the Right."

The office of Judge Christian Riss is an oasis of comfort in the Lyons courthouse, a decrepit-looking place where the washroom walls are smothered with racist, anti-Arab graffiti. Riss is in his mid-thirties but looks younger. His manner is formal, and he properly refuses to "interpret" the case. His job, he says, is to conduct an investigation then decide whether there is enough evidence to lay charges.

The investigation took Riss and his assistants all over France, to Israel, and to North America, as witnesses were located then brought to Lyons to identify the accused. It was not an easy task. Needless to say, most of Barbie's victims were long dead; and those who had survived were old. Forty-year-old memories might be vague, though it was also true that the sort of memories the survivors carried in their hearts were not likely to fade with time. Riss's job was logistically difficult as well. Outside of the Barbie case, he was personally responsible for investigating 150 other files. Some saw this as evidence that the government was trying to drown the Barbie trial, hoping that the prisoner might die in the meantime, but Riss and others insisted that such a caseload was normal within the French judicial structure. In any event, Riss complained, and in June 1984 the rest of his caseload was removed, and he was free to concentrate on Barbie.

Initially, Riss decided that eight separate charges could be brought against Barbie. They were:

1. The massacre of 22 hostages in the cellar of the Gestapo building during the summer of 1943. When the French police were called in to remove the bodies, they discovered that 178 bullets had been pumped into the 22 people.
2. The arrest and torture of 19 individuals during the summer of 1943.
3. The roundup of 86 people in the offices of the Lyons UGIF on rue Sainte-Catherine, February 9, 1943, and their subsequent deportation. In a telegram to Gestapo headquarters in Paris, Barbie informed his superiors that the prisoners had been sent to Drancy. One of them was the father of French Minister of Justice Robert Badinter.
4. The shooting of 42 people, including 40 Jews, in 1943–44. All had been held at Montluc as hostages for reprisal killings.
5. The roundup, torture and subsequent deportation of railway workers at the SNCF depot at Oullins, August 9, 1944.
6. The deportation to Auschwitz and Ravensbrück of 650 people, half Jews, half *résistants*, in the last convoy to leave Lyons, on August 11, 1944. The convoy list for this train was typed up in Lyons and later found in Auschwitz, and the train went there directly, without going through Drancy. Barbie claims that he sent the train to Drancy as usual, but that it changed direction en route, without his knowledge, because the French railway lines were being sabotaged. This particular train was indeed attacked, and traveled around in circles, but it eventually managed to reach the French-German border at Belfort. And that was that.
7. The shooting of 70 Jews at Bron, a suburb of Lyons, on August 17, 1944, as well as numerous other Jews and two priests at Saint-Genis-Laval on August 20, 1944. At this stage the Gestapo was emptying the prisons before the arrival of the Allies. It has been suggested that many murders were committed at this point because the prisoners had been horribly tortured and mutilated.
8. The arrest and deportation of 55 Jews, including 52 children, from a children's refuge at Izieu. (These figures represented original estimates in 1945.)

Klaus Barbie denied everything.

After two years of investigation, Judge Riss announced in early January 1985 that only three of the original eight charges would be retained. There were several reasons for his decision. Charges that might possibly be interpreted as dealing with the Resistance were dropped as inadmissible. So were the charges that could be interpreted as coming under the very broad terms of Barbie's earlier trials, in 1952 and 1954. Jean Moulin, for example, remained out of the question. Although Barbie had never actually been charged with the torture and subsequent death of France's greatest Resistance hero, the presumed act was a war crime and consequently prescribed. Finally, Judge Riss had to allow that it had been very difficult to find living witnesses whose memories could be trusted. Barbie would be charged only with those crimes that could be fully authenticated and/or documented. These were: the deportation of the Lyons UGIF committee; the deportation of 650 individuals to Auschwitz and Ravensbrück on August 11, 1944; and the deportation of the children of Izieu.

Not everyone was happy. The historical show trial originally desired by both the Resistance and the Jews would probably not take place. At a meeting in Lyons of lawyers representing civil suits being brought against Barbie, someone suggested meanly that the minister of justice had retained the rue Sainte-Catherine charge "out of personal vengeance." The Jews of Lyons were equally chagrined. "We want the trial of Klaus Barbie to be an *example* of nazism, but now we're afraid he'll only be judged for what he did in such and such a case, and that the larger aspect will be lost," said Dr. Marc Aron, head of the local Jewish Congress (CRIF). "Individual facts will emerge, but the overall determination of the Nazis to destroy the Jews will not. And *that's* what's important."

Without a doubt, the cornerstore of the prosecution would rest upon the example of the unfortunate children of Izieu.

In the spring of 1943, the Oeuvre de secours aux enfants (OSE), a Jewish organization dedicated to hiding and smuggling Jewish children out of France, established a clandestine children's colony in the remote mountains of the Ain region with the generous help of a local prefect. In the tiny village of Izieu, with its scattering of gray stone houses and its sparse population of one hundred and thirty people, the forty-two children and their adult guardians were welcomed and protected. All the children, aged between four and seventeen, had already suffered terrible traumas. Many of their parents had already been deported, and most of the children had already spent time in the French holding camps.

For several months the children of Izieu enjoyed a relatively normal life, just like summer camp. They drew pictures for their lost parents and wrote them letters, many of which have been preserved. As of September 1943, however, their situation grew more precarious. Danger stalked even the most remote corners of the mountain countryside. A Jewish doctor in the region was arrested. The children would need to be dispersed once again.

On April 3, 1944, Madame Sabina Zlatin left for Montpellier to try to arrange a safer hideaway. While she was away she received an unsigned telegram, which later turned out to be from the prefect. "Sickness in the house. Contagious," it said. Madame Zlatin felt a sharp pain of recognition. She understood that the Gestapo had struck.

It was 9:00 A.M. on the morning of April 6, 1944, a beautiful, sunny day. As the two trucks and two cars carrying armed Gestapo police turned into the property, the children were eating a breakfast of hot chocolate and bread. When the screaming and the imploring was over and the children had been tossed into the trucks "like parcels," according to an eyewitness, the half-full bowls of chocolate would testify to the rapidity of the Gestapo action.

How had Klaus Barbie's Gestapo come to know of the existence of forty-two children in a distant mountain commune? Barbie had been informed, of course: very likely by someone in the village, or close by. Barbie's act was nonetheless exceptional. During the whole of the German Occupation, in the whole of France, only one other ss officer raided a Jewish children's home.[7]

With the exception of a teenage boy who jumped out of a window and hid in the bushes, everyone present in the Izieu colony that day was taken. As the open trucks approached a neighboring community down the road, the local population gathered around in anger. Why *children*? they demanded to know. Who were they harming? Why were they being guarded by police pointing guns?

There was a local village child in the convoy, a non-Jew who had been visiting the Izieu community. He recognized his aunt in the crowd and began to cry. His aunt began to scream. The Gestapo realized that the child was not a Jew and agreed to let him "kiss his aunt goodbye." Then he melted into the crowd and was saved.

One person survived to tell the rest of the story. Leah Feldblum, who was twenty-six years old and a counselor at the Izieu colony, described the subsequent events to Serge Klarsfeld some forty years later. "The fifty-one prisoners were driven to Lyons where they were incarcerated at Montluc for the night. Everyone was interrogated individually. The next day the adults and the older boys were hand-cuffed, and the entire contingent was loaded on to a passenger train for the transfer to Drancy. On April 13, three-quarters of the children were deported to Auschwitz along with four of the adults [including Feldblum]. The others followed . . .[8]

On April 6, 1944 at 8:20 P.M., Klaus Barbie sent a telegram to SD headquarters in Paris.

In the morning hours, the Jewish children's home . . . in Izieu-Ain was closed down. A total of 41 children, aged from 3 to 13, were arrested. Furthermore, the entire Jewish personnel, consisting of 10 people, including five women, was arrested. It was not possible to seize money or other valuables.

Transport to Drancy will take place 7.4.44.

By order, Barbie, SS-Obersturmführer.[9]

This telegram was going to be the central piece of evidence at Barbie's trial. Barbie and his lawyer, Vergès, later claimed that Barbie's signature on the telegram had been falsified, presumably by Klarsfeld. "That's ridiculous," retorted Klarsfeld. "We will bring in handwriting analysts to prove you wrong. You know that that telegram will convict your client."

According to Klarsfeld, it is impossible to know whether Klaus Barbie was actually present at Izieu on April 6, 1944. There are conflicting eyewitness reports. The important issue is his authority for the action. Barbie was head of the Gestapo, even though the Jewish Affairs sub-section was directed by an underling. Furthermore, no one in the Lyons Gestapo could have signed the telegram for Barbie without his explicit authority.

Among the children taken away on that day were Mina Halaunbrenner, age eight, and Claudine Halaunbrenner, age five. Both were daughters of Itta Halaunbrenner, who, forty years later in La Paz, would chain herself to a bench with Beate Klarsfeld to publicize the presence of Klaus Barbie in Bolivia.

There were five children in the Halaunbrenner family: Léon, born in Galicia, Poland, in 1929; Alexandre, born in France in 1932; Mina, born in 1935; Claudine, born in 1939; and Monique, born in 1942.

Their parents, Itta and Jacob, were Polish Jews who had escaped to France as refugees in the early 1930s.

In 1942, the family lived in Paris, in the Jewish immigrant district of the Marais. By summer, Jacob had escaped over the Demarcation Line into the unoccupied zone and was looking for a *passeur* to bring the rest of the family out. He was successful, and by October they were all together in a village near Angoulême. But within days the French gendarmes had arrested the family in their hotel and dispatched them to Nexon, one of the Jewish internment camps created by the Vichy government. For the next ten months, they were shunted from Nexon to the camp at Rivesaltes to the camp at Gurs. The males were separated from the females. There were barbed wire, hunger, dysentery, bitter cold and typhoid.

With the help of a sympathetic local prefect, the Halaunbrenner family was released into "supervised custody" near Lyons in August 1943. They escaped and moved into the city, where an uncle and his sons had already taken up residence. By this time Klaus Barbie had been on the job for more than eight months, and the situation in Lyons was tense. The Halaunbrenners were warned about informers and surprise roundups. It was best to move frequently, said their relatives.

Returning home at eleven o'clock one morning, Alexandre and his father saw the Gestapo in front of their house. Barbie was there, and three other men. They had been waiting for two hours. They were looking for Joseph, the uncle's son, whom they suspected of being in the Resistance. Joseph no longer lived there, but Barbie wasn't taking no for an answer. He and his men waited and waited: until six o'clock in the evening.

At 6:00 P.M. Léon Halaunbrenner returned home from work. Léon was only fourteen, but he looked older. Barbie was sure he was Joseph. He grabbed Léon and his father, Jacob. "It's only an interrogation session," one of the men assured everyone.

Itta Halaunbrenner also grabbed hold of her son. "He's just a boy; he's just a boy," she screamed. Barbie struck her with the butt of his revolver. That night no one slept.

The next day, Itta was in the street with her four children, waiting for her husband and her son to return. Alexandre saw the Gestapo in the distance. He knew enough to realize that when they sent the big truck it was to pick up a lot of people. "Ma, they're coming to get us," he whispered in terror. They flattened themselves against the wall inside a neighboring doorway. Then they ran, Itta carrying Monique, who was less than a year old; they ran to a clandestine synagogue Alexandre knew of.

There they were taken in charge by the UGIF. Monique was hidden in a municipal nursery among other infants. Mina and Claudine were sent to Izieu. The rest of the family was hidden for several days in a convent, then provided with false identity cards. Itta's new name was Maria Sterleska. She was still Polish — no one could camouflage that accent — but now she was Christian. Itta picked up Monique and found a place for the family to live. She supported the children by buying flour on the black market and baking little pastries that Alexandre sold in the cafés of Lyons.

A month after the disappearance of Jacob and Léon, Itta and Alexandre returned to the old house to see if any of the neighbors had any news. A woman came forward in tears. "Your husband died in the hospital," she said. Itta and Alexandre looked at each other. How could he have died in the hospital? What did he die *of*? They did the rounds of every hospital in Lyons. Eventually someone suggested they try the morgue.

Jacob Halaunbrenner's body was still there. On November 24, 1943, he had been machine-gunned in the cellar of the Gestapo headquarters at the Ecole de Santé. His body was torn to shreds.

They received a postcard from Léon, from Montluc, through the auspices of the Red Cross. Then nothing. Later they learned that he had been transferred to Drancy, then deported to the salt mines of Upper Silesia. Several months later he died, of starvation and exhaustion.

Until April 1944, there was regular news from Izieu through UGIF and the OSE. When that stopped as well, Itta and the children knew something must have happened. But it was not until August 25 and the liberation of Lyons that they had any confirmation. Alexandre saw it in the local paper. The children's colony at Izieu had been denounced and everyone deported.

For years Itta Halaunbrenner hoped her daughters would return. Other survivors were returning, why not them? It was 1949 before she learned that only the able-bodied had survived the first day at Auschwitz. The old, the young and the infirm were gassed within minutes of their arrival.

After the war ended, the French government sent out death certificates to the surviving family members of those Jews who had been deported to Auschwitz. Adult or child, they all said the same thing. "Died at Drancy," with the date of deportation, followed by the ludicrous inscription: *"Mort pour la France."*

In the Jewish section of the Père Lachaise cemetery in Paris, some families have copied the formula. Other headstones are more explicit. Over the empty graves is written: *"Murdered at Auschwitz."*

For decades, no one ever mentioned that the children of Izieu were deported because and only because they were Jews. The community of Izieu put up a road monument that spoke of the "martyrdom of innocents" and the "sacred place" where they had lived. A local newspaper further obscured the truth by reporting indignantly that they were arrested because their parents were "Jews, or communists or simply Gaullists," implying that the Jewish children were enemy *résistants* of a sort, just like the others.[10] There was nothing malicious intended, but the fact that chidren were murdered solely because they were of Jewish birth was not something people wished to draw attention to. The question of who in the tiny community had betrayed them was too emotionally charged.

It was important to establish that the children of Izieu were deported as part of the Final Solution and not as part of an attack on the soldiers of the Resistance. Over a thirteen-year period, Serge Klarsfeld traced survivors of their families—in France, Israel, Canada, the United States and South America. Every one of the children deported from Izieu turned out to be Jewish. The one child the Gestapo allowed to escape into the custody of his aunt was a gentile.

Many of the survivors, including Alexandre and Itta Halaunbrenner, will testify for the prosecution at the trial of Klaus Barbie; and for Klarsfeld, the Izieu children's file remains the *raison d'être* of the entire Barbie affair.

"For more than thirteen years I have been living with the children of Izieu. It is for these children, and for two of their mothers who are still living, that we located, unmasked and were successful in having Barbie brought back for trial," Klarsfeld said on April 8, 1984, at a commemorative ceremony in Izieu.

"Klaus Barbie not only arrested and tortured the most famous member of the French Resistance. He also voluntarily ended the lives of more than forty Jewish children who represented no danger to the German authorities and who wanted only to survive. When he cabled his superiors on April 6, 1944, Barbie signed his name to a crime that would grow steadily more notorious.

"We do not know whether the memory of these children calls for vengeance or not, but we are sure that it was important to end the exceptional impunity from which Barbie has benefited for forty years. The trial of Klaus Barbie is above all a necessary act that will finally bring to a term the suffering of so many families."

Not everyone was quite so sure. By March 1985, the lawyers for the prosecution had never once met together. Jacques Vergès had been waging the Barbie trial in the press for more than a year, but, with the exception of Klarsfeld's occasional interventions, the prosecution lawyers had yet to be heard from.

"Vergès is going to make mincemeat out of them," warned an observer. "They don't even *understand* his strategy, let alone know how to confront it."

In spite of Klarsfeld's apparent confidence, the unfolding of the Klaus Barbie trial was anything but evident. Whatever the outcome, Jacques Vergès could hardly lose. He would succeed — indeed, had already succeeded — in making all the important points he wanted to make: about the Resistance, about the government, about "Zionists," and about what was, in his opinion, a prejudiced interpretation of the crimes-against-humanity legislation that included the Holocaust but excluded the abominations of the Algerian war. Whatever happened to Klaus Barbie, his trial would serve as an important legal precedent that lawyers both inside and outside France would watch with interest.

· 12 ·

UNHEALED WOUNDS

Spring 1985. The countdown to the Barbie trial had begun. The minister of justice announced that the trial would *not* be televised live. It would likely be filmed, however, for educational purposes; to be shown to schoolchildren after a twenty-year period had elapsed. (Twenty years would give everyone plenty of time to decide whether what went on at the Barbie trial was "suitable" for classroom lessons.) There was talk of a glass booth for the accused, *à la* Eichmann. Security checks, warned the newspapers, would be imposed on everyone. The trial itself might be held outside of Lyons, out of fairness to Barbie. And only a small percentage of the hundreds of journalists who had applied for accreditation would be accepted in the courtroom.

Tension was building. In April, leaders of the Jewish community and various human rights associations expressed their concern about the forthcoming trial in a public forum. Charles Korman from LICRA, Théo Klein, president of the French Jewish Congress (CRIF), Henri Noguères, historian and past president of the League for the Rights of Man, Charles Libman, Serge Klarsfeld's associate in the Barbie prosecution, and writer Bernard-Henri Lévy "debated" the subject, which was entitled "Understanding the Barbie Trial." A major focus of concern was not Barbie *per se* but his lawyer, Jacques Vergès. Vergès was decidely unpopular in this circle. "There won't be anyone to actually *defend* Vergès," acknowledged Korman a bit warily before the discussion opened.

The discussion was held within the context of the fourth International Jewish Film Festival, which was taking place in Paris at the time. Three days before the event, a bomb exploded during the projection of a not-unrelated film, *Eichmann, Man of the Third Reich*. Miraculously, no one was killed: the seats around the area where the bomb had been planted were apparently unoccupied. But the recurrence of

217

anti-Semitic terror in Paris was, in a word, terrifying. Was it the neo-Nazis, friends of Eichmann and Barbie? Was it Abu Nidal's ultramilitant Palestinians? Was it the Islamic Jihad movement of Lebanon attacking "Israel" in a Paris movie theater that would naturally be full of French Jews? Was it an anti-Semitic branch of a newly revitalized French xenophobia? Was it the act of an isolated racist? Or a psychopath?

No one knew the answer.

The countdown to the trial had begun; but the atmosphere in France had changed drastically since Klaus Barbie was first "welcomed" by the joyous clamor of the populace. The fortunes of the Mitterrand government were in serious decline—had been, in effect, since the day the socialists were elected to office in May 1981. It is predictably harder to be in power than in opposition, but the French socialists had more than the usual antigovernment hostility to deal with. In a country where supporters of the political Left were known as "the people of the Left," and where left-wing ideology had appropriated the liberal values of the French Revolution and captured the minds and hearts of millions of people, the election of a socialist government created fairy-tale expectations among left-leaning elements of the population. For voters on the other side of the political spectrum, the election of the "Union of the Left," as the socialist-communist governing coalition was called, was, of course, nothing short of a disaster for France, both ideologically and practically.

When the socialists came to power, the historical ideas of the "Left" were immediately subjected to reevaluation. Fundamental concepts of class struggle and the destruction of capitalism were suddenly as absent from the speeches of François Mitterrand and his entourage as they were from the political philosophies of Ronald Reagan and Margaret Thatcher. The emotional content of leftist commitment was replaced by "modernization" in a race to nudge the creaky structures of France into the late twentieth century before new technologies consigned the entire nation to the realm of the dinosaurs. There were, of course, those that mourned the passage. "The Left . . . ought to break with capitalism. It has already broken with socialism," lamented journalist Laurent Joffrin. "It has exchanged French socialism, the badge of the people of the Left, for a soulless motto: modernization . . . [The socialists] thought they were sailing the ship of History. Instead they are rowing in the galley of business management."

"The politics of the Left can be resuméd in the following way:

whatever is socialist does not work: whatever works is not socialist," he continued. "Is it any wonder that [the compass of] the Left has lost the north?"

By July 1984 when the Communist party left the government coalition, the "people of the Left" had become a fiction. The departure did not win the communists votes; indeed, as the months progressed, their popularity dipped to its lowest postwar level. The old pro-Soviet line was less and less meaningful to a population that was looking admiringly at what they called the "liberal" (i.e., conservative) economic policies of the United States under Ronald Reagan and unhappily comparing the strong American dollar to their own faltering currency. The steadfast refusal of the PCF to tolerate internal reform did not help matters, and the Twenty-Fifth Party Congress[2] in which the progressives were purged from the political bureau and elsewhere was the object of dismayed analysis.

In any case, public-opinion polls suggested that the historical Left-Right dichotomy might be breaking down. In January 1985, 38 percent of people questioned were not sure whether the policies of Prime Minister Laurent Fabius were "Left" or "Right." And 27 percent of the population refused to classify themselves as being on one side or the other. Significantly, only 28 percent of people questioned thought one had to favor the "struggle against capitalism" in order to vote Left. On the other hand, 50 percent thought the traditional values of "justice, generosity and fraternity" remained all-important indicators.[3]

The Left needed to redefine its traditional basis in order to maintain its own constituency, for every political signpost pointed to defeat in the upcoming legislative elections of March 1986. In this respect, after months of doom and gloom, the Klaus Barbie trial began to look politically advantageous once again. There were dangers, of course: there might be a few prominent socialists among the wartime collaborators Barbie and Vergès had promised to drag out of the closet. And the still-controversial Algerian war, replete with its own hidden history of compromise, had in fact been initiated by a socialist government. But if 50 percent of the electorate believed that "justice, generosity and fraternity" remained the hallmarks of the Left, then this "trial of nazism" was worth the risk. Fifty percent was a magic number. Fifty percent could win an election.

The socialists would have to fight an uphill battle to do well in the 1986 elections, and the opportunity to attack the "Right" through the Barbie trial might turn out to be crucial. Since Barbie's return to France in February 1983, a new, extreme right-wing movement with a strongly xenophobic base had emerged on a national scale, and by spring 1985 it had picked up substantial electoral support. France had not sloughed off the worldwide economic slump with the rapidity of some other western countries, and unemployment had risen steadily since 1981 to more than 10 percent of the work force at the end of 1984.[4] With a socialist government seemingly unable to stem the tide, the extreme right-wing — called the Front National — appropriated the unemployment issue. The main thrust of their attack was directed against immigrants — Arab immigrants. *They* were taking jobs away from *real* French people. *They* were responsible for crime in the streets. The catalog of charges and insinuations was disturbingly familiar, only now the object of overt scorn was the Arab rather than the Jew. Like Jekyll and Hyde, the other face of *les deux France* was coming into view once again. The old, historical schism was clearly alive and well.

The success of the Front National and its leader, Jean-Marie Le Pen, took most people by surprise. Le Pen's party had been formed in 1972, but few had been paying attention. In 1972 overt racism and anti-Semitism were still socially taboo, and neo-Nazi revisionists were only just beginning their campaign to soften public opinion for an attack on the historical reality of Auschwitz. But the identity of the founding members of the Front National might have given pause to anyone with a memory for recent history. Le Pen himself had a political background of extreme right-wing activity, including support for the neo-Luddite Poujadist movement of the 1950s and a controversial term in an Algerian "interrogation center" during the war (he was accused of having participated in torture sessions).[5] As well, the founding committee included: a former member of the extreme right-wing OAS, the organization that had threatened de Gaulle with a military coup during the Algerian war; a former executive assistant of Jean-Louis Tixier-Vignancourt, the man who had directed French radio and cinema from Vichy, where he was described as "enjoying Jew baiting and looking for chances to cast more insults at Léon Blum;"[6] a leader of a militant student organization with the uncomfortable title of the New Order; and writers from such extreme right-wing publications as *Défense de l'Occident* ("Defense of the West").

The Front National was "there" during the decade of the 1970s without being particularly frightening. But fear did grip thousands of people on October 16, 1983, when they learned of an extraordinary public meeting that was taking place in Paris in the context of "French Friendship Day."

On that Sunday afternoon, in the auditorium of the Mutualité, more than 2,000 people listened to and applauded speakers representing every extreme right-wing organization in France; and some very familiar ideas found a new public forum. "Four superpowers are colonizing France: Marxists, Freemasons, Jews and Protestants," proclaimed the director of a pro-family organization[7] in a startling evocation of Action Française and the 1930s. He then proceeded to identify each "superpower" with a government cabinet minister, with special emphasis on the "Jewish ministers." "Judaism is the source of all or part of the government's policies," he announced. "And let us not forget that the Jews are at the two poles of contemporary society. They are the source of finance capital as well as being the most vehement detractors of our society . . . "

The political editor of *Présent*,[8] the pro-Front National newspaper, confided that the attitudes of Jews caused him to "question certain things." He would like to say more, he continued, but the antihate laws of 1972 prevented him from saying what was really on his mind. The result of such laws, he concluded, was that "the only community in France that is not protected is the French community."

The author of a 1982 book, *Dreyfus, the Scum*,[9] said that [Arab] immigrants "breed like rabbits" and raised the horrifying specter of a "Moslem President" of the Republic. A newspaper editor attacked a female television news announcer for being Belgian, and said that a highly placed government functionary "looked like a Turk."[10]

The organizer of the event, Bernard Antony, aka Romain Marie, also had his word to say.[11] Murder International and the Communist International both were composed essentially of Jews, he announced. However, such comments could in no way be construed as anti-Semitism. "The Jews are being abusive when they claim that the extreme Right is anti-Semitic. *We* could reply that communism is Jewish!" he explained in a remarkable non sequitur.[12]

A certain number of right-wing associations had booths at the "Friendship Day" assembly: the capital punishment lobby; a highly politicized organization of independent business people and farmers;[13]

and a federation of former Algerian colonials.[14] But the individual most in evidence was none other than Marshal Philippe Pétain, whose picture adorned souvenir posters, buttons, plates and ashtrays.

A century of conservative ideology was being reborn: from anti-Dreyfus, to Action Française, to Marshal Pétain, to Algérie Francaise, to the new anti-Arab xenophobia of the 1980s. The historical landmarks remained the same; and the passion remained intact.

Aside from having said almost thirty years ago that Jewish Prime Minister Pierre Mendès France filled him with "a patriotic and almost physical revulsion," Jean-Marie Le Pen is careful never to say anything directly racist or anti-Semitic; indeed, he has a habit of taking anyone who suggests that he is either one or the other to court. What he does do, and brilliantly, is two-directional. First, he opens the racist terrain to others (such as his supporters quoted above) without rejecting what they say. Second, through a billboard campaign built on innuendo, he leaves his "real" meaning open to the imagination of the reader. Le Pen's billboard messages prior to the cantonal (regional) elections of March 1985 were instructive. The most common slogan was *"La France et les Français d'abord"* (France and the French first), a direct appeal to latent xenophobia, and one that conveyed the familiar idea that no "immigrant" could ever be "French" regardless of the vagaries of official naturalizations. To be "French" was something more mystical, in the blood-and-soil mode, as Front National supporter André Figueras (not Le Pen himself) explained in some detail. To be "French" was to be "a product of French civilization, culture and language," he said. "Thus it is not by delivering French citizenship to children who happen to be born here of just any parents that one can, with a magic wand, create 'French' people ... By adding a heavy dose of a foreign substance to a basic substance, which is naturally and historically French, one will [finish by] denaturing the basic substance."[15]

Le Pen's other billboard messages were even more subliminal. "Le Pen says aloud what everyone thinks to himself," said one. Another displayed a picture of the leader with a gag over his mouth. "They're trying to keep him quiet," read the caption.

Le Pen himself was direct both about the presumed connection between the presence of "immigrants" (i.e., "non-French") in the country and both unemployment and delinquency and about his belief in the essential, "natural" inequalities between various peoples. In his program he recommended the rescinding of French nationality for the second generation (a move that recalled the policies of Vichy France with regard to the Jews) and called for a stronger, more authoritative government. But his billboards went further. At a psychological level they liberated latent racism and dissolved social taboos that had been in effect since the Liberation. For the first time in decades it became respectable to make racist remarks and even to call oneself a racist.

This respectability was demonstrated in February 1984, when Le Pen was the invited guest on a popular television program.[16] With a smile, and in a neutral voice, he described his views as "pure common sense." And as he spoke, a historical memory was triggered in living rooms all over France. Large numbers of people who felt they, or their parents, or their grandparents had been betrayed forty years earlier when the national religion of Pétainism was disavowed and gagged *(just like Le Pen on his billboards)* experienced a shock of recognition.

The next day, another television station ran a special program on racism and invited viewers to write letters on the subject.[17] The French media were not unaccustomed to hate mail, but this time there was a significant difference. People signed their letters. "I'm a racist and proud of it," wrote one woman. "I have nothing against inferior races, but I don't have to associate with them either," explained another correspondent. Still others claimed that the "inferior races" were themselves anti-French (i.e., "racist"). Therefore, they felt justified . . . And so on. Overnight, ultraconservative France had removed its "gag."

On June 17, 1984, the Front National captured an astounding 11 percent of the votes at the European Elections, establishing Jean-Marie Le Pen as a major player on the political stage of France. The other event of that day was the decline of the Communist party. The Front National and the communists had received approximately the same measure of support.

For the better part of the next year, rivers of newspaper ink were devoted to the Le Pen phenomenon, much of it speculating as to how he would do in the regional elections of March 1985. Most disconcerting was the public quandary of the center-right parties, the neo-Gaullist RPR (Rassemblement pour la République) and the UDF (Union pour la Démocratie Française). Basic political opportunism suggested a possible alignment with the Front National in an attempt to defeat the government. On the other hand, no one was unaware of the implications of such an alignment, or of the fact that it might backfire among moderate voters. As a compromise, the RPR in particular hardened its line on immigration and crime, co-opting some of the Front National platform.

In March 1985, the Front National ran 1,500 candidates in 1,900 constituencies and won 8.69 percent of the vote. The result was less spectacular than that of the previous June, but substantial all the same. In the second runoff vote the following week, Front National supporters followed instructions and voted massively for the center-right-parties. When the tally came in, the combined Right had won 53.51 percent of the vote, and the combined Left had won 46.28 percent. (The communists joined their erstwhile enemies, the socialists, for the occasion.)

Respectability. Large numbers of people liberated from restrictive inhibitions. A tiny minority pushed over the edge. Within days of the March elections a young Moroccan was murdered in Menton, and an eighteen-year-old Algerian was murdered in Miramas, both places where the Front National had strong support. "We killed him because we don't like Arabs," casually acknowledged one of the two men who shot the youth from a moving car.

The new phenomenon was that some people openly approved. "He was a toad, a pure *beur*[18] who chose to live here and make trouble in France, just like a lot of his coreligionists," commented a local police officer, a man who clearly believed his own personal gag had been removed in spite of the job he held. Some days later a national newspaper published a letter from a reader who was "shocked" at the public outcry *against* the murder "of that pimp." "If it is racist to want to preserve the future of our country ... then I am a racist," she wrote.[19]

The bombing of the Jewish film festival in Paris occurred on the same weekend the two murders took place. "Words are not innocent," headlined *Le Monde*, commenting on a year of Front National ideology in the national press.

A nearly 10-percent vote for the extreme Right did not mean that a new Vichy France was about to assume the reins of power, but it did mean that a softening of public opinion had occurred and that the center-right parties would need to acknowledge Front National policies if they hoped to co-opt some of Le Pen's support. On the other hand, the success of Jean-Marie Le Pen gave the governing socialists a golden opportunity to redefine who they were and what they traditionally stood for. On the night of the March elections, Lionel Jospin, secretary general of the PS, opened fire on national television. "The last rise of a xenophobic party in this country ended in a bloodbath. Vichy France was the blackest moment in French history," he stormed.[20] And on April 19, 1985, François Mitterrand created a historic precedent by becoming the first president of the republic to address a meeting of the League for the Rights of Man. Dignified, relaxed (he was among friends) and patriotic (he wore a red, white and blue tricolored tie), Mitterrand reminded the assembly that the French Revolution of 1789 had introduced the idea of human dignity and equality for the very first time and that, in spite of the rise of racism in the country, the French were the inheritors of that important moment in history. "The demarcation line divides those who believe in liberty, equality and fraternity from those who do not. The line is that of the republic itself," he said, alluding to the historical conflict between *les deux France.*

But the socialists were not entirely free of ambiguity in the epic battle of good against evil. Within two weeks of the March regional elections, François Mitterrand decided to alter the electoral rules, which established a win by majority, in favor of proportional representation on the basis of the vote. The change was defended—and defensible—on grounds of fairness. But the timing was suspicious. The law would prevent political parties from blocking together (e.g., prevent the Right from forming a combined majority over the Left) and would likely benefit the socialists in the 1986 elections. Small parties—including the Front National—would thus have a chance to take seats in the National Assembly. Indeed, according to calculations, the Front National would take fifty seats under the new system.

While the socialists were reminding the electorate that *they* were the party of "justice, generosity and fraternity," not to mention *liberté, égalité, fraternité,* and while the Klaus Barbie "trial of nazism" was preparing to burst forth on to the public stage (benefiting the political Left and doubtless harming the Right), few were likely to forget that the socialists were also the party that had first opened the doors of the National Assembly to the Front National.

In this fragile political environment, the Barbie trial, with its uniquely Jewish content, was bound to be exceptionally delicate. No one, least of all the Jews, could count on much popular support. The trial was going to remind conservative France of things it did not want to hear about, at a time when the Right felt particularly powerful.

"The trial will present the French with a historical problem that has, unfortunately, become contemporary again," commented Théo Klein, head of the French Jewish Congress (CRIF). "That through silence, indifference and even collaboration the leaders of France and a part of the French population were able to arrest and deport another part of the population in acts that led to their death. Forty years later it is still hard to understand. The prefects and public servants who carried out the task, or let it happen, were the same people, before, during and after the war. In 1940, I felt deeply and very painfully that I was no longer a member of society, although my family had lived in France for centuries.

"It is important that we relive this period, because thanks to the excesses of Mr. Le Pen, we are now experiencing a similar rejection of one part of the population. The Barbie trial must demonstrate that once the way is opened to discrimination and hatred, no one can predict where the path will lead. The limits are never clearly traced in advance."

Théo Klein is a thoughtful man. The possibility that the Barbie trial may fail to produce the desired effect, that it may on the contrary, actually restimulate anti-Semitism among elements of the French population who do not wish to be reminded of what they did, or did not do, during the Occupation has not escaped his attention. Nor has he avoided thinking about the possible consequences of an attack, by the Jewish community, on current xenophobia. He says, with some hesitation, that if anyone had asked his opinion about whether Klaus Barbie should be brought back to France and tried, he is not sure he would have been in favor. He says, too, that as a lawyer he regards the law of crimes against humanity without legal prescription with unease. But fact is fact. Barbie is in France and, if he lives long enough, will be tried. Whatever concerns have been evoked must now be viewed from a moral and not a political point of view, Klein argues.

"It is true that from the moment we say, publicly, that the racist phenomenon currently directed against Arabs also concerns us as Jews, we are opening the door to a possible attack on ourselves as well, but we have to know what we want and where we stand. We know that racism and anti-Semitism come from the same roots. If we say, 'It's

not us this time,' and abandon those who are the new objects of hatred, who will come to *our* aid when we need it? On what grounds will
we be able to ask for help?"

Not everyone shared Klein's moral courage, but his ambivalence
over the forthcoming trial certainly represented the thinking of the
thousands of French Jews whose initial nervousness over the return of
Klaus Barbie has grown rather than subsided over the past two years.
As a result, Serge and Beate Klarsfeld are not necessarily heroes in
every household. But the Klarsfelds' commitment to a public exposure
of a taboo-ridden past remains steadfast. The dead will not rest until
Barbie, Leguay and Bousquet have been brought to trial and forced to
bear witness to their acts.

Unhealed wounds. For Serge Klarsfeld and his supporters, France
ceased to be "France" when the Vichy government came into being.
The France of the Revolution, in which all men were free and equal, in
which there was a place for Jews, ceased to be. And although the Pétain
regime ended forty years ago, that France would never live again until
the ghost of those years had been exorcised: until the French themselves, both Christians and Jews, collectively renounced the devil and
reaffirmed the essential plurality of the nation. Until then, and as long
as "Vichy" remained a loaded, taboo word, Jews like Klarsfeld could
not feel totally secure.

Hence, for Klarsfeld, the betrayal of the Jews is "the darkest hour
in French history," for during that hour France betrayed herself. Hence
the Barbie trial, with its emphasis on the "trial of nazism" and on the
deportation of Jewish children, whom no one helped and whose identity as Jews — the sole and unique reason for their destruction — was
glossed over after the event. Hence the even more important trials of
Leguay and Bousquet, *French* instruments of a shame that was never
fully acknowledged over four succeeding decades.

Unhealed wounds. No group was prouder to be French than the
French Jews. France was the land of the Enlightenment: France had
shone a beacon of liberal tolerance all over the world and touched the
sensibilities of mankind. To be French was a religion in itself to the
assimilated Jews of France.

That was why they were so blind to the implications of Vichy. In
his recently published diary, [21] Raymond-Raoul Lambert, head of the
UGIF in the southern zone until he and his entire family were deported
to Auschwitz, described his total bewilderment. Lambert was entirely

and thoroughly French. All his points of reference — his cultural, literary and historical antecedents — were French; and thus he was unable to assimilate the "impossible" fact of a rejection by his own nation.

On October 2, 1940, when he read that the Vichy government was preparing new laws regarding the Jews, Lambert wrote in his diary: "It is possible that within a few days I shall be diminished as a citizen, and that my sons, who are French by birth, by culture, and by faith will be cruelly cast outside the French community . . . Is this possible? I can't believe it. France is no longer France . . . "[22]

On October 19, he wrote: "Racism has become the law of the new State. All my illusions crumble, and I am afraid for myself and for my country . . . In the future this revocation of the Declaration of the Rights of Man will appear as a new Revocation of the Edict of Nantes; . . . but I will never leave the country for which I almost gave my life.[23]

"Last night I cried like a man who has suddenly been abandoned by the woman he has loved throughout life, by the unique tutor of his thoughts, and by the commander of his actions."[24]

The importance of Raymond-Raoul Lambert's diary is that the wounds it reveals turn out to be the same or similar to those that torture Serge Klarsfeld. "France is no longer France," wrote Lambert, referring, of course, to only one of the "two Frances," to the France where he, as a Jew, could live. For Klarsfeld, France will be "France" once more when the dark corners of the Nazi presence and the role of Vichy have been illuminated — and repudiated. There is disappointment as well as bitterness in his comment: "We always give these people a chance to say they regret and they never do." But that disappointment does not mean Klarsfeld will give up. Too much is at stake: the desire to live comfortably as a Jew in France, in the wake of a Jewish father's deportation from France; and in the final analysis, France itself, as he sees it — the France he must believe in.

Serge has taken it upon himself to right the balance in France. His wife, Beate, has taken it upon herself to right the balance in her native Germany. She believes that neither she nor her children can be proud of the country she loves until it, too, has publicly routed out its Nazi war criminals. Beate Klarsfeld has shouldered the griefs of her nation.

It might appear that she is having more success than her husband. On April 21, 1985, Helmut Kohl became the first German chancellor to visit the site of a Nazi concentration camp and from there to speak about the Holocaust. Before hundreds of survivors of Bergen-Belsen, Kohl spoke painfully of "shame" and "historical responsibility." "A reconciliation with the survivors and the descendants of the victims is only possible if we accept our history as it really was; if we, as Germans, recognize our shame and our historical responsibility; and if we perceive the necessity to take action against everything that diminishes freedom and human dignity," he said with emotion.[25] His government had recently passed legislation to make Holocaust revisionist "history" an offense.

The ghosts of Vichy France have yet to be so boldly confronted. Unhealed wounds.

In April 1985, a Jewish community newspaper in Paris[26] published an open letter to *Le Figaro*. The author, Claude Lévy, was a man of some distinction who had been honored with several military and academic titles.

In his letter, Mr. Lévy said that the previous July, on the fortieth anniversary of the Liberation, he had wished to place a memorial notice in *Le Figaro* commemorating the death of his parents who were arrested in 1944 by the Gestapo of Klaus Barbie and deported to Auschwitz. In the text of his notice, Lévy said that his parents had been denounced by an informer. He requested that one think of them on this fortieth anniversary, "and of the 80,000 Jewish deportees from France who were exterminated on the orders of the German Nazis and the French Vichy government [sic] ."

Lévy's suggestion that Jews were exterminated (rather than deported) on orders from Vichy France was historically inaccurate. According to the associate editor of *Le Figaro*, Jacques Jacquet-Francillon, the paper considered the remark a political "commentary" and refused to publish on that basis. But Lévy's subsequent letter, in which he charged *Le Figaro* with "discrimination" and spoke of the "pain and shame" inherent in the way his parents came to be arrested and die, remained eloquent evidence of forty years of suffering.

Unhealed wounds — on both sides. For the majority of French men and women who had placed their faith in the hero of Verdun, Philippe Pétain, in the name of France and the timeless values of work, family and country, the *épuration* or postwar purge of the collaboration was in itself a trauma that had never healed. Going to bed a Pétainist and waking up a Gaullist was a fiction that had allowed daily life to continue, but it did not dull the cutting edge of sorrow. That sorrow

was transmitted within the bosom of many families, as was a continued defense of the Marshal and the values of his regime. Consider, for
example, a woman of sixty in the north of France whose father, an
important industrialist, was tried by the postwar regime for collaboration on both an economic and political level (he was acquitted, as
were the majority of middle-class industrialists). Forty years later, she
maintained both the traditional defense (Pétain and her papa were really *résistants* playing a double game) and the fanatical anticommunism
that marked the earlier period. In 1984 she was prepared to defend
apartheid in South Africa as "a bulwark against communism," just as,
forty years earlier, she and her family had defended the anti-Jewish
laws of Vichy on the same spurious grounds. Her vision of France
remains profoundly xenophobic. Although the Jews in her city have
been integrated for four centuries, she is not quite sure they are French.
Indeed, she is moderately suspicious of *all* French people who live outside her own immediate region.

Her daughter, a sensitive women in her mid-thirties, has dropped
the ideology, but held on to the sorrow. Unlike her mother, she is able
to give voice to the shame that stained France when France deported
the Jews. "With the exception of the few people who fought in the
active Resistance, there is hardly a family in France that does not continue to feel some discomfort," she said quietly.

For the few on the Right who remain both adamant and activist,
there is, in France, an association dedicated to the memory of the Marshal. And Jacques Isorni, Pétain's lawyer at the time of his trial for
treason, recently published his *Mémoires*, a laudatory book about the
Marshal. Pierre Laval's son-in-law has also published a book in an
attempt to exonerate the memory of the former premier.[27]

Unhealed wounds: the Algerian war. The same population that
had actively supported Pétain was at the forefront of Algérie Française
a decade later. (A generation later many of them rallied behind Jean-
Marie Le Pen.) The events of the Algerian war also proved indigestible
and, like the collaboration, kept reappearing to embarrass individuals
and governments. Twenty years after the end of the war, the fact that
torture had been used as an "interrogation" tool was only beginning
to seep into general public consciousness, and the subject remained so
controversial that Jacques Vergès was able to use it as a "strategy of
disruption" in his ongoing defense of Klaus Barbie. The colonials who
were forced to return to France at the end of the Algerian war also

bore wounds that had never healed. Algeria was their ancestral home, and the privileges they had enjoyed there were now lost forever. It was hardly a surprise that they supported the Front National in large numbers. On a psychological level, it was intolerable to see Algerians in France when Algerians had, in effect, kicked them out of Algeria.

Unhealed wounds: the Resistance. The Resistance got a lot of good press; indeed, postwar France was built on its successes. But internal rivalries and betrayals continued to rankle. The communists never stopped hating René Hardy and Henri Frenay. And, in spite of two trials and two acquittals, many others continued to hold Hardy responsible for the capture of Jean Moulin. There was also the problem of Moulin himself. No one had ever "paid for" his death. And now that Barbie was within killing distance, so to speak, it seemed that he would not even be confronted with that tragic event in France's history. Indeed, the entire Resistance was going to be excluded from the trial, and all those people like Jean Gay who had been tortured and deported by Barbie were to be left frustrated and hungry for justice, or revenge, or both.

The psychology of this interminable, ongoing cycle of repressed history was important and could be traced in large measure to the practice of amnesty. Amnesty had a practical face — in the sense that it allowed governments to shut the door on the past and get on with business as usual; and a humane face — in that it presumably "forgave" large groups of people. It was also an important tool in other sorts of societies where people were imprisoned uniquely for their ideas, as Amnesty International demonstrated. But in France, far from being a means of avoiding "hatred," as writer Raymond Bourgine had put it,[28] amnesty seemed to be a surefire way of keeping hostility alive forever. A country seemingly in love with psychiatric theory maintained a legal structure that ignored in macrocosm what was amply known in microcosm. At the level of the individual psyche, repression and taboo had a habit of causing ulcers or worse. The same was true on a larger scale; and France, as it happened, had a severe case of chronic indigestion. Each national crisis created more "mud," as they called it: mud that must never be stirred. In consequence, anger, sorrow and shame could never be adequately acknowledged, and playwrights could write comic allegories about supposedly dead bodies that continued to grow, to the profound embarrassment of host and guest alike. In 1984, Bernard-Henri Lévy wrote a novel[29] some would call allegorical in which the hero, Benjamin, is the son of the collaboration and the stepson of the Resistance, which becomes rigid and right-wing in its middle age. Benjamin's shameful natural parentage is hidden from him until a "devil" who is, quite overtly, Maître Jacques Vergès, reveals the truth.[30] Benjamin is eventually destroyed by his personal history.

It was precisely this repression that made it possible for the real Jacques Vergès to make threats about putting "France" on trial — "France" being the France of the collaboration and the Algerian war.

The concomitant legal structure of prescription created related problems. As with amnesty, the intentions were laudable, but the reality often turned out to be otherwise. If a crime is no longer a crime after ten years have elapsed, in that the accused can no longer be brought to trial, then the criminal who has been canny enough to avoid being caught becomes a victor, and the victim of his crime must forever remain a victim. If such a victim can no longer hold out hope that justice may one day prevail, then the very concept of justice as an agreed-upon means of righting the social balance has been eroded. The accused may eventually, of course, be acquitted. That is not the point. What *is* important is that he or she remain subject to judgment, without temporal term, within the legal forum, in accordance with the values the society claims to uphold.

When there is little hope of bringing a crime to trial because of a general amnesty, or because ten years have passed since the crime was committed, a kind of lassitude regarding the specificity of different crimes seems to set in. A horrendous crime may be trivialized by the assertion that it is no more or less horrendous than another. Such an attitude distorts a vision of justice.

Nowhere was this distortion more evident than in the general attitude to Klaus Barbie and his trial. With the probable exception of those like the Halaunbrenner family whose lives had been forever and unalterably destroyed by Barbie, few seemed to care about the trial of the *accused*. The legal arguments over what constituted a "crime against humanity," which is not subject to prescription, as opposed to a "war crime," which is, were problematic and important, but they were of concern chiefly to Barbie's lawyer, who wanted to discredit the basis for the trial, and to groups — like the Resistance — who wanted to be represented at the trial. Every interest group wanted to be present at an event that was going to attract international attention, but few seemed to see, as Hannah Arendt saw so long ago in the case of Eichmann, that justice would be served only if the accused was the unique focus of the proceedings. If the trial of the individual Nazi was unimportant because he was "old," "pathetic" or a "mere ss captain," then any attempt to try "nazism" through him was a meaningless enterprise. If it was too late to judge a Nazi because his crimes have since been eclipsed by crimes committed in Algeria, Vietnam, Cambodia, El Salvador, Nicaragua and a host of other places, then none of the foregoing crimes were worth worrying about any more than the old Nazi was worth worrying about, and humanity might just as well throw up its collective hands in despair. The affirmation that justice might still matter could come only from the fair application of justice. This meant that the individual human being who had acted of his own free will must be judged for what he had done. Not for more than he had done, but not for less, either. In the final analysis, what other choice was there in the struggle against collective dehumanization but the determination not to ignore it in the individual? Anything else amounted to unconscious complicity with the act.

If Klaus Barbie lived long enough to enter a French courtroom, he would find himself engaged in a drama with two men whose lives had been shaped by a beginning as tragic as his own. Barbie was the product of a long evolution in German history, but specifically of having grown to adulthood in a strange world where hatred was a cardinal virtue outside the family and violence was a staple within. For the rest of his life he developed his talents according to the "ideals" imprinted in his youth. Pride lay in never having "betrayed" his past, in never having examined his values according to any other criteria.

By his side, his lawyer, the enigmatic Jacques Vergès, a man whose earliest memories were stained by racial scandal and the ambiguity of his personal status, a man for whom violence had become a norm to be approved or condemned according to its "political" content, a man for whom crime had the esthetic quality of great art. Like his client, Vergès had never "betrayed" — or reconsidered — the lessons learned in youth. Like his client, he had spent an entire lifetime composing variations on a theme that remained constant.

And facing Barbie, his mortal enemy, Serge Klarsfeld, the Jew responsible for the fact of his presence here in this courtroom. Klarsfeld, the man whose life also was determined one day long ago, when, trembling behind a false wall, he heard them take away a beloved father who never returned.

The world would be watching their struggle.

NOTES

Chapter 1

1. *L'Express*, February 7, 1983.
2. Charles Millon, in *Le Figaro*, February 14, 1983.
3. *Le Nouvel Observateur*, February 18, 1983.
4. Miriam Worms, in *Le Nouvel Observateur*, February 18, 1983.
5. *The Guardian*, April 10, 1983.
6. *Le Figaro*, February 7, 1983.
7. *Le Nouvel Observateur*, February 11, 1983.
8. Ibid.

Chapter 2

1. Susan Sontag, "Fascinating Fascism," in *A Susan Sontag Reader* (New York: Farrar, Straus, Giroux, 1982).
2. Johann Gottlieb Fichte, *Reden an die Deutsche Nation*, Berlin, 1808, p. 488, quoted in Lucy S. Dawidowicz, *The War Against the Jews: 1933–1945* (New York: Holt, Rinehart and Winston, 1975), p. 34.
3. Gordon A. Craig, *Germany: 1866–1945* (New York: Oxford University Press, 1978).
4. Quoted in Barbara W. Tuchman, *The Proud Tower: A Portrait of the World Before the War, 1890–1914* (New York: Macmillan, 1966). p. 357.
5. Friedrich Ludwig Jahn, *Deutsches Volkstum*, 1810, quoted in Dawidowicz, *The War Against the Jews* p. 35.
6. *Kreuzzeitung*, June 1875, quoted in Craig, *Germany: 1866–1945*, p. 84.
7. Maurice Joly, *Dialogue in Hell Between Machiavelli and Montesquieu*.
8. By Sir John Radcliffe (pseudonym for Herman Goedsche).
9. For a fascinating account of the history of the *Protocols*, I refer the reader to Herman Bernstein, *The Truth About "The Protocols of Zion"* (New York: Ktav, 1935, 1971).
10. Craig, *Germany: 1866–1945*, p. 103.
11. Dawidowicz, *The War Against the Jews*, p. 47.
12. Ibid.
13. From records of the Staatliches Friedrich Wilhelms Gymnasium, Trier.
14. For an excellent examination of this issue, see Lucy S. Dawidowicz, *The Holocaust and the Historians* (Cambridge, Mass.: Harvard University Press, 1981).
15. Quoted in George Lachman Mosse, ed., *Nazi Culture: Intellectual, Cultural and Social Life in the Third Reich* (New York: Grosset and Dunlop, 1966), p. 265.
16. Craig, *Germany: 1866–1945*, p.662.
17. Mosse, *Nazi Culture*, p. 103.
18. Geoffrey Cocks, *Psychotherapy in the Third Reich* (Oxford: Oxford University Press, 1985).
19. Andrew Mollo, *To the Death's Head True: The Story of the ss* (London: Methuen, 1982), p. 36.

20. Ibid., pp. 35, 36.
21. Interview with Alfredo Serra, 1973.
22. Beate Klarsfeld, *Wherever They May Be* (New York: Vanguard Press, 1975), p. 218.
23. Quoted in Brendan Murphy, *The Butcher of Lyon: The Story of the Infamous Nazi, Klaus Barbie* (New York: Empire Books, 1983), p. 143.
24. German document, quoted in Raul Hilberg, *The Destruction of the European Jews* (Chicago: Quadrangle Books, 1961), p. 372.
25. At the war's end, fewer than 20,000 Dutch Jews remained alive. Of these, 8,000 were Jews in mixed marriages who escaped deportation, and 7,000 were Jews in hiding.

Chapter 3

1. In writing this chapter, I have referred extensively to several excellent historical studies: Robert O. Paxton, *Vichy France: Old Guard and New Order* (1972: French edition, Paris: Les Editions du Seuil, 1973); Michael R. Marrus and Robert O. Paxton, *Vichy France and the Jews* (New York: Schocken Books, 1983. Original edition, Paris: Calmann-Lévy, 1981); Serge Klarsfeld, *Vichy–Auschwitz: Le rôle de Vichy dans la solution finale de la question juive en France, 1942* (Paris: Fayard, 1982); Jean-Denis Bredin, *L'Affaire* (Paris: Julliard, 1983); Hannah Arendt, *Antisemitism* (New York: Harcourt Brace Jovanovich, 1951).
2. Quoted in Bredin, *L'Affaire*, p. 488.
3. François Mauriac, *Cinq ans de ma vie* (Paris: Maspero, 1962), quoted in Bredin, *L'Affaire*, p. 484.
4. Quoted in Tuchman, *The Proud Tower*, p. 217.
5. Quoted in Bredin, *L'Affaire*, p. 375.
6. Henri Giscard d'Estaing, *D'Esterhazy à Dreyfus* (Paris: Plon, 1950), quoted in Bredin, *L'Affaire*, p. 467.
7. Jean-Pierre Peter, "Dimensions de l'Affaire Dreyfus," *Annales* ESC, XVI, 6 (November–December 1961), quoted in Bredin, *L'Affaire*, p. 469.
8. Tuchman, *The Proud Tower*, p. 250.
9. Arendt, *Antisemitism*, p. 110.
10. Marrus and Paxton, *Vichy France and the Jews*, p. 39.
11. David Schoenbrun, *Soldiers of the Night: The Story of the French Resistance* (Toronto: Clarke Irwin, 1980), pp. 29–30.
12. Television documentary, "France Régions," October 18, 1984.
13. Marrus and Paxton, *Vichy France and the Jews*, p. 197.
14. *France, revue de l'Etat nouveau*, June 1942.
15. Raymond Aron, *Mémoires: 50 ans de réflexion politique* (Paris: Julliard, 1983), p. 178.
16. S. Klarsfeld, *Vichy–Auschwitz*, p. 99.
17. Ibid., p. 101.
18. Marrus and Paxton, *Vichy France and the Jews*, p. 206.
19. S. Klarsfeld, *Vichy–Auschwitz*, p. 109.
20. Marrus and Paxton, *Vichy France and the Jews*, p. 231.
21. S. Klarsfeld, *Vichy–Auschwitz*, p. 113.
22. Marrus and Paxton, *Vichy France and the Jews*, p. 246.
23. Quoted in Serge Klarsfeld, *Memorial to the Jews Deported from France, 1942–1944* (New York: Beate Klarsfeld Foundation, 1983), p. 332.

24. Aron, *Mémoires*, pp. 157, 744.
25. Interview with Richard Wertenschlag, February 11, 1985.
26. Quoted in Hilberg, *Destruction of the European Jews*, pp. 398–99.
27. S. Klarsfeld, *Memorial*, p. 202. Marrus and Paxton point out, in *Vichy France and the Jews*, that at the time of this letter, the leadership was actually still trying to verify the existence of gas chambers and a general plan of extermination.
28. S. Klarsfeld, *Vichy–Auschwitz*, p. 422.
29. Ibid., p. 153.
30. Television documentary, "France Régions", October 18, 1984.

Chapter 4

1. Quoted in Henri Amouroux, *L'Impitoyable Guerre civile* (Paris: Robert Laffont, 1983), p. 93.
2. Quoted in *Le Petit Parisien*, July 10, 1942.
3. For many right-wingers, the choice between resistance and collaboration was not as clear-cut as it has sometimes been made out to be.
4. Quoted in Amouroux, *L'Impitoyable Guerre*, p. 332.
5. See notes to Chapter 2.
6. Statistics on the collaboration and the Resistance from Pascal Ory, *Les Collaborateurs* (Paris: Les Editions du Seuil, 1976); and interview with Pascal Ory.
7. André Halimi, *La Délation sous l'occupation* (Paris: Alain Moreau, 1983), Introduction.
8. Quoted in Amouroux, *L'Impitoyable Guerre*, p. 312.
9. Free translation by the author.
10. Evidence provided October 5, 1967, by state prosecutor Thomas, quoted in Marcel Ruby, *La Résistance à Lyon*, 2 vols. (Lyons: Les Editions L'Hermès, 1979), p. 59.
11. The documents vary between these figures.
12. Raymond Samuel adopted the name Aubrac as a *nom de guerre* and kept it after the war.
13. See Chapter 3.
14. Quoted in Amouroux, *L'Impitoyable Guerre*, p. 362.
15. The last convoy of Jews to leave France for Auschwitz was sent directly from Lyons, by Barbie, on August 11, 1944.
16. B. Klarsfeld, *Wherever They May Be*, p. 219.
17. The trial of Abel Bonnard, minister of education under Vichy.

Chapter 5

1. March 5, 1939.
2. Jean Moulin, *Premier combat* (Paris: Les Editions de Minuit, 1947), p. 107.
3. Ibid.

Chapter 6

1. See Chapter 3.
2. B. Klarsfeld, *Wherever They May Be*, p. 216.
3. Former SS officer Wilhelm Wellnitz, quoted in Ibid., p. 219.
4. L'Union générale des Israélites de France, the French Jewish Council instituted by the Vichy government and not the Germans.
5. Quoted in B. Klarsfeld, *Wherever They May Be*, p. 227.

6. Ibid., p. 221.
7. Ibid., p. 227.
8. September 8, 1971, quoted in Ibid., p. 223.
9. This statement confirms that as late as 1944 French Jewish leaders were unaware or disbelieving of the death camps.
10. As noted, Barbie's commander in chief, Dr. Werner Knab, had also come to Lyons from a death squad in Kiev.
11. B. Klarsfeld, *Wherever They May Be*, p. 247.
12. Robert Wilson, *The Confessions of Klaus Barbie* (Vancouver, B.C.: Arsenal Pulp Press, 1984).
13. A son, Klaus-Jorg, was born in 1946.
14. "Europe No. 1."
15. Ironically, 1972 was also the year Pompidou amnestied *milicien* Paul Touvier.
16. The Germans made four copies of the passenger list of each convoy. One copy had been collecting dust in the CDJC archives since the war.
17. Canada and the United States have also stripped former Nazi and pro-Nazi criminals of fraudulently obtained citizenship.
18. From a source in the Siles Zuazo government, quoted in Murphy, *The Butcher of Lyon*, p. 27.

Chapter 7

1. Quoted in *Le Monde*, January 10, 1984.
2. *Le Journal Rhône-Alpes*, November 1983.
3. *Le Figaro*, February 9, 1983.
4. Interview with Jacques Vergès, November 10, 1983.
5. According to de la Servette, he had already planned to force Barbie's hand on the fifteenth, and Decourtray's announcement on the fourteenth was a coincidence.
6. Quoted in *Le Monde*, October 1, 1983.
7. *Nationalzeitung*, Basel, November 7, 1964.
8. *Le Monde*, March 20, 1965; cf. Centre d'information et de documentation moyen-orient, Brussels, December 15, 1969.
9. Quoted in *L'Hebdo*, Lausanne, March 19, 1982.
10. *L'Hebdo*, Lausanne, March 19, 1982; cf. sworn testimony by Genoud, September 13, 1982.
11. Hannah Arendt, *Eichmann in Jerusalem* (New York: The Viking Press, 1963), p. 15.
12. Frank Garbely.
13. *Le Matin*, Lausanne, March 12, 1982.
14. Sworn testimony, December 12, 1983.
15. *Le Monde*, March 20, 1965.
16. Centre d'information et de documentation moyen-orient, Brussels, December 15, 1969.
17. Television documentary, "L'Espion qui vient de l'extrême droite," Antenne 2, April 26, 1984.
18. Archives, Comité d'action de la résistance, January 6, 1966.
19. *Nationalzeitung*, Basel, November 7, 1964.
20. *L'Hebdo*, Lausanne, March 19, 1982.
21. Ibid.

22. At the time of writing, a trial for libel was pending in Switzerland against *Le Monde* and *L'Express*.
23. Lev Korneiev, *Along the Path of Aggression and Racism*, see Léon Poliakov, *De Moscou à Beyrouthe: Essai sur la désinformation* (Paris: Calmann-Lévy, 1983), p. 75; and cf. also *Le Monde*, June 16, 1983.
24. Centre d'information et de documentation moyen-orient.
25. Source a former collaborator. On February 14, 1985, Simon Wiesenthal confirmed that Degrelle was still alive and well and living in Spain.
26. Centre d'information et de documentation moyen-orient, December 15, 1969.
27. Ibid.
28. *Le Matin*, Lausanne, March 12, 1982.
29. *Il Mattino*, Naples, n.d., quoted in Wilson, *Confessions of Klaus Barbie*, p. 36.
30. Jacques Vergès, *Pour en finir avec Ponce Pilate* (Paris: Le Pré aux Clercs, 1983).

Chapter 8

1. May 30, 1946. Paul Vergès was sentenced to five years.
2. *Révolution* I:1 (May 1963).
3. Interview with Vergès, December 26, 1984.
4. *Valeurs Actuelles*, September 19, 1983; *L'Express*, November 18, 1983.
5. The British approach to "empire" was no less pompous, but it was less ideological. The British were more pragmatic and prepared to allow a higher degree of local autonomy.
6. Bernard Droz and Evelyne Lever, *Histoire de la guerre d'Algérie* (Paris: Les Editions du Seuil, 1982), p. 21, passim.
7. Hervé Hamon and Patrick Rotman, *Les Porteurs de valises* (Paris: Albin Michel, 1979), p. 79, passim.
8. Ibid., p. 94.
9. Georges Arnaud, *Mon Procès* (Paris: Les Editions de Minuit, 1961), quoted in Hamon and Rotman, *Les Porteurs de valises*, p. 282.
10. Ibid., p. 288.
11. The truth about the famous letter emerged later. The letter was a forgery, as Sartre was out of the country, but it had been written with his consent and was approved after the fact.
12. Quoted in Hamon and Rotman, *Les Porteurs de valises*, pp. 282–83.
13. Quoted in Droz and Lever, *Histoire de la guerre d'Algérie*, p. 62.
14. Ibid., p. 155.
15. Thirty years later, as president of the Republic, Mitterrand's attitude to an independence movement in New Caledonia was noticeably more conciliatory.
16. Raymond Aron was one of the most lucid European political thinkers of the twentieth century. He was a liberal who was opposed to ideology, a very difficult and unpopular position to uphold in France.
17. Jacques Mansour Vergès, *Pour les fidayine* (Paris: Les Editions de Minuit, 1969).
18. Claire Sterling, *The Terror Network* (New York: Holt, Rinehart and Winston, 1981), p. 39.
19. *L'Humanité*, September 25, 1963.

20. Quoted in *Revue Actuel*, April 1984.
21. *Le Monde*, September 19, 1963.
22. According to Russell scholar John G. Slater of the University of Toronto, it is unlikely that Russell was even aware of the letter that went out over his name.
23. *Revue Actuel*, April 1984.
24. *Le Monde*, March 20, 1964.

Chapter 9

1. Centre de documentation juive, Paris DXXIII–1309, 1310, 1313, quoted in Poliakov, *De Moscou à Beyrouthe*, p. 54.
2. Ibid., p. 54, passim.
3. September 8, 1960. Quoted in Hamon and Rotman, *Les Porteurs de valises*, p. 289.
4. November 26, 1955. Quoted in Poliakov, *De Moscou à Beyrouthe*, pp. 85–86.
5. Ibid., p. 94.
6. Johannes von Leers, Leopold Gleim and Ludwig Heiden.
7. "L'Espion qui vient de l'extrême droite," Antenne 2, April 26, 1984.
8. Oriana Fallaci, *Interview with History* (Boston: Houghton Mifflin 1977).
9. *Revue Actuel*, April 1984.
10. Quoted in Ibid.
11. Gabriel Padon, cited in *Le Monde*, March 11, 1966.
12. *Le Matin*, Lausanne, March 12, 1982.
13. Sterling, *The Terror Network*, pp. 111–17.
14. *L'Hebdo*, Lausanne, March 19, 1982.
15. David Irving, quoted in "L'Espion qui vient de l'extrême droite," Antenne 2, April 26, 1984.
16. *L'Express*, June 12–18, 1967.
17. Vergès, *Pour les fidayine*, p. 17.
18. *L'Hebdo*, Lausanne, March 19, 1982.
19. *Le Monde*, March 7–8, 1982.
20. *L'Hebdo*, Lausanne, March 19, 1982.
21. *L'Express*, April 23, 1982.
22. Oriana Fallaci interview, March 1972, quoted in Sterling, *The Terror Network*, p. 113.
23. *Le Quotidien*, cited in radio interview, "Le Tribunal des flagrants délires," June 7, 1983.
24. Vergès, *Pour en finir avec Ponce Pilate*, pp. 121–22.
25. *Valeurs Actuelles*, February 27, 1984.
26. *L'Express*, July 4, 1983.
27. Interview with Vergès, December 24, 1984.
28. Quoted in *Le Point*, February 10, 1985. This is precisely what happened in February 1985 when Direct Action (French) and the Red Army Faction (German) publicly coordinated their activities.
29. *Le Quotidien*, March 5, 1985.
30. The Hoffmann group was a nucleus of six members or former members of the ANS (Aktionsgruppe Nationaler Sozialisten) who specialized during the early 1980s in attacks on American army bases in West Germany.
31. Quoted in the 1984 documentary about the far Right that was broadcast in

France (as "L'Espion qui vient de l'extrême droite") and in Britain (as "The Other Face of Terror").

32. *Die Wochenzeitung*, June 29, 1984.
33. The Orient Trading Company.
34. "L'Espion qui vient de l'extrême droite."

Chapter 10

1. *Valeurs Actuelles*, September 19, 1983.
2. Ibid.; and *L'Express*, July 4, 1983.
3. *Revue Actuel*, April 1984.
4. Jacques Vergès, *De la stratégie judiciaire* (Paris: Les Editions de Minuit, 1968).
5. *L'Express*, July 4, 1983.
6. *L'Express*, November 18, 1983.
7. Vergès, *Pour en finir avec Ponce Pilate*.
8. Vergès, *De la stratégie judiciaire*, pp. 203–204.
9. Interview with Vergès, November 27, 1984.
10. Vergès, *De la stratégie judiciaire*, pp. 204–205.
11. Interview with Vergès, November 10, 1983.
12. Quoted in *Le Quotidien*, July 4, 1983.
13. *Vertiges*, June 1984.
14. Ory, *Les Collaborateurs*.
15. *Le Dauphiné Libéré*.
16. Maurice Rajsfus, *Les Juifs dans la collaboration: l'UGIF, 1941–1944* (Paris: Etudes et documentations internationales, 1980), p. 232.
17. CDJC, XXVIII–3–28, quoted in Rajsfus, Ibid., pp. 254–55.
18. Xavier Vallat made it very clear that he had candidates in reserve for just such an exigency. Rajsfus, Ibid., p. 369.
19. Procès-Verbal, July–August 13, 1944. CDJC, CDXXX–38. Quoted in Rajsfus, Ibid., pp. 373–82.
20. Telephone interview, November 16, 1983.
21. Yves Jouffa investigated the archives in Lyons in February 1985 and was able to document the falsity of this charge.
22. *Le Matin*, Lausanne, May 21, 1984.
23. *Hommes et Libertés*, 29–30 (December 1983).
24. Henri Noguères, *La Vérité aura le dernier mot* (Paris: Les Editions du Seuil, 1985).
25. Lucie Aubrac, *Ils partiront dans l'ivresse* (Paris: Les Editions du Seuil, 1984).
26. *L'Express*, July 4, 1983.

Chapter 11

1. *L'Express*, February 11, 1983.
2. Raymond Bourgine, "La civilisation de l'amnistie," *Valeurs Actuelles*, March 19, 1979.
3. Ibid.
4. Ibid.
5. Interview with Voguet, March 13, 1985.
6. Interview with Mireille Bertrand, November 16, 1983.
7. Alois Brunner raided the UGIF children's homes in Paris in July 1944.

8. Serge Klarsfeld, *Les Enfants d'Izieu: une tragédie juive* (Paris: S. Klarsfeld, 1985), p. 33.
9. CDJC, VII–10.
10. *Les Allobroges*, April 7, 1946.

Chapter 12

1. Laurent Joffrin, *La Gauche en voie de disparition* (Paris: Les Editions du Seuil, 1984), p. 7.
2. February 1985.
3. Poll conducted by SOFRES for *Libération*, January 9–12, 1985.
4. 10.3 percent, National Statistics Institute (INSEE).
5. *Libération*, February 12, 1985.
6. Maurice Martin du Gard, *Chronique de Vichy*, p. 55, quoted in Marrus and Paxton, *Vichy France and the Jews*, p. 20.
7. Arnaud de Lassus, director of Action familiale et scolaire.
8. Jean Madiran.
9. André Figueras, *Ce canaille de Dreyfus* (Paris: Publications A. Figueras, 1982).
10. François Brigneau, editor in chief of *Présent* and editorial writer for *Minute*.
11. Romain Marie represented a 1930s-style integrist Catholic movement that supported the Front National. He was subsequently elected to the European Parliament for the Front National.
12. Sources for this meeting from *Le Monde*, August 19, 1983, as well as Edwy Plenel and Alain Rollat, *L'Effet Le Pen* (Paris: La Decouverte/Le Monde, 1984).
13. Centre national des indépendents et paysans (CNIP).
14. La Fédération pour l'unité des réfugiés et des rapatriés (FURR).
15. *R.L.P.-Hebdo*, no. 117. Quoted in Alain Rollat, *Les Hommes de l'extrême droite* (Paris: Calmann-Lévy, 1985), excerpted in *L'Evénement du Jeudi*, April 4–10, 1985.
16. "L'Heure de vérité," Antenne 2, February 13, 1984.
17. "L'Edition spéciale," TF 1, February 14, 1984.
18. Term for second-generation Algerian born in France.
19. *Le Figaro*, April 11, 1985.
20. Antenne 2, March 10, 1985.
21. Raymond-Raoul Lambert, *Carnet d'un témoin*. Richard Cohen, ed. (Paris: Fayard, 1985).
22. Ibid., p. 83.
23. Lambert was awarded the Legion of Honor for service during World War I.
24. Lambert, *Carnet d'un témoin*, pp. 84–85.
25. Associated Press wire service, quoted in *Le Figaro*, April 22, 1985.
26. *Information Juive*.
27. René de Chabrun, *Pierre Laval: Traitor or Patriot?* (New York: Scribner's 1984).
28. Bourgine, "La civilisation de l'amnistie."
29. Bernard-Henri Lévy, *Le Diable en tête* (Paris: Les Editions Grasset, 1984).
30. At a seminar held at the Sorbonne in autumn 1984, Lévy identified his character as "someone like Jacques Vergès."

BIBLIOGRAPHY

Author's Note: This list does not claim to be exhaustive. However, it does represent the works I found most useful in the preparation of this book.

Amouroux, Henri. *L'Impitoyable Guerre civile*. Paris: Robert Laffont, 1983.

Ardagh, John. *France in the 1980s*. Harmondsworth, Middlesex: Penguin Books and Secker and Warburg, 1982.

Arendt, Hannah. *Antisemitism*. New York: Harcourt Brace Jovanovich, 1951.

———. *Eichmann in Jerusalem*. New York: The Viking Press, 1963.

Aron, Raymond. *Mémoires: 50 ans de réflexion politique*. Paris: Julliard, 1983.

Aron, Robert. *Histoire de l'épuration*. Paris: Fayard, 1967.

Bernstein, Herman. *The Truth About "The Protocols of Zion."* New York, Ktav Publishing House, 1935, 1971.

Bower, Tom. *Klaus Barbie, Butcher of Lyons*. London: Michael Joseph, 1984.

Bredin, Jean-Denis. *L'Affaire*. Paris: Julliard, 1983.

Carsten, F.H. *The Rise of Fascism*. London: Batsford 1967.

Craig, Gordon A. *Germany: 1866–1945*. New York: Oxford University Press, 1978.

Dawidowicz, Lucy S. *The Holocaust and the Historians*. Cambridge, Mass.: Harvard University Press, 1981.

———. *The War Against the Jews: 1933–1945*. New York: Holt, Rinehart and Winston, 1975.

De Hoyos, Ladislas. *Barbie*. Paris: Robert Laffont, 1984.

Delperrie de Bayac, Jacques. *Histoire de la milice*. Paris: Fayard, 1969.

Droz, Bernard, and Evelyne Lever. *Histoire de la guerre d'Algérie*. Paris: Les Editions de Seuil, 1982.

Hamon, Hervé, and Partick Rotman. *Les Porteurs de valises*. Paris: Albin Michel, 1979.

Hilberg, Raul. *The Destruction of the European Jews*. Chicago: Quadrangle Books, 1961.

Joffrin, Laurent. *La Gauche en voie de disparition*. Paris: Les Editions du Seuil, 1984.

Klarsfeld, Beate. *Wherever They May Be*. New York: Vanguard Press, 1975.

Klarsfeld, Serge. *Les Enfants d'Izieu: une tragédie juive*. Paris: Serge Klarsfeld, 1985.

————. *Vichy–Auschwitz: Le rôle de Vichy dans la solution finale de la question juive en France, 1942.* Paris: Fayard, 1982.

Lambert, Raymond-Raoul. *Carnet d'un témoin.* Richard Cohen, ed. Paris: Fayard, 1985.

Marrus, Michael R., and Robert O. Paxton. *Vichy France and the Jews.* New York: Schocken Books, 1983. Original edition, Paris: Calmann-Lévy, 1981.

Mollo Andrew. *To the Death's Head True: The Story of the* ss. London: Thames/ Methuen, 1982.

Mosse, George Lachman, ed. *Nazi Culture: Intellectual, Cultural and Social Life in the Third Reich.* New York: Grosset and Dunlop, 1966.

Moulin, Jean. *Premier combat.* Paris: Les Editions de Minuit, 1947.

Murphy, Brendan. *The Butcher of Lyon: The Story of the Infamous Nazi, Klaus Barbie.* New York: Empire Books, 1983.

Ory, Pascal. *Les Collaborateurs.* Paris: Les Editions du Seuil, 1976.

Paxton, Robert O. *Vichy France: Old Guard and New Order.* French edition, Paris: Les Editions du Seuil, 1973.

Plenel, Edwy, and Alain Rollat. *L'Effet Le Pen.* Paris: La Découverte/Le Monde, 1984.

Poliakov, Léon. *De Moscou à Beyrouthe: Essai sur la désinformation.* Paris: Calmann-Lévy, 1983.

Rajsfus, Maurice. *Les Juifs dans la collaboration: l'*UGIF, *1941–1944.* Paris: Etudes et documentations internationales, 1980.

Ruby, Marcel. *La Contre Résistance à Lyon.* Lyons: Les Editions L'Hermès, 1981.

————. *La Résistance à Lyon.* 2 Vols. Lyons: Les Editions L'Hermès, 1979.

Schoenbrun, David. *Soldiers of the Night: The Story of the French Resistance.* Toronto: Clarke Irwin, 1980.

Sterling, Claire. *The Terror Network.* New York: Holt, Rinehart and Winston, 1981.

Tannenbaum, Edward R. *The Action Française: Diehard Reactionaries in Twentieth-Century France.* New York: John Wiley, 1962.

Tuchman, Barbara W. *The Proud Tower: A Portrait of the World Before the War, 1890–1914.* New York: Macmillan, 1966.

Vergès, Jacques. *De la stratégie judiciaire.* Paris: Les Editions de Minuit, 1968.

————. *Pour en finir avec Ponce Pilate.* Paris: Le Pré aux Clercs, 1983.

————. *Pour les fidayine.* Paris: Les Editions de Minuit, 1960.

INDEX